OUR EARTH

Sandy Creek
NEW YORK

An Imprint of Sterling Publishing
387 Park Avenue South
New York, NY 10016

ISBN 978-1-4351-4904-5

Manufactured in GuangDong, China
Lot #:
10 9 8 7 6 5 4 3 2 1
06/13

OUR EARTH

THE ULTIMATE REFERENCE RESOURCE FOR THE WHOLE FAMILY, WITH OVER 500 PHOTOGRAPHS AND ILLUSTRATIONS

Sandy Creek
NEW YORK

CONTENTS

WONDERFUL WORLD

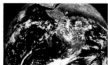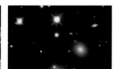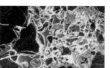

Our Earth, and the universe around, awaits you! In this book packed with astounding images and amazing facts, you can explore at leisure our incredible planet, its ancient rocks, violent natural phenomena such as earthquakes and volcanoes, its varied weather and climate, and wonderfully diverse plant life. Your journey of discovery also takes you beyond the Earth, to the stars and planets of the infinite cosmos.

This book has five informative sections, covering the Solar System, Geology and the Earth's Formation, the Power of Nature, the World of Plants, and Weather and Climate. Fact-filled and lavishly illustrated, here is the story of our world and its place in the universe: from the far-distant stars to the inner secrets of trees and flowers.

Our Solar System

Long ago, some people believed the stars were bonfires in the sky, and that the universe was a plate resting on the shell of a giant turtle. Most early scientists, like the ancient Greek astronomer Ptolemy, believed the Earth was at the center of the universe. As knowledge grew, people wondered what lay beyond the Earth, and to explore the heavens they first built telescopes and then sent spacecraft into outer space. Here are brilliant images of the cosmos to marvel at—spectacular photos of the stars and planets will delight you as you discover how our planet Earth fits into the bigger picture.

In the Milky Way Galaxy alone, scientists calculate there are more than 100 billion stars. Such mind-boggling statistics provoke the question: is it possible that our Sun is the only star with a planet that cradles life? In this section of the book, you can learn more about our neighbors in the solar system—the Sun's family of planets. Using space probes and telescopes, scientists are learning more about the planets and their moons, showing us images of dramatic volcanoes and craters, and revealing individual oddities. Explore the mysteries of the asteroids, comets, far-distant Pluto, and the recently discovered frozen miniworlds of the

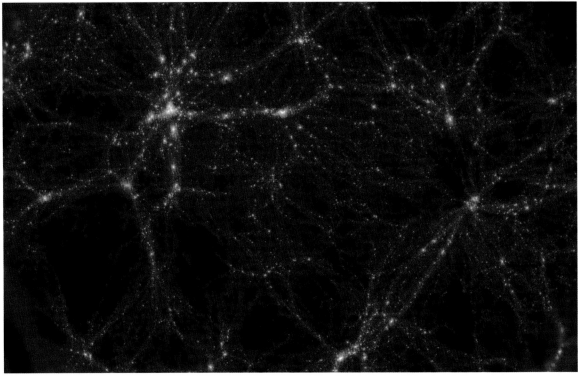

DARK MATTER
The visible objects in the cosmos represent only a small fraction of the total matter within the universe. Most of it is invisible even to the most powerful telescopes. Galaxies and their stars move as they do because of the gravitational forces exerted by this material.

Kuiper belt. All these are wonders for you to explore, and you can also enjoy star-maps of the constellations, the star-groups that since ancient times have served as guides for navigation, calendars, and storytelling. Every page reveals more about the universe and its secrets.

Geology and Formation

If the Earth were a plane, rocks would be its "flight recorders." Rocks store information about the past, and geology (the study of rocks) helps scientists reconstruct the long history of the Earth. Rock material originated within the clouds of dust and gases that orbited around the Sun over four billion years ago, and rocks have been silent witnesses to the cataclysms our planet has experienced over the epochs. Rock evidence shows how the planet's surface has changed over more than 4 billion years. Even insignificant rocks contain evidence about life millions of years ago. For ancient civilizations, stones symbolized eternity, but stones endure because their material is recycled time and again. Fifty million years from now, landscapes will be not as we know them—not the Andes, nor the Himalayas, nor the ice of Antarctica, nor the Sahara Desert. Weathering and erosion, slow and relentless, never stops. Yet still there will be rocks, their chemical composition, shape, and texture recording the passage of geological events. In this section of *Our Earth*, you will delight in stunning images of rocks and mountains, seemingly the same yet slowly changing.

Discover the fascinating world of

minerals, with their amazing physical and chemical properties. The Earth's crust and the oceans contain minerals without which our lives would be very different: Such as coal, petroleum, and natural gas, and metal ores used in so many ways—such as aluminum for cans; copper for electric cables; and titanium, mixed with other durable metals in alloys, to make high-speed airplanes and spacecraft.

The Power of Nature

This section of *Our Earth* describes the forces of nature that shape our planet, unleashed by movements of rocks deep underground. In full color, here are images of cities, shaken by earthquakes and volcanoes, natural phenomena that can unleash rivers of fire, destroy cities and alter landscapes. Undersea earthquakes can cause tsunamis, waves that spread across the ocean with the speed of an airplane. See for yourself the scale of tsunami destruction, when on December 26, 2004, an undersea quake hit the Indian Ocean, causing tsunami waves that flooded coastal areas of eight Asian nations, causing about 230,000 deaths.

Many ancient civilizations thought of mountain volcanoes as dwelling places of gods, to explain their awesome fury. Volcanoes spew out lava flows that can change lush landscape into barren wilderness. Hot lava destroys everything in its path, while gas and ash hurled into the air by a volcanic eruption can kill people, animals, and plants. Yet, amazingly, life re-emerges, for lava and ash cool and in time make soil unusually fertile. For this reason many farmers live near "smoking mountains," in spite of the danger. No human can control the

TORRES DEL PAINE
Torres del Paine National Park is located in Chile between the massif of the Andes and the Patagonian steppes.

MT. KILAUEA
Shield volcano in Hawaii. One of the most active shield volcanoes on Earth.

forces of nature. All people can do is live, rebuild, and live again.

Storms and volcanic eruptions are predictable, but not earthquakes, which without warning can spread destruction and death. Throughout its history, Earth has been shaken by earthquakes. Some have done immense damage, such as the earthquake that rocked San Francisco in 1906, registering 8.3 on the Richter scale, and felt as far away as Oregon to the north. In California, as elsewhere, the earthquake risk remains.

A World of Plants
There are approximately 300,000 plant species in the world, living in a variety of regions, from the frozen Arctic tundra to the lush tropical rainforests.

Without plants, there would be no animal life. Plants made the Earth's atmosphere breathable, and are vital sources of food, medicines, and raw materials. The great forests are precious natural resources, and act as the planet's "lungs." How plants use photosynthesis to convert sunlight into carbohydrates such as sugars and starches is almost magical, as are plants' abilities to adapt to different environments, through adaptations such as deep roots, water-retaining stems, and prickly leaves to survive in deserts. Why plants invest so much energy into producing flowers is another amazing story, and in this section of *Our Earth*, discover how plant fertilization takes place. Did you know that pollination is aided by the wind and insects and that some flowers are pollinated only by one

AMANITA MUSCARIA
The quintessential toadstool has unpleasant psychoactive effects. Depending on the dose, they range from dizziness, muscle cramps, and vomiting to amnesia.

species of insect? Here is a wealth of fascinating information, with spectacular images and illustrations that take you inside the heart of a tree, to reveal the functions of its tissues down to the tiny veins in its leaves.

The first plants on our planet helped to convert bare rock into soil. What happened next, and how plants spread worldwide during the Carboniferous Period is a fascinating early chapter in the Earth's prehistory. In this section's overview of plants, there is an explanation of the differences between plants, algae, and fungi.

Plants have always been vital to human diet, and more so since the first farmers began planting crops. The selective breeding of plants is ages-old, but is now moving at an even faster rate. Staple food crops—such as rice, corn, wheat, rye, barley, oats, soyabeans, lentils, and chickpeas—are grown worldwide. Plants produce many other products (such as medicines), and provide billions of people with the essentials of life.

Weather & Climate
"The flutter of a butterfly's wings in Brazil can unleash a tornado in Florida." That was the conclusion in

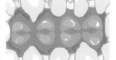

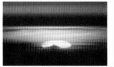

1972 of Edward Lorenz, an expert in math and meteorology—the study of weather and climate. He was trying to find a way of predicting meteorological phenomena that put people at risk. The Earth's atmosphere is such a complicated system that many scientists define it as chaotic.

No wonder any weather forecast is subject to rapid change. Weather affects people's lives in many ways, and not just when people who planned to go to the beach have to shut themselves up in the basement until a hurricane passes. Wild weather and severe climate disturbance can be catastrophic. People who live in regions subject to tornadoes, hurricanes, or tropical storms, live in fear of disruption and destruction.

Natural phenomena, such as tornadoes, hurricanes, and cyclones, become disasters when they strike populated areas or devastate farmland. Experience shows that we have to learn to live with these events and plan ahead for what might happen when they occur.

In this section you will find useful information about the factors that determine weather and climate, and the methods that are used to make the forecasts and predictions. This science helps people plan for and live with adverse weather events, and you will be able to understand why long-term forecasts are so complicated. Such key topics, and more, are all here, to inform and arouse your curiosity about the mighty forces that affect life on Earth.

BRIEF FLASH
Electrical storms are produced in large cumulonimbus-type clouds, which typically bring heavy rains in addition to lightning and thunder. The discharge takes place from the cloud toward the ground after the stepped leader, a channel of ionized air, extends down to the ground.

1 OUR SOLAR SYSTEM

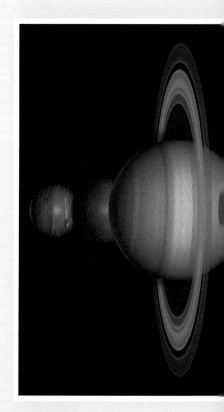

26

48

Our Solar System

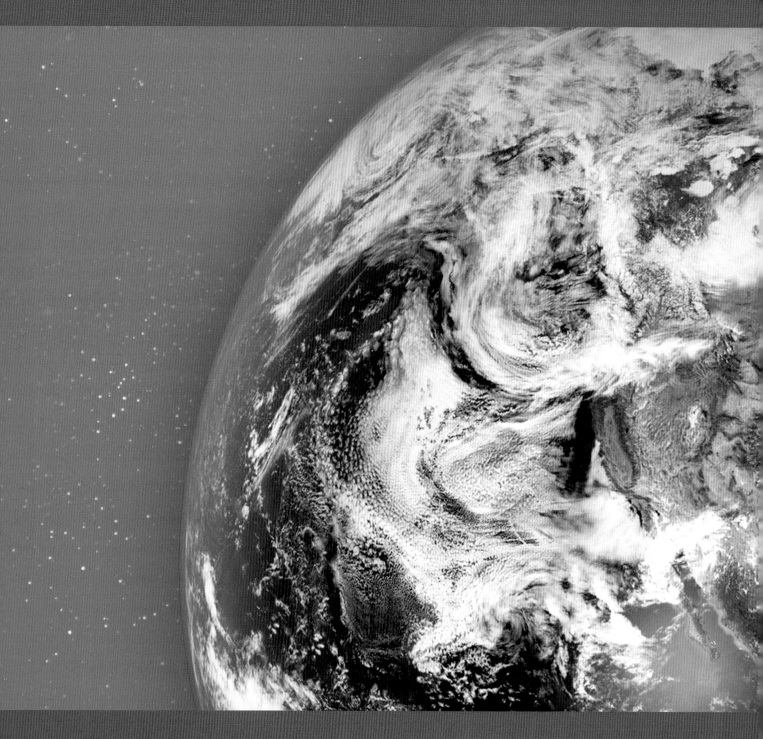

Among the millions and millions of stars that form the Milky Way galaxy, there is a medium-sized one located in one of the galaxy's arms—the Sun. To ancient peoples, the Sun was a god; to us, it is the central source of energy that generates heat, helping life exist. This star, together

OLYMPUS MONS, ON MARS
Olympus Mons is the largest volcano of the solar system. It is about two-and-a-half times as high as Mount Everest.

with the planets and other bodies that spin in orbits around it, make up the solar system, which formed about 4.6 billion years ago. The planets that rotate around it do not produce their own light. Instead, they reflect sunlight. After the Earth, Mars is the most explored planet, and home to the largest volcano in the entire solar system.

The Instant of Creation

I t is impossible to know precisely how, out of nothing, the universe began to exist. According to the "Big Bang" theory—the theory most widely accepted in the scientific community—in the beginning, there appeared an infinitely small and dense burning ball that gave rise to space, matter, and energy. This happened 13.7 billion years ago. The great, unanswered question is what caused a small dot of light—filled with concentrated energy from which matter and antimatter were created—to arise from nothingness. In very little time, the young universe began to expand and cool. Several billion years later, it acquired the form we know today.

Energetic Radiation

The burning ball that gave rise to the universe remained a source of permanent radiation. Subatomic particles and antiparticles annihilated each other. The ball's high density spontaneously produced matter and destroyed it. Had this state of affairs continued, the universe would never have undergone the growth that scientists believe followed cosmic inflation.

HOW IT GREW

Cosmic inflation was an expansion of the entire universe. The Earth's galactic neighborhood appears fairly uniform. Everywhere you look, the types of galaxies and the background temperature are essentially the same.

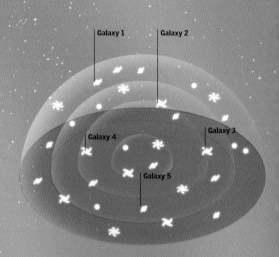

Galaxy 1　Galaxy 2　Galaxy 3　Galaxy 4　Galaxy 5

TIME	**0**	**10^{-43}** sec	**10^{-38}** sec
TEMPERATURE		10^{32} °F (and C)	10^{29} °F (and C)

1 Scientists theorize that, from nothing, something infinitely small, dense, and hot appeared. All that exists today was compressed into a ball smaller than the nucleus of an atom.

2 At the closest moment to zero time, which physics has been able to reach, the temperature is extremely high. Before the universe's inflation, a superforce governed everything.

3 The universe is unstable. Only 10–38 seconds after the big bang, the universe increases in size more than a trillion trillion trillion times. The expansion of the universe and the division of its forces begin.

ELEMENTARY PARTICLES

In its beginnings, the universe was a soup of particles that interacted with each other because of high levels of radiation. Later, as the universe expanded, quarks formed the nuclei of the elements and then joined with electrons to form atoms.

ELECTRON
Negatively charged elemental particle

PHOTON
Massless elemental luminous particle

GRAVITON
It is believed to transmit gravitation.

GLUON
Responsible for the interactions between quarks

QUARK
Light, elemental particle

Cosmic Inflation Theory

Although big bang theorists understood the universe as originating in an extremely small, hot, and condensed ball, they could not understand the reason for its staggering growth. In 1981, physicist Alan Guth proposed a solution to the problem with his inflation theory. In an extremely short period of time (less than a thousandth of a second), the universe grew more than a trillion trillion trillion times. Near the end of this period of expansion, the temperature approached absolute zero.

WMAP (WILKINSON MICROWAVE ANISOTROPY PROBE)

NASA's WMAP project maps the background radiation of the universe. In the image, hotter (red-yellow) regions and colder (blue-green) regions can be observed. WMAP makes it possible to determine the amount of dark matter.

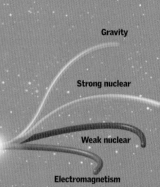

HOW IT DID NOT GROW

Had the universe not undergone inflation, it would be a collection of different regions, each with its own particular types of galaxies and each clearly distinguishable from the others.

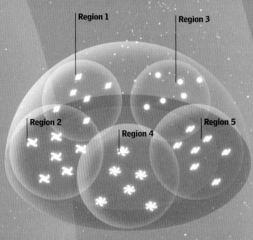

Region 1

Region 3

Region 2

Region 4

Region 5

THE SEPARATION OF FORCES

Before the universe expanded, during a period of radiation, only one unified force governed all physical interactions. The first distinguishable force was gravity, followed by electromagnetism and nuclear interactions. Upon the division of the universe's forces, matter was created.

Gravity

Strong nuclear

SUPERFORCE

Weak nuclear

Electromagnetism

EXPANSION

10^{-12} sec

10^{15} °F (and C)

4 The universe experiences a gigantic cooldown. Gravity has already become distinguishable, and the electromagnetic force and the strong and weak nuclear interactions appear.

10^{-4} sec

10^{12} °F (and C)

5 Protons and neutrons appear, formed by three quarks apiece. Because all light is trapped within the web of particles, the universe is still dark.

5 sec

9×10^{9}°F (5×10^{9}°C)

6 The electrons and their antiparticles, positrons, annihilate each other until the positrons disappear. The remaining electrons form atoms.

3 min

2×10^{9} °F (1×10^{9} °C)

7 The nuclei of the lightest elements, hydrogen and helium, form. Protons and neutrons unite to form the nuclei of atoms.

1 sec

The neutrinos separate from the initial particle soup through the disintegration of neutrons. Though having extremely little mass, the neutrinos might nevertheless form the greatest part of the universe's dark matter.

FROM PARTICLES TO MATTER

The quarks, among the oldest particles, interact with each other by forces transmitted through gluons. Later protons and neutrons will join to form nuclei.

Quark

Gluon

1 A gluon interacts with a quark.

2 Quarks join by means of gluons to form protons and neutrons.

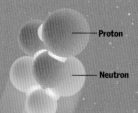

Proton

Neutron

3 Protons and neutrons unite to create nuclei.

The Transparent Universe

With the creation of atoms and overall cooling, the once opaque and dense universe became transparent. Electrons were attracted by the protons of hydrogen and helium nuclei, and together they formed atoms. Photons (massless particles of light) could now pass freely through the universe. With the cooling, radiation remained abundant but was no longer the sole governing factor of the universe. Matter, through gravitational force, could now direct its own destiny. The gaseous lumps that were present in this process grew larger and larger. After 100 million years, they formed even larger objects. Their shapes not yet defined, they constituted protogalaxies. Gravitation gave shape to the first galaxies some 500 million years after the big bang, and the first stars began to shine in the densest regions of these galaxies. One mystery that could not be solved was why galaxies were distributed and shaped the way they were. The solution that astronomers have been able to find through indirect evidence is that there exists material called "dark matter" whose presence would have played a role in galaxy formation.

1 GASEOUS CLOUD
The first gases and dust resulting from the Big Bang form a cloud.

2 FIRST FILAMENTS
Because of the gravitational pull of dark matter, the gases joined in the form of filaments.

DARK MATTER

The visible objects in the cosmos represent only a small fraction of the total matter within the universe. Most of it is invisible even to the most powerful telescopes. Galaxies and their stars move as they do because of the gravitational forces exerted by this material, which astronomers call dark matter.

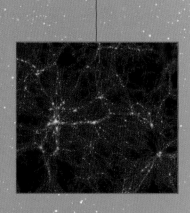

EVOLUTION OF MATTER

What can be observed in the universe today is a great quantity of matter grouped into galaxies. But that was not the original form of the universe. What the big bang initially produced was a cloud of uniformly dispersed gas. Just three million years later, the gas began to organize itself into filaments. Today, the universe can be seen as a network of galactic filaments with enormous voids between them.

TIME (IN YEARS)	**380,000**	**500 million**
TEMPERATURE	**4,900°F (2,700°C)**	**-405°F (-243°C)**

8 380,000 years after the Big Bang, atoms form. Electrons orbit the nuclei, attracted by the protons. The universe becomes transparent. Photons travel through space.

9 Galaxies acquire their definitive shape: islands of millions and millions of stars and masses of gases and dust. The stars explode as supernovas and disperse heavier elements, such as carbon.

FIRST ATOMS

Hydrogen and helium were the first elements to be formed at the atomic level. They are the main components of stars and planets. They are by far the most abundant elements in the universe.

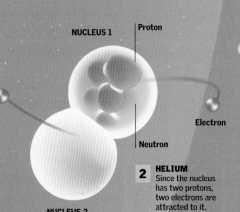

NUCLEUS 1

Proton

Electron

Neutron

NUCLEUS 2

1 HYDROGEN
An electron is attracted by and orbits the nucleus, which has a proton and a neutron.

2 HELIUM
Since the nucleus has two protons, two electrons are attracted to it.

3 CARBON
With time, heavier and more complex elements were formed. Carbon, the key to human life, has six protons in its nucleus and six electrons orbiting it.

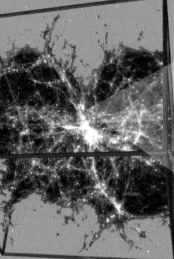

3 **FILAMENT NETWORKS**
The universe has large-scale filaments that contain millions and millions of galaxies.

THE UNIVERSE TODAY

Irregular galaxy

Star cluster

Star

Nebula

Spiral galaxy

Quasar

Barred spiral galaxy

Elliptical galaxy

Galaxy cluster

9.1 billion
THE EARTH IS CREATED
Like the rest of the planets, the Earth is made of material that remained after the formation of the Sun. The Earth is the only planet known to have life.

9 billion

-432°F (-258°C)

10 Nine billion years after the Big Bang, the solar system emerged. A mass of gas and dust collapsed until it gave rise to the Sun. Later the planetary system was formed from the leftover material.

13.7 billion

-454°F (-270°C)

11 The universe continues to expand. Countless galaxies are surrounded by dark matter, which represents 22 percent of the mass and energy in the universe. The ordinary matter, of which stars and planets are made, represents just 4 percent of the total. The predominant form of energy is also of an unknown type. Called "dark energy," it constitutes 74 percent of the total mass and energy.

TIMESCALE

The vast span of time related to the history of the universe can be readily understood if it is scaled to correspond to a single year—a year that spans the beginning of the universe, the appearance of humans on the Earth, and the voyage of Columbus to America. On January 1 of this imaginary year—at midnight—the big bang takes place. *Homo sapiens* appear at 11:56 P.M. on December 31, and Columbus sets sail on the last second of the last day of the year. One second on this timescale is equivalent to 500 true years.

BIG BANG
occurs on the first second of the first day of the year.

THE SOLAR SYSTEM
is created on August 24 of this timescale.

COLUMBUS'S ARRIVAL
takes place on the last second of December 31.

JANUARY

DECEMBER

Anatomy of Galaxies

Galaxies are rotating groups of stars, gas, and dust. More than 200 years ago, philosopher Immanuel Kant postulated that nebulae were island-universes of distant stars. Even though astronomers now know that galaxies are held together by gravitational force, they have not been able to decipher what reasons might be behind galaxies' many shapes. The various types of galaxies range from ovals of old stars to spirals with arms of young stars and bright gases. The center of a galaxy has the greatest accumulation of stars. The Milky Way Galaxy is now known to be so big that rays of light, which travel at 186,000 miles (300,000 km) per second, take 100,000 years to cross from one end to the other.

Star Cities

The first galaxies formed 100 million years after the big bang. Billions of these great conglomerates of stars can be found throughout space. The two most important discoveries concerning galaxies are attributed to the astronomer Edwin Hubble. In 1926, he pointed out that the spots, or patches, of light visible in the night sky were actually distant galaxies. Hubble's discovery put an end to the view held by astronomers at the time that the Milky Way constituted the universe. In 1929, as a result of various observations of the spectrum of light radiated by the stars in the galaxies, Hubble noted that the light from the galaxies showed a redshift (Doppler effect). This effect indicated that the galaxies were moving away from the Milky Way Galaxy. Hubble concluded that the universe is expanding. But the expansion of the universe does not imply that galaxies are growing in numbers. On the contrary, galaxies can collide and

COLLISION
300 million light-years from the Earth, these two colliding galaxies form a pair. Together they are called "The Mice" for the large tail of stars emanating from each galaxy. With time, these galaxies will fuse into a single, larger one. It is believed that in the future the universe will consist of a few giant stars.

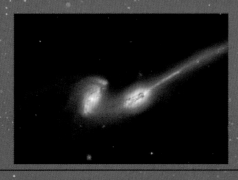

1

1.2 BILLION YEARS
ago, the Antennae (NGC 4038 and NGC 4039) were two separate spiral galaxies.

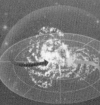

2

300 MILLION YEARS
later, the galaxies collided at great speed.

MILKY WAY

Seen from its side, the Milky Way looks like a flattened disk, swollen at the center. Around the disk is a spherical region, called a "halo", containing dark matter and globular clusters of stars. From June to September, the Milky Way is especially bright, something that would make it more visible viewed from above than from the side.

CLASSIFYING GALAXIES ACCORDING TO HUBBLE

ELLIPTICAL

These galaxies are elliptical in shape and have little dust and gas. Their masses fall within a wide range.

SPIRAL

In a spiral galaxy, a nucleus of old stars is surrounded by a flat disk of stars and two or more spiral arms.

IRREGULAR

Irregular galaxies have no defined shape and cannot be classified. They contain a large amount of gases and dust clouds.

SUBCLASSIFICATIONS

E0   E3   E5   E7

SUBCLASSIFICATIONS

Galaxies are subdivided into different categories according to their tendency toward round shapes (in the case of elliptical galaxies), as well as by the presence of an axis and the length of their arms (in the case of spiral and barred spiral galaxies). An E0 galaxy is elliptical but almost circular, and an E7 galaxy is a flattened oval. An Sa galaxy has a large central axis and coiled arms, and an Sc galaxy has a thinner axis and more extended arms.

Galactic Clusters

Galaxies are objects that tend to form groups or clusters. Acting in response to gravitational force, they can form clusters of galaxies of anywhere from two to thousands of galaxies. These clusters have various shapes and are thought to expand when they join together. Abell 2151 (The Hercules cluster), shown here, is located approximately 500 million light-years from Earth. Each dot represents a galaxy that includes billions of stars.

merge. When two galaxies collide, they can distort each other in various ways. Over time, there are fewer and fewer galaxies. Some galaxies exhibit very peculiar shapes. The Sombrero Galaxy, shown above in the center of the page, has a bright white core surrounded by thin spiral arms.

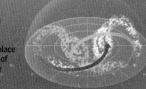

3

300 MILLION YEARS
go by until the collision takes place and the shapes of the galaxies are distorted.

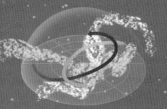

4

300 MILLION YEARS
later, the stars in the spiral arms are expelled from both galaxies.

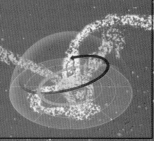

5

NOW
two jets of expelled stars stretch far from the original galaxies.

Stellar Metropolis

For a long time, our galaxy (called the Milky Way because of its resemblance to a stream of milk in the night sky) was a true enigma. It was Galileo Galilei who, in 1610, first pointed a telescope at the Milky Way and saw that the weak whitish strip was composed of thousands and thousands of stars that appeared to almost touch each other. Little by little, astronomers began to realize that all these stars, like our own Sun, were part of the enormous ensemble—the galaxy that is our stellar metropolis.

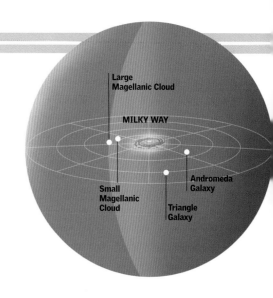

Large Magellanic Cloud

MILKY WAY

Small Magellanic Cloud

Andromeda Galaxy

Triangle Galaxy

Structure of the Milky Way

The Milky Way, containing more than 100 billion stars, has two spiral arms rotating around its core. The Sagittarius arm, located between the Orion arm and the center of the Milky Way, holds one of the most luminous stars in the galaxy, Eta Carinae. The Perseus arm, the main outer arm of the Milky Way, contains young stars and nebulae. The Orion arm, extending between Perseus and Sagittarius, houses the solar system within its inner border. The Orion arm of the Milky Way is a veritable star factory, where gaseous interstellar material can give birth to billions of stars. Remnants of stars can also be found within it.

Rotation

The speeds of the rotation of the various parts of the Milky Way vary according to those parts' distances from the core of the galaxy. The greatest number of stars is concentrated in the region between the Milky Way's core and its border. Here the speed of rotation is much greater because of the attraction that the objects in this region feel from the billions of stars within it.

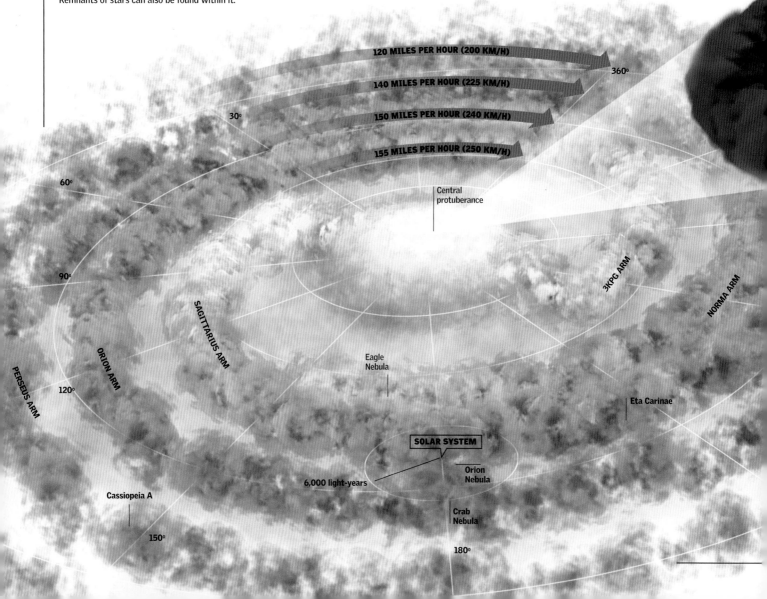

120 MILES PER HOUR (200 KM/H)

140 MILES PER HOUR (225 KM/H)

150 MILES PER HOUR (240 KM/H)

155 MILES PER HOUR (250 KM/H)

360°

30°

Central protuberance

60°

90°

3KPG ARM

NORMA ARM

SAGITTARIUS ARM

120°

ORION ARM

PERSEUS ARM

Eagle Nebula

Eta Carinae

SOLAR SYSTEM

Orion Nebula

6,000 light-years

Cassiopeia A

Crab Nebula

150°

180°

Central Region

Because the Milky Way is full of clouds of dust and rock particles, its center cannot be seen from outside the galaxy. The Milky Way's center can be seen only through telescopes that record infrared light, radio waves, or X-rays, which can pass through the material that blocks visible light. The central axis of the Milky Way contains ancient stars, some 14 billion years old, and exhibits intense activity within its interior, where two clouds of hot gas have been found: Sagittarius A and B. In the central region, but outside the core, a giant dark cloud contains 70 different types of molecules. These gas clouds are associated with violent activity in the center of our galaxy and contain the heart of the Milky Way within their depths. In general, the stars in this region are cold and range in color from red to orange.

HOT GASES
The hot gases originating from the surface of the central region may be the result of violent explosions in the accretion disk.

BRIGHT STARS
Bright stars are born from gas that is not absorbed by the black hole. Most of them are young.

BLACK HOLE
Many astronomers believe that a black hole occupies the center of the Milky Way. Its strong gravitational force would trap gases in orbit around it.

SAGITTARIUS B2
The largest dark cloud in the central region of the Milky Way, Sagittarius B2 contains enough alcohol to cover the entire Earth.

MAGNETISM
The center of the Milky Way is surrounded by strong magnetic fields, perhaps from a rotating black hole.

GAS SPIRALS
A ring of gas spirals around the galaxy's center. Its speed demonstrates that the gas is trapped by a strong gravitational force, which is much more powerful than the gravity of stars in the core.

The Exact Center

The core of the Milky Way galaxy is marked by very intense radio-wave activity that might be produced by an accretion disk made up of incandescent gas surrounding a massive black hole. The region of Sagittarius A, discovered in 1994, is a gas ring that rotates at very high speed, swirling within several light-years of the center of the galaxy. The speed of its rotation is an indication of the powerful gravitational force exerted from the center of the Milky Way, a force stronger than would be produced by the stars located in the region. The hot, blue stars that shine in the center of the Milky Way may have been born from gas not yet absorbed by the black hole.

270°

OUTER RING
A ring of dark clouds of dust and molecules that is expanding as a result of a giant explosion. It is suspected that a small object in the central region of the Milky Way might be its source.

A Diverse Galaxy

The brightest portion of the Milky Way that appears in photographs taken with optical lenses (using visible light) is in the constellation Sagittarius, which appears to lie in the direction of the center of the Milky Way. The bright band in the nighttime sky is made up of stars so numerous that it is almost impossible to count them. In some cases, stars are obscured by dense dust clouds that make some regions of the Milky Way seem truly dark. The objects that can be found in the Milky Way are not all of one type. Some, such as those known as the "halo population", are old and are distributed within a sphere around the galaxy. Other objects form a more flattened structure called the "disk population." In the spiral arm population, we find the youngest objects in the Milky Way. In these arms, gas and interstellar dust abound.

CARINA ARM

240°

OUTER ARM

10°

100,000
LIGHT-YEARS
The diameter of the Milky Way is large in comparison with other galaxies but not gigantic.

THE MILKY WAY IN VISIBLE LIGHT

THE CONSTELLATION SAGITTARIUS
Close to the center of the Milky Way, Sagittarius shines intensely.

DARK REGIONS
Dark regions are produced by dense clouds that obscure the light of stars.

SECTORS
Many different sectors make up the Milky Way.

STARS
So many stars compose the Milky Way that it is impossible for us to distinguish them all.

A Very Warm Heart

The Sun at the center of the solar system is a source of light and heat. This energy is produced by the fusion of atomic hydrogen nuclei, which generate helium nuclei. The energy that emanates from the Sun travels through space and initially encounters the bodies that populate the solar system. The Sun shines thanks to thermonuclear fusion, and it will continue to shine until its supply of hydrogen runs out in about six or seven billion years.

Very Gassy

The Sun is a giant ball of gases with very high density and temperature. Its main components are hydrogen (90%) and helium (9%). The balance of its mass is made up of trace elements, such as carbon, nitrogen, and oxygen, among others. Because of the conditions of extreme temperature and pressure on the Sun, these elements are in a plasma state.

CHARACTERISTICS

CONVENTIONAL PLANET SYMBOL

ESSENTIAL DATA

Average distance from Earth	**93 million miles (150 million km)**
Equatorial diameter	**864,000 miles (1,391,000 km)**
Mass*	**332,900**
Gravity*	**28**
Density	**0.81 ounce per cubic inch (1.4 g per cu cm)**
Average temperature	**9,932°F (5,500°C)**
Atmosphere	**Dense**
Moons	**None**

*In both cases, Earth = 1

CONVECTIVE ZONE extends from the base of the photosphere down to a depth of 15 percent of the solar radius. Here energy is transported up toward the surface by gas currents (through convection).

RADIATIVE ZONE This portion of the Sun is traversed by particles coming from the core. A proton can take a million years to cross this zone.

14,400,000°F
(8,000,000°C)

Nuclear Fusion Of Hydrogen

The extraordinary temperature of the nuclear core helps the hydrogen nuclei join. Under conditions of lower energy, they repel each other, but the conditions at the center of the Sun can overcome the repulsive forces, and nuclear fusion occurs. For every four hydrogen nuclei, a series of nuclear reactions produce one helium nucleus.

1 NUCLEAR COLLISION Two hydrogen nuclei (two protons) collide and remain joined. One changes into a neutron, and deuterium forms, releasing a neutrino, a positron, and a lot of energy.

Proton
Positron
Neutrino
Neutron

Deuterium

Photon

2 PHOTONS The deuterium formed collides with a proton. This collision releases one photon. This high-energy photon needs 30,000 years to reach the photosphere.

HELIUM NUCLEUS

Deuterium 1
Deuterium 2

3 HELIUM NUCLEI The group of two protons and a neutron collides with another such group. A helium nucleus forms, and a pair of protons is released.

Proton 1
Proton 2

Surface and Atmosphere

The visible portion of the Sun is a sphere of light, or "photosphere," made of boiling gases emanating from the solar core. The gas flares form plasma, which passes through this layer. Later the gas flares enter a vast gas layer called the "solar atmosphere." The density of this layer decreases toward its outermost region. Above the photosphere lies the solar atmosphere—the chromosphere and the corona. The energy generated at the core moves through the surface of the photosphere and solar atmosphere for thousands of years in search of an exit into space.

SUNSPOTS
are regions of gases that are generally colder (7,232°F [4,000°C]) than the photosphere (10,112°F [5,600°C]). For that reason, they appear dark.

PENUMBRA
Peripheral region. It is hotter and brighter than the umbra.

PHOTOSPHERE
The visible surface of the Sun, a boiling tide, is thick with gases in a plasma state. In its uppermost layer, its density decreases and its transparency increases, and the solar radiation escapes from the Sun as light. The spectrographic study of this layer has allowed scientists to confirm that the main components of the Sun are hydrogen and helium.

10,112°F (5,600°C)

UMBRA
Central region. It is the coldest and darkest part.

900,000°F (500,000°C)
Maximum temperature of the chromosphere

CHROMOSPHERE
Above the photosphere, and of less density, lies the chromosphere, a layer 3,110 miles (5,000 km) thick. Its temperature ranges from 8,100°F (4,500°C) to 900,000° F (500,000°C) with increasing altitude.

CORE
The core occupies only 2 percent of the total volume of the Sun, but in it is concentrated about half the total mass of the Sun. The great pressures and temperatures in the core produce thermonuclear fusion.

27,000,000°F (15,000,000°C)

SPICULES
Vertical jets of gas that spew from the chromosphere, usually reaching 6,200 miles (10,000 km) in height. They originate in upper convection cells and can rise as high as the corona.

MACROSPICULES
This type of vertical eruption is similar to a spicule, but it usually reaches up to 25,000 miles (40,250 km) in height.

1,800,000°F (1,000,000°C)
The temperature in the corona

CORONA
Located above the chromosphere, it extends millions of miles into space and reaches temperatures nearing 1,800,000°F (1,000,000°C). It has some holes, or low-density regions, through which gases flow into the solar wind.

SOLAR WIND
Consists of a flux of ions emitted by the solar atmosphere. The composition is similar to that of the corona. The Sun loses approximately 1,800 pounds (816 kg) of matter per second in the form of solar wind.

SOLAR PROMINENCES
Clouds and layers of gas from the chromosphere travel thousands of miles until they reach the corona, where the influence of magnetic fields causes them to take on the shape of an arc or wave.

SOLAR FLARES
These eruptions come out of the solar atmosphere and can interfere with radio communications on Earth.

Our Nearest Neighbors

This chapter will help you become better acquainted with our neighbors in the solar system—the other planets—and the most important characteristics that distinguish them. All this information that explores the mysteries of space is accompanied by recent images captured by the newest telescopes. They

reveal many details about the planets and their satellites, such as the volcanoes and craters found on the surface of some of them. Certainly, the opportunity to compare other worlds near to ours will help us understand that for the time being there is no better place than the Earth to live.

Attracted by a Star

P lanets and their satellites, asteroids and other rocky objects, and an incalculable number of comet-like objects, some more than 1 trillion miles (1.6 trillion km) from the Sun, make up the solar system. In the 17th century, astronomer Johannes Kepler proposed a model to interpret the dynamic properties of the bodies of the solar system. According to this interpretation, the planets complete elliptical trajectories, called "orbits," around the Sun. In every case, the movement is produced by the influence of the gravitational field of the Sun. Today, as part of a rapidly developing field of astronomy, it is known that planet or planet-like bodies also orbit other stars.

Outer Planets

◢ Planets located outside the asteroid belt. They are enormous gas spheres with small solid cores. They have very low temperatures because of their great distance from the Sun. The presence of ring systems is exclusive to these planets. The greatest of them is Jupiter: 1,300 Earths could fit inside it. Its mass is 2.5 times as great as that of the rest of the planets combined.

ORBITS

In general, the planets orbit in one common plane, called the "ecliptic."

Earth's orbit
Venus's orbit
Mercury's orbit
Mars's orbit
Main belt

Jupiter's orbit
Saturn's orbit
Uranus's orbit
Neptune's orbit

The rotation of most planets around their own axes is in counterclockwise direction. Venus and Uranus, however, revolve clockwise.

NEPTUNE
DIAMETER   30,775 MILES (49,528 KM)
MOONS   13

Triton   Proteus   Nereid

URANUS
DIAMETER   31,763 MILES (51,118 KM)
MOONS   27

Titania   Oberon   Umbriel   Ariel   Miranda   Puck

SATURN
DIAMETER   74,898 MILES (120,537 KM)
MOONS   50+

Titan   Rhea   Iapetus   Tethys

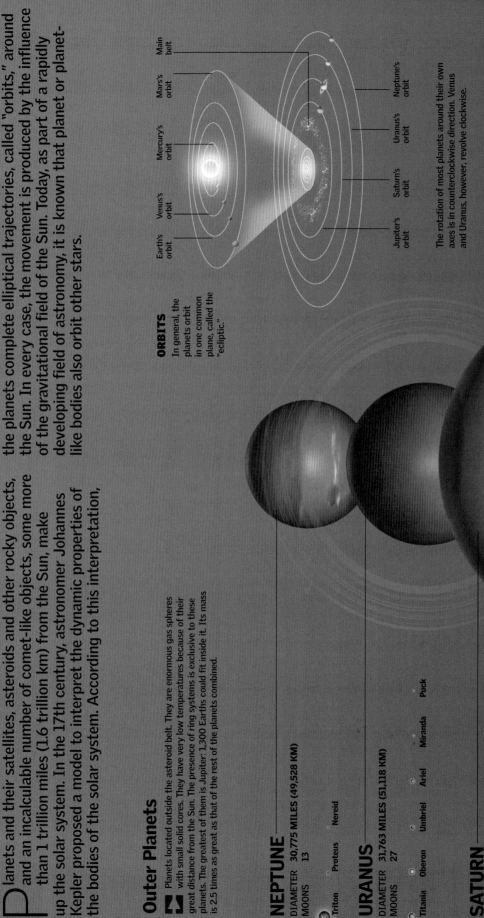

Early ideas suggested that the planets formed gradually, beginning with the binding of hot dust particles. Today, scientists suggest that the planets originated from the collision and melding of larger-sized bodies, called "planetesimals."

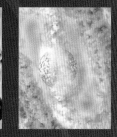

1 ORIGIN

Remains from the formation of the Sun created a disk of gas and dust around it, from which the planetesimals formed.

2 COLLISION

Through collisions among themselves, planetesimals of different sizes joined together to become more massive objects.

3 HEAT

The collisions produced a large amount of heat that accumulated in the interior of the planets, according to their distance from the Sun.

SOLAR GRAVITY

The gravitational pull of the Sun upon the planets not only keeps them inside the solar system, but also influences the speed with which they revolve in their orbits around the Sun. Those closest to the Sun revolve in their orbits much faster than those farther from it.

JUPITER

DIAMETER 88,846 MILES (142,984 KM)
MOONS 60+

Ganymede Callisto Io Europa

Asteroid Belt

The border between the outer and inner planets is marked by millions of rocky fragments of various sizes that form a band called the asteroid belt. Their orbits are influenced by the gravitational pull exerted on them by the giant planet Jupiter. This effect also keeps them from merging and forming a planet.

Inner Planets

Planets located inside the asteroid belt. They are solid bodies in which internal geologic phenomena, such as volcanism, which can modify their surfaces, are produced. Almost all of them have an appreciable atmosphere of some degree of thickness, according to individual circumstances, which plays a key role in the surface temperatures of each planet.

MARS

DIAMETER 4,217 MILES (6,787 KM)
MOONS 2

Phobos Deimos

EARTH

DIAMETER 7,926 MILES (12,756 KM)
MOONS 1

MOON

VENUS

DIAMETER 7,520 MILES (12,103 KM)
MOONS 0

MERCURY

DIAMETER 3,031 MILES (4,878 KM)
MOONS 0

S U N

Mercury, an Inferno

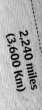

M ercury is the planet nearest to the Sun and is therefore the one that
has to withstand the harshest of the Sun's effects. Due to its proximity to the Sun,
Mercury moves at great speed in its solar orbit, completing an orbit every 88 days. It has
almost no atmosphere, and its surface is dry and rugged, covered with craters caused by the impact
of numerous meteorites; this makes it resemble the Moon. Numerous faults, formed during the
cooling of the planet when it was young, are also visible on the surface. Constantly baked by its
neighbor, the Sun, Mercury has an average surface temperature of 333°F (167°C).

A Scar-covered Surface

The surface of Mercury is very similar to that of the Moon. It is possible to find
craters of varying sizes. The largest one has a diameter of some 810 miles (1,300
km). There are also hills and valleys. In 1991, radio telescopes were able to detect possible
evidence of the presence of frozen water in Mercury's polar regions, information that
Mariner 10 had been unable to gather. *Mariner 10*, the only mission sent to Mercury,
flew by the planet three times between 1974 and 1975. The polar ice was found at
the bottom of very deep craters, which limit the ice's exposure to the Sun's rays.
The spacecraft *Messenger*, launched in 2004, has since March 17, 2011, circled
Mercury twice a day and collected thousands of images to provide new
information about Mercury's surface and magnetic field.

CALORIS CRATER
The largest impact crater in the
solar system, it has a diameter of
810 miles (1,300 km).

The crater
was
flooded
with lava.

When the projectile that formed
the crater struck, Mercury was still
forming. The extensive waves that
extended from the site of impact
formed hills and mountain ranges.

BEETHOVEN
is the second largest crater
on Mercury. It is 400 miles
(644 km) in diameter. Its floor
was flooded by lava and later
marked by meteorite impacts.

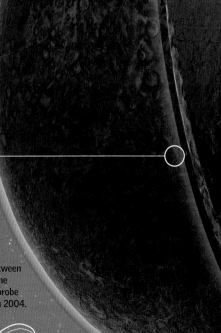

330 miles
(530 km)

2,240 miles
(3,600 km)

Missions to Mercury

The space probe *Mariner 10* was the first to reach Mercury. Between
1974 and 1975, the craft flew by the planet three times and came
within about 200 miles (320 km) of the surface. *Messenger*, a space probe
scheduled to study Mercury between 2008 and 2011, was launched in 2004.

MARINER 10

MESSENGER
The probe passed by
Mercury twice in 2008
and once in 2009 before
beginning to orbit the planet.
On March 18, 2010 —
starting at 12:45 a.m. UTC—
Messenger transitioned from
orbiting the Sun to being the
first spacecraft ever to orbit
the planet Mercury.

Composition and Magnetic Field

Like the Earth, Mercury has a magnetic field, although a much weaker one. The magnetism results from its enormous core made of solid iron. The mantle that surrounds the core is believed to be a fine layer of iron and sulfur.

29%
Sodium

22%
Hydrogen

6%
Helium

43%
Others

EXTREMELY THIN ATMOSPHERE

Mercury's atmosphere is almost nonexistent and consists of a very thin layer that cannot protect the planet either from the Sun or from meteorites. During the day, when Mercury is closer to the Sun, the planet's temperature can surpass 842°F (450°C). At night, temperatures can plummet to -297°F (-183°C).

During the night, the heat of Mercury's rocks is lost rapidly, and the planet's temperature drops.

During the day, the Sun directly heats the rock.

-297°F
(-183°C)

842°F
(450°C)

CRUST
Made of silicate rocks, Mercury's crust is similar to the crust and mantle of the Earth. It has a thickness of approximately 60 miles (100 km).

CORE
Dense, large, and made of iron, its diameter may be as great as 2,240 to 2,300 miles (3,700–3,800 km).

MANTLE
Made up mostly of silica-based rocks

333°F
(167°C)

Baked by its neighbor the Sun, Mercury is the planet with the greatest thermal fluctuations in the solar system. Its average temperature is 333°F (167°C), but when it gets closer to the Sun, the temperature can climb to 842° F (450°C). At night, it drops to -297°F (-183°C).

CHARACTERISTICS

**CONVENTIONAL
PLANET SYMBOL**

ESSENTIAL DATA

Average distance from the Sun	**36,000,000 miles (57,900,000 km)**
Solar orbit (Mercurian year)	**88 days 00 hours**
Equatorial diameter	**3,032 miles (4,880 km)**
Orbital speed	**29.75 miles per second (47.87 km/s)**
Mass*	**0.06**
Gravity*	**0.38**
Density	**3.14 ounces per cubic inch (5.43 g/cu cm)**
Average temperature	**333°F (167°C)**
Atmosphere	**Almost nonexistent**
Lunas	

*In both cases, Earth = 1

AXIS INCLINATION

0.1°
One rotation lasts 59 days.

Rotation and Orbit

Mercury rotates slowly on its axis and takes approximately 59 Earth days to complete a turn, but it only needs 88 days to travel in its orbit. To an observer in Mercury, these two combined motions would give a combined interval of 176 days between two sunrises. A person observing the sunrise from position 1 would have to wait for the planet to make two orbits around the Sun and make three rotations on its own axis before seeing the next sunrise.

ORBIT OF MERCURY AROUND THE SUN

3 2

4

1

SUN

5

6 7

Each number corresponds to a position of the Sun in the sky as seen from Mercury.

VIEW FROM MERCURY

3 Reaches the zenith (noon) and stops

4 Recedes a bit

5 Stops again

6 Resumes its original path toward the horizon

7 Decreases toward the sunset

2 Rises and increases its size

1 The Sun rises.

HORIZON OF MERCURY

Venus, Our Neighbor

Venus is the second closest planet to the Sun. Similar in size to the Earth, it has a volcanic surface, as well as a hostile atmosphere governed by the effects of carbon dioxide. Although about four billion years ago the atmospheres of the Earth and Venus were similar, the mass of Venus's atmosphere today is 100 times greater than the Earth's. Its thick clouds of sulfuric acid and dust are so dense that stars are invisible from the planet's surface. Viewed from the Earth, Venus can be bright enough to be visible during the day and second only to the moon in brightness at night. Because of this, the movements of Venus were well-known by most ancient civilizations.

CHARACTERISTICS

CONVENTIONAL PLANET SYMBOL ♀

ESSENTIAL DATA

Average distance from the Sun	67,000,000 miles (108,000,000 km)
Solar orbit (Venusian year)	224 days 17 hours
Equatorial diameter	7,520 miles (12,100 km)
Orbital speed	22 miles per second (35 km/s)
Mass*	0.8
Gravity*	0.9
Density	3.03 ounces per cubic inch (5.24 g/cu cm)
Average temperature	860°F (460°C)
Atmosphere	Very thick
Moons	None

*In both cases, Earth = 1

AXIS INCLINATION

177°

Rotates on its own axis every 243 days.

GREENHOUSE EFFECT
Only 20 percent of the Sun's light reaches the surface of Venus. The thick clouds of dust, sulfuric acid, and carbon dioxide that constitute Venus's atmosphere reflect the remaining light, leaving Venus in permanent darkness.

SOLAR RADIATION
Venus is kept hot by its thick atmosphere, which retains the energy of the Sun's rays.

864°F (462°C)

INFRARED RAYS
The surface of Venus radiates infrared radiation. Only 20 percent of the Sun's rays pass through Venus's thick clouds of sulfuric acid.

Composition

The overwhelming presence of carbon dioxide in the Venusian atmosphere induces a greenhouse effect, increasing the surface temperature to 864° F (462°C). Because of this, Venus is hotter than Mercury, even though Venus is farther from the Sun and reflects all but 20 percent of the Sun's light. The surface temperature of Venus is relatively constant, averaging 860° F (460°C). The atmospheric pressure on Venus is 90 times greater than that on the Earth.

ATMOSPHERE
Venus's glowing appearance is caused by the planet's thick, suffocating atmosphere, which is made up of carbon dioxide and sulfuric clouds that reflect sunlight.

60 miles (100 km)

IS THE THICKNESS OF THE ATMOSPHERE.

Carbon dioxide **97%**

Nitrogen and traces of other gases **3%**

SULFURIC ACID

Venus lacks water. A U.S. robot probe sent to Venus in 1978 found some evidence that water vapor could have existed in the atmosphere hundreds of millions of years ago, but today no trace of water remains.

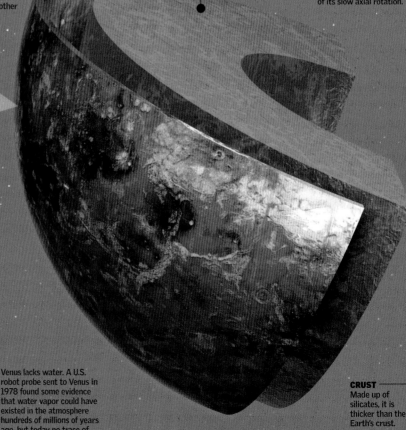

MANTLE
Made of molten rock, it constitutes most of the planet. It traps the solar radiation and is 1,860 miles (3,000 km) thick.

14,400°F (8,000°C)

CORE
It is believed that Venus's core is similar to the Earth's, containing metallic elements (iron and nickel) and silicates. Venus has no magnetic field—possibly because of its slow axial rotation.

CRUST
Made up of silicates, it is thicker than the Earth's crust.

VENUS'S PHASES

As Venus revolves around the Sun, its solar illumination varies as is seen from the Earth depending upon its position in relation to the Sun and the Earth. Thus, Venus has phases similar to the Moon's. During its elongations, when Venus is farthest from the Sun in the sky, Venus appears at its brightest.

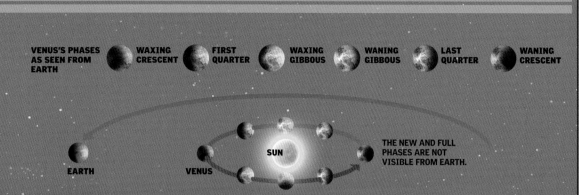

VENUS'S PHASES AS SEEN FROM EARTH

WAXING CRESCENT

FIRST QUARTER

WAXING GIBBOUS

WANING GIBBOUS

LAST QUARTER

WANING CRESCENT

EARTH

VENUS

SUN

THE NEW AND FULL PHASES ARE NOT VISIBLE FROM EARTH.

Surface

The Venusian surface has not remained the same throughout its life. The current one is some 500 million years old, but the rocky landscape visible today was formed by intense volcanic activity. Volcanic rock covers 85 percent of the planet. The entire planet is crisscrossed by vast plains and enormous rivers of lava, as well as a number of mountains. The lava flows have created a great number of grooves, some of which are very wide. The brightness of Venus's surface is the result of metallic compounds.

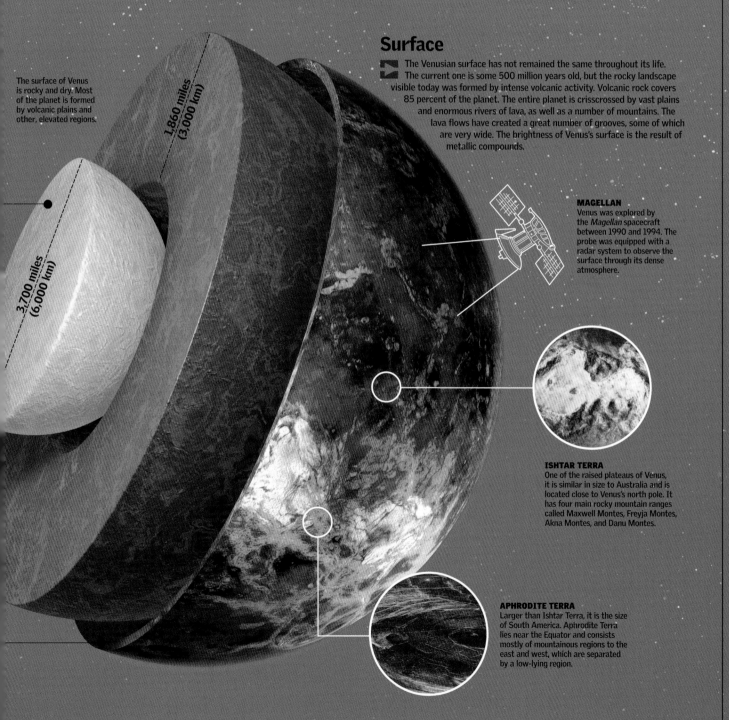

The surface of Venus is rocky and dry. Most of the planet is formed by volcanic plains and other, elevated regions.

1,860 miles (3,000 km)

3,700 miles (6,000 km)

MAGELLAN
Venus was explored by the *Magellan* spacecraft between 1990 and 1994. The probe was equipped with a radar system to observe the surface through its dense atmosphere.

ISHTAR TERRA
One of the raised plateaus of Venus, it is similar in size to Australia and is located close to Venus's north pole. It has four main rocky mountain ranges called Maxwell Montes, Freyja Montes, Akna Montes, and Danu Montes.

APHRODITE TERRA
Larger than Ishtar Terra, it is the size of South America. Aphrodite Terra lies near the Equator and consists mostly of mountainous regions to the east and west, which are separated by a low-lying region.

Red and Fascinating

Mars is the fourth planet from the Sun. Of all the planets, Mars most closely resembles the Earth. It has polar ice caps, and the tilt of its axis, period of rotation, and internal structure are similar to those of the Earth. Known as the "Red Planet" because of the reddish iron oxide that covers its surface, Mars has a thin atmosphere composed essentially of carbon dioxide. Mars does not have water, though it did in the past, and there is evidence some water might exist underground. Many spacecraft have been sent to explore Mars, in part because it is the planet other than Earth most likely to have developed some form of life, and it will probably be the first planet humans leave the Earth to visit.

Martian Orbit

Because Mars's orbit is more elliptical than that of Earth, Mars's distance from the Sun varies widely. At its perihelion, or closest approach to the Sun, Mars receives 45 percent more solar radiation than at its aphelion, or farthest point. Temperatures on Mars range from -220°F to 63°F (-140°C to 17°C).

-220°F
(-140°C)
IN WINTER

SUN   EARTH   MARS

63°F
(17°C)
IN SUMMER

Composition

Mars, a rocky planet, has an iron-rich core. Mars is almost half the size of the Earth and has a similar period of rotation, as well as clearly evident clouds, winds, and other weather phenomena. Its thin atmosphere is made up of carbon dioxide, and its red color comes from its soil, which is rich in iron oxide.

CRUST
is thin and made up of solid rock. It is 31 miles (50 km) thick.

Moons

Mars has two moons, Phobos and Deimos. Both have a lower density than Mars and are pitted with craters. Phobos has a diameter of 17 miles (27 km), and Deimos has a diameter of 9 miles (15 km). Deimos orbits Mars in 30 hours at an altitude of 14,627 miles (23,540 km), and Phobos orbits Mars in eight hours at an altitude of 5,840 miles (9,400 km). Astronomers believe that the moons are asteroids that were captured by Mars's gravity.

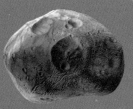

DEIMOS

DIAMETER	9 MILES (15 KM)
DISTANCE FROM MARS	14,627 MILES (23,540 KM)

PHOBOS

DIAMETER	17 MILES (27 KM)
DISTANCE FROM MARS	5,840 MILES (9,400 KM)

Terra Sirenum

MISSIONS TO MARS
After our own Moon, Mars has been a more attractive target for exploratory missions than any other object in the solar system.

1965 MARINER 4
The first mission sent to Mars, it made only brief flyovers.

1969 MARINER 6 AND 7
studied the southern hemisphere and equator of Mars.

1971 MARINER 9
photographed the Olympus volcano for the first time.

1973 MARS 4, MARS 5, MARS 6, AND MARS 7
Russian spacecraft successfully sent to Mars

1976 VIKING 1 AND 2
searched for traces of life. They were the first spacecraft to land on Martian soil.

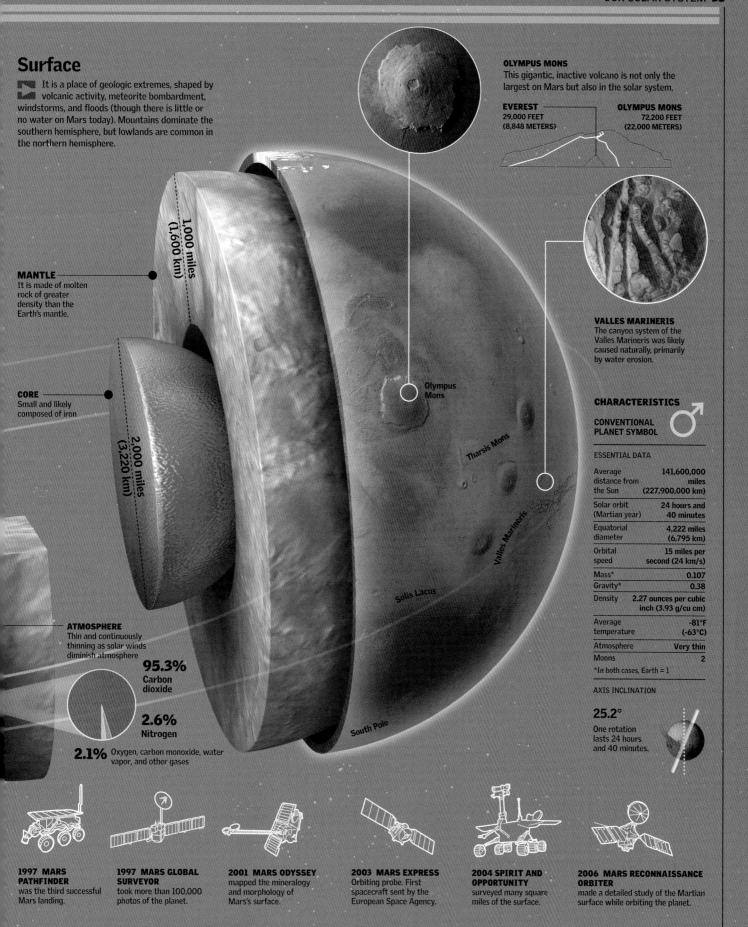

Surface

It is a place of geologic extremes, shaped by volcanic activity, meteorite bombardment, windstorms, and floods (though there is little or no water on Mars today). Mountains dominate the southern hemisphere, but lowlands are common in the northern hemisphere.

OLYMPUS MONS
This gigantic, inactive volcano is not only the largest on Mars but also in the solar system.

EVEREST
29,000 FEET
(8,848 METERS)

OLYMPUS MONS
72,200 FEET
(22,000 METERS)

MANTLE
It is made of molten rock of greater density than the Earth's mantle.

1,000 miles
(1,600 km)

CORE
Small and likely composed of iron

2,000 miles
(3,220 km)

VALLES MARINERIS
The canyon system of the Valles Marineris was likely caused naturally, primarily by water erosion.

Olympus Mons

Tharsis Mons

Valles Marineris

Solis Lacus

South Pole

CHARACTERISTICS

CONVENTIONAL PLANET SYMBOL ♂

ESSENTIAL DATA

Average distance from the Sun	141,600,000 miles (227,900,000 km)
Solar orbit (Martian year)	24 hours and 40 minutes
Equatorial diameter	4,222 miles (6,795 km)
Orbital speed	15 miles per second (24 km/s)
Mass*	0.107
Gravity*	0.38
Density	2.27 ounces per cubic inch (3.93 g/cu cm)
Average temperature	-81°F (-63°C)
Atmosphere	Very thin
Moons	2

*In both cases, Earth = 1

AXIS INCLINATION

25.2°
One rotation lasts 24 hours and 40 minutes.

ATMOSPHERE
Thin and continuously thinning as solar winds diminish atmosphere

95.3%
Carbon dioxide

2.6%
Nitrogen

2.1% Oxygen, carbon monoxide, water vapor, and other gases

1997 MARS PATHFINDER
was the third successful Mars landing.

1997 MARS GLOBAL SURVEYOR
took more than 100,000 photos of the planet.

2001 MARS ODYSSEY
mapped the mineralogy and morphology of Mars's surface.

2003 MARS EXPRESS
Orbiting probe. First spacecraft sent by the European Space Agency.

2004 SPIRIT AND OPPORTUNITY
surveyed many square miles of the surface.

2006 MARS RECONNAISSANCE ORBITER
made a detailed study of the Martian surface while orbiting the planet.

Jupiter, Gas Giant

Jupiter is the largest planet in the solar system. Its diameter is 11 times that of the Earth, and its mass is 300 times as great. Because the speed of Jupiter's rotation flattens the planet at its poles, its equatorial diameter is greater than its polar diameter. Jupiter rotates at 25,000 miles per hour (40,000 km/hr). One of the most distinctive elements of Jupiter's atmosphere is its so-called Great Red Spot, a giant high-pressure region of turbulence that has been observed from the Earth for more than 300 years. The planet is orbited by numerous satellites and has a wide, faint ring of particles.

Composition

Jupiter is a giant ball of hydrogen and helium that have been compressed into liquid in the planet's interior and into metallic rock in its core. Not much is known about Jupiter's core, but it is believed to be bigger than the Earth's core.

INNER MANTLE
Surrounds the core. It is made of liquid metallic hydrogen, an element only found under hot, high-pressure conditions. The inner mantle is a soup of electrons and nuclei.

CHARACTERISTICS

CONVENTIONAL PLANET SYMBOL ♃

ESSENTIAL DATA

Average distance from the Sun	483,000,000 miles (777,300,000 km)
Solar orbit (Jovian year)	11 years 312 days
Equatorial diameter	88,700 miles (142,750 km)
Orbital speed	8 miles per second (13 km/s)
Mass*	318
Gravity*	2.36
Density	0.77 ounce per cubic inch (1.33 g/cu cm)
Average temperature	-184°F (-120°C)
Atmosphere	Very dense
Moons	62

*In both cases, Earth = 1

AXIS INCLINATION

3.1°

One rotation lasts 9 hours and 55 minutes.

ATMOSPHERE
measures 620 miles (1,000 km).

7,500 miles (12,000 km)

28,000 miles (45,000 km)

CORE
Its size is about 10 times larger than the Earth's core.

17,000 (28,000

54,000°F
(30,000°C)

OUTER MANTLE
Made of liquid molecular hydrogen. The outer mantle merges with the atmosphere.

The Moons of Jupiter

Jupiter has 62 moons. Many of them have not been officially confirmed and do not even have names. Jupiter's rotation is gradually slowing because of the moons' tidal effects.

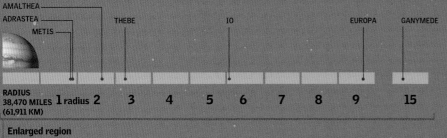

AMALTHEA
ADRASTEA
METIS
THEBE
IO
EUROPA
GANYMEDE

RADIUS
38,470 MILES
(61,911 KM)

1 radius 2 3 4 5 6 7 8 9 15

Enlarged region

CALLISTO
LEDA HIMALIA LYSITHEA ELARA
ANANKE CARME PASIPHAË SINOPE

26   160/63/67   302 322 335/8

GALILEAN MOONS

Of Jupiter's 62 moons, four are visible from Earth with binoculars. These are called the Galilean moons in honor of their discoverer, Galileo Galilei. Astronomers believe that Io has active volcanoes and that Europa has an ocean underneath its icy crust.

EUROPA
2,000 MILES
(3,220 KM)

GANYMEDE
3,270 MILES
(5,263 KM)

IO
2,264 MILES
(3,644 KM)

CALISTO
2,986 MILES
(4,806 KM)

Winds

The winds on Jupiter blow in contiguous bands and opposing directions. The bands' small differences in temperature and chemical composition give the planet its multicolored appearance. Jupiter's inclement environment, in which winds blow at more than 370 miles per hour (600 km/h), can cause large storms, such as the Great Red Spot in the southern hemisphere of the planet. The Great Red Spot, which is 16,155 miles (26,000 km) long, is believed to be composed mainly of ammonia gas and clouds of ice.

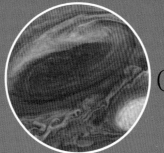

16,160 miles
(26,000 km)

GREAT RED SPOT

RINGS

Jupiter's rings are made of dust from the planet's four inner moons. These rings were first seen in 1979 by the space probe *Voyager 1* and later by *Voyager 2.*

OUTER GOSSAMER RING
INNER GOSSAMER RING
MAIN RING
HALO

RING MATERIAL

JUPITER'S MAGNETISM

Jupiter's magnetic field is 20,000 times stronger than the Earth's. Astronomers believe the field is caused by the electrical currents that are created by the rapid rotation of metallic hydrogen. Jupiter is surrounded by a huge magnetic bubble, the "magnetosphere." The magnetosphere's tail reaches more than 370,000,000 miles (600,000,000 km)—beyond the orbit of Saturn.

ATMOSPHERE
surrounds the inner liquid layers and the solid core. It is 620 miles thick (1,000 km).

Jupiter's magnetosphere is the largest object in the solar system. It varies in size and shape in response to the solar wind, which is composed of the particles continuously radiated from the Sun.

89.8%
Hydrogen

10.2%
HELIUM
With traces of methane and ammonia

400,000,000 miles
(644,000,000 km)

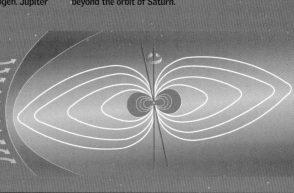

The Lord of the Rings

Saturn is the solar system's second largest planet. Like Jupiter, it is a large ball of gas surrounding a small, solid core. Saturn was the most distant planet discovered before the invention of the telescope. To the naked eye, it looks like a yellowish star, but with the help of a telescope, its rings are clearly visible. Ten times farther from the Sun than the Earth, Saturn is the least dense planet. If an ocean could be found large enough to hold it, Saturn would float.

Rings

Saturn's rings, the brightest rings in the solar system, are made of rock and ice and orbit Saturn's Equator. The rings are probably remains of destroyed comets that were trapped by Saturn's gravitational field.

ENCKE DIVISION
A small gap that separates ring A into two parts

F RING
The farthest visible ring

A RING
Saturn's outer ring

CASSINI DIVISION
3,100 miles (5,000 km) wide, it is located between the A and B rings.

B RING
Saturn's brightest and widest ring

C RING
Saturn's only transparent ring

D RING
The closest ring to the surface of Saturn—so near that it almost touches the planet

RINGS G AND E

310 miles (500 km)

9,100 miles (14,650 km)

15,800 miles (25,430 km)

10,900 miles (17,540 km)

5,300 miles (8,530 km)

2,200 miles (3,540 km)

THICKNESS AND WIDTH
Although Saturn's rings are very wide, their thickness is sometimes less than 33 feet (10 m).

The Moons of Saturn

Saturn has more than 45 moons, making Saturn's family of moons one of the largest in the solar system. The sizes of the moons vary from Titan's 3,200 miles (5,150 km) to tiny Calypso's 10 miles (16 km).

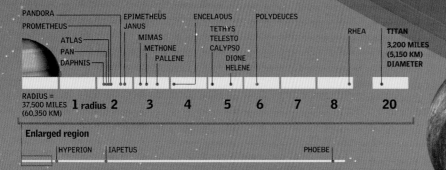

PANDORA
PROMETHEUS
ATLAS
PAN
DAPHNIS

EPIMETHEUS
JANUS
MIMAS
METHONE
PALLENE

ENCELADUS
TETHYS
TELESTO
CALYPSO
DIONE
HELENE

POLYDEUCES

RHEA

TITAN
3,200 MILES (5,150 KM) DIAMETER

RADIUS = 37,500 MILES (60,350 KM)   1 radius   2   3   4   5   6   7   8   20

Enlarged region

HYPERION   IAPETUS   PHOEBE

25   61   220

TITAN
Titan's diameter is larger than Mercury's. It has an atmosphere that is mostly made of nitrogen.

Surface

Like Jupiter, Saturn has a surface of clouds that form bands because of the planet's rotation. Saturn's clouds are less turbulent and less colorful than Jupiter's. The higher, white clouds reach temperatures of -220°F (-140°C). A layer of haze extends above the clouds.

HAZE

WHITE CLOUDS

DEEP AND ORANGE CLOUDS

BLUISH CLOUDS

WINDS
Saturn's winds generally reach speeds of about 220 miles per hour (355 km/h), causing strong storms.

Gaseous Exterior

Saturn and Jupiter differ very little in their composition. Both are gaseous balls surrounding solid cores. What sets Saturn apart are its rings, formed by clustered pieces of ice that range in size from small particles to large chunks. Each particle in a ring is a satellite orbiting Saturn. From the Earth, the massed debris seems to form large structures, but each discrete piece actually has its own orbit.

ATMOSPHERE

<1%
Sulfur gives it a yellowish appearance.

2%
Helium

97%
Hydrogen

COMPONENTS
The main components of Saturn's atmosphere are hydrogen (97%) and helium (2%). The rest is composed of sulfur, methane, and other gases.

CHARACTERISTICS

CONVENTIONAL PLANET SYMBOL ♄

ESSENTIAL DATA

Average distance from the Sun	887,000,000 miles (1,427,000,000 km)
Solar orbit (Saturnine year)	29 years 154 days
Equatorial diameter	74,940 miles (120,600 km)
Orbital speed	6 miles per second (10 km/s)
Mass*	95
Gravity*	0.92
Density	0.4 ounce per cubic inch (0.7 g/cu cm)
Average temperature	-193°F (-125°C)
Atmosphere	Very dense
Moons	More than 45

*In both cases, Earth = 1

AXIS INCLINATION

26.7°
One rotation lasts 10 hours and 39 minutes.

18,600 miles (30,000 km)

OUTER MANTLE
This layer is formed by liquid molecular hydrogen.

ATMOSPHERE
Mainly hydrogen and helium

8,700 miles (14,000 km)

INNER MANTLE
It is made up of liquid metallic hydrogen.

19,900 miles (32,000 km)

CORE
Composed of rock and metallic elements, such as silicates and iron

21,600°F (12,000°C)

Uranus Without Secrets

To the unaided eye, Uranus looks like a star at the limit of visibility. It is the seventh farthest planet from the Sun and the third largest planet in the solar system. One peculiarity distinguishing it from the other planets is its anomalous axis of rotation, tilted nearly 98 degrees around the plane of its orbit, so that one or the other of Uranus's poles points toward the Sun. Astronomers speculate that, during its formation, Uranus may have suffered an impact with a protoplanet, which could have altered Uranus's tilt. Uranus's orbit is so large that the planet takes 84 years to completely orbit the Sun. Uranus's period of rotation is 17 hours and 14 minutes.

Magnetic Field

Uranus generates a magnetic field 50 times more powerful than Earth's. This field is not centered on the planet, but is offset and tilted 60 degrees from Uranus's axis. If this were the case on Earth, the magnetic north pole would be located in Morocco. Unlike other planets, Uranus's magnetic field originates in the planet's mantle, not its core.

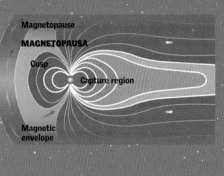

Magnetopause

MAGNETOPAUSA

Cusp

Capture region

Magnetic envelope

Some scientists suggest that Uranus's anomalous magnetic field may indicate that the convection of Uranus's core has stopped because of cooling—or, perhaps, that the planet is currently undergoing a magnetic inversion, as has happened on the Earth.

Composition

Uranus's core is made of abundant amounts of silicates and ice. The planet is almost four times larger than the Earth, and its atmosphere is made up of hydrogen, helium, and methane. Uranus has an almost horizontal tilt, causing it to have very long seasons.

CORE
Made up of silicates and ice

INNER MANTLE
Probably icy water, methane, and ammonia. (According to some models, the materials of the mantle and core do not form layers.)

OUTER MANTLE
Composed primarily of hydrogen and helium, as well as a small amount of methane

ATMOSPHERE
Uranus's atmosphere is made up of hydrogen, methane, helium, and small amounts of acetylene and other hydrocarbons.

5,000 miles (8,000 km)

6,000 miles (10,000 km)

10,000 miles (16,000 km)

CHARACTERISTICS

CONVENTIONAL PLANET SYMBOL

ESSENTIAL DATA	
Average distance from the Sun	1,780,000,000 miles (2,865,000,000 km)
Solar orbit (Uranian year)	84 years 4 days
Equatorial diameter	31,763 miles (51,118 km)
Orbital speed	4 miles per second (6.4 km/s)
Mass*	14.5
Gravity*	0.89
Density	0.8 ounce per cubic inch (1.4 g/cu cm)
Average temperature	-346°F (-210°C)
Atmosphere	Less dense
Moons	27

* In both cases, Earth = 1

AXIS INCLINATION

97.9°

One rotation lasts 17 hours and 14 minutes.

-346°F
(-210°C)
AVERAGE TEMPERATURE

85%
Hydrogen

3%
Methane

12%
Helium

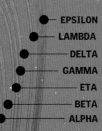

EPSILON
LAMBDA
DELTA
GAMMA
ETA
BETA
ALPHA

4
5
6
1986 U2R

Rings

Like all giant planets of the solar system, Uranus has a ring system, but it is much darker than Saturn's and more difficult to see. The planet's 11 rings, which orbit the planet's equator, were discovered in 1977. In 1986, they were explored by *Voyager 2*.

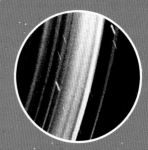

Satellites

Uranus has 27 moons. The first four were discovered in 1787, and another ten were identified in 1986 by the space probe *Voyager 2*. Uranus's moons were named in honor of characters from the works of William Shakespeare and Alexander Pope, a naming convention that distinguishes them from the other moons in the solar system. Some of Uranus's moons are large, but most measure only dozens of miles.

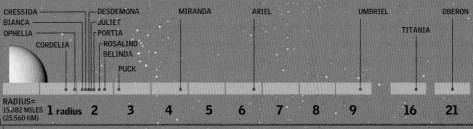

CRESSIDA
BIANCA
OPHELIA
CORDELIA
DESDEMONA
JULIET
PORTIA
ROSALIND
BELINDA
PUCK
MIRANDA
ARIEL
UMBRIEL
TITANIA
OBERON

RADIUS=
15,882 MILES
(25,560 KM)

1 radius **2** **3** **4** **5** **6** **7** **8** **9** **16** **21**

Enlarged region

2001U3 (FRANCISCO)
CALIBAN STEPHANO TRINCULO SYCORAX
2003U3 (MARGARET)
PROSPERO SETEBOS

169 **283 314 339** **482** **580** **654 698**

MOONS

Uranus has small, dark moons, discovered by *Voyager 2*, as well as bigger moons, such as Miranda, Ariel, Umbriel, Oberon, and Titania. These last two are approximately 930 miles (1,500 km) in diameter.

Miranda, only 293 miles (472 km) in diameter, is the smallest of Uranus's five main moons. It has an irregular surface with grooves and a bright mark.

TITANIA
980 MILES
(1,577 KM)

UMBRIEL
730 MILES
(1,175 KM)

MIRANDA
293 MILES
(472 KM)

ARIEL
720 MILES
(1,159 KM)

OBERON
946 MILES
(1,522 KM)

Surface

For a long time, Uranus was believed to have a smooth surface. The Hubble Space Telescope, however, showed that Uranus is a dynamic planet that has the solar system's brightest clouds and a fragile ring system that wobbles like an unbalanced wheel.

REFRACTION OF RAYS

1 In Uranus, sunlight is reflected by a curtain of clouds that lie underneath a layer of methane.

ATMOSPHERE
SUNLIGHT

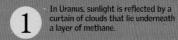

URANUS

2 When sunlight passes through this layer, the methane absorbs the red light waves and lets the blue light waves pass through, producing the planet's hue.

ATMOSPHERE
SUNLIGHT

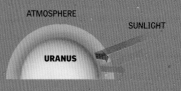

URANUS

Neptune: Deep Blue

Seen from our planet, Neptune appears as a faint, blue point invisible to the naked eye. Images sent to Earth by *Voyager 2* show the planet as a remarkably blue sphere, an effect produced by the presence of methane in the outer part of Neptune's atmosphere. The farthest of the gaseous planets, Neptune is 30 times farther from the Sun than the Earth is. Its rings and impressive clouds are noteworthy, as is its resemblance to Uranus. Neptune is of special interest to astronomers because, before its discovery, its existence and location were predicted on the basis of mathematical calculations.

Moons

Neptune has 13 natural satellites: all are named. Triton and Nereid were the first moons observed by telescope from Earth. The 11 remaining moons were observed from space by the U.S. space probe *Voyager 2.* All the names of Neptune's satellites correspond to ancient Greek marine deities.

THALASSA — DESPINA — PROTEUS — HALIMEDE PSAMATHE SAO LAOMEDEIA NESO TRITON NEREID
NAIAD — GALATEA
LARISSA

NEPTUNE'S RADIUS = 15,388 MILES (24,765 KM)

1 2 3 4 5 6 7 8 9 10 11 12 13 14 222
radius

TRITON
Its diameter is 1,681 miles (2,705 km). Triton orbits Neptune in a direction opposite that of the other moons. Its surface has dark stripes formed by the material spewed from its geysers and volcanoes.

-391°F
(-235°C)

is its temperature, making Triton one of the coldest bodies in the solar system.

Rings

Uranus has faint rings of dust. When they were discovered from the Earth, astronomers thought the rings formed incomplete arcs. The ring names honor the first scientists to study Neptune.

GALLE

LE VERRIER

LASSELL

ARAGO

ADAMS
Located 39,000 miles (62,765 km) from the planet's core, this ring has three prominent arcs, or sections, named Liberty, Fraternity, and Equality.

00 miles hour (0 km/h)

COMPOSITION
Neptune's rings are dark, like those of Uranus and Jupiter. Their composition is unknown, and they are believed to be unstable. Liberty, which makes up part of the outer ring, could vanish before the 22nd century.

Surface

White methane clouds surround Neptune, circulating at some of the fastest speeds in the solar system. Neptune's winds reach 1,200 miles per hour (2,000 km/h) from east to west, swirling against the direction of the planet's rotation.

Winds

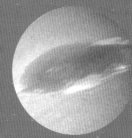

THE GREAT SPOT
This giant storm, called the Great Dark Spot, was first seen on the surface of Neptune in 1989 and was as large as the Earth. By 1994, it had disappeared.

Hard Heart

According to some models, Neptune has a rocky silicate core, covered by a mantle of icy water, ammonia, hydrogen, and methane. According to some models, however, the materials of the mantle and core do not form layers.

12,000 miles (20,000 km)

CORE
Made up of silicates and ice

6,000 miles (10,000 km)

ATMOSPHERE
Banded, like the atmospheres of the other gas giants, Neptune's atmosphere forms a cloud system at least as active as Jupiter's.

INNER MANTLE
Probably icy water, methane, and ammonia

OUTER MANTLE
Composed primarily of hydrogen and helium, as well as a small amount of methane

3,000 miles (5,000 km)

89.8%
Hydrogen

10.2%
Helium

CHARACTERISTICS

CONVENTIONAL PLANET SYMBOL ♆

ESSENTIAL DATA	
Average distance from the Sun	2,800,000,000 miles (4,500,000,000 km)
Solar orbit (Neptunian year)	164 years 264 days
Equatorial diameter	30,800 miles (49,570 km)
Orbital speed	3.4 miles per second (5.5 km/s)
Mass*	17.2
Gravity*	1.12
Density	1 ounce per cubic inch (1.7 g/cu cm)
Average temperature	-328°F (-200°C)
Atmosphere	Dense
Moons	13

*In both cases, Earth = 1

AXIS INCLINATION
28.3°
One rotation lasts 16 hours and 36 minutes.

Pluto: Now a Dwarf

Pluto stopped being the ninth planet of the solar system in 2006 when the International Astronomical Union decided to change the classification of cold, distant Pluto to that of dwarf planet. This tiny body in our solar system has never had an imposing profile, and it has not yet been possible to study it closely. All that is known about Pluto comes through observations made from the Earth or Earth orbit, such as those made by the Hubble Space Telescope. Despite the lack of information gathered about Pluto, it is notable for its unique orbit, the tilt of its axis, and its location within the Kuiper belt. All these characteristics make Pluto especially intriguing.

PLUTO

ROTATION AXIS

CHARON

A Double World

Pluto and its largest satellite, Charon, have a very special relationship. They have been called double planets—the diameter of Charon is about that of Pluto. One theory hypothesizes that Charon was formed from ice that was torn from Pluto when another object collided with the dwarf planet.

Surface

Only a little is known about Pluto, but the Hubble Space Telescope showed a surface covered by a frozen mixture of nitrogen and methane. The presence of solid methane indicates that its temperature is less than -333°F (-203°C), but the dwarf planet's temperature varies according to its place in orbit, ranging between 30 and 50 astronomical units from the Sun.

SYNCHRONIZED ORBITS

The orbital arrangement of Pluto and Charon is unique. Each always faces the other, making the two seem connected by an invisible bar. The synchronization of the two bodies is such that an observer on one side of Pluto would be able to see Charon, but another observer standing on the other side of the planet could not see this moon due to the curvature of the planet.

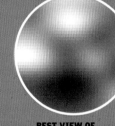

BEST VIEW OF PLUTO AVAILABLE

Moons

In addition to Charon, which was discovered in 1978, Pluto is orbited by two additional moons, Nix and Hydra, first observed in 2005. Unlike the surface of Pluto, which is made of frozen nitrogen, methane, and carbon dioxide, Charon appears to be covered with ice, methane, and carbon dioxide. One theory holds that the matter that formed this satellite was ejected from Pluto as a result of a collision, an origin similar to that ascribed to Earth's moon.

DENSITY

Charon's density is between 0.7 and 0.8 ounce per cubic inch (1.2 and 1.3 g/cu cm), indicating that its composition does not include much rock.

730 miles
(1,175 km)

Charon's diameter–half of Pluto's

Composition

Scientific calculations have deduced that 75 percent of Pluto consists of a mixture of rocks and ice. This frozen surface is made up of 98 percent nitrogen, as well as traces of solidified carbon monoxide and methane. Recently scientists have concluded that

Pluto is an object that belongs to the Kuiper belt, a group of objects left over from the formation of the outer planets. In addition to large amounts of frozen nitrogen, Pluto has simple molecules containing hydrogen and oxygen, the building blocks of life.

MANTLE
The mantle is a layer of frozen water.

ATMOSPHERE
Pluto's very thin atmosphere freezes and falls to the dwarf planet's surface as Pluto moves toward its aphelion.

CRUST
The crust of this dwarf planet is made of methane and water frozen on the surface.

1,100 miles (1,770 km)

140 miles (225 km)

CORE
The core is made of iron, nickel, and silicates.

98%
NITROGEN

2%
METHANE
With some traces of carbon monoxide

CHARACTERISTICS

CONVENTIONAL PLANET SYMBOL

P

ESSENTIAL DATA

Average distance from the Sun	3,700,000,000 miles (5,900,000,000 km)
Solar orbit (Plutonian year)	247.9 years
Equatorial diameter	1,400 miles (2,253 km)
Orbital speed	3 miles per second (4.8 km/s)
Mass*	0.002
Gravity*	0.067
Density	1.2 ounces per cubic inch (2.08 g/cu cm)
Average temperature	-382°F (-230°C)
Atmosphere	Very thin
Moons	3

* In both cases, Earth = 1

AXIS INCLINATION

122°
One rotation lasts 6.387 Earth days.

6,387
terrestrial days is the time Pluto takes to complete one rotation.

A PECULIAR ORBIT

Pluto's orbit is noticeably elliptical, and it is tilted 17° from the plane of the planets' orbits. The distance between Pluto and the Sun varies from 2,500,000,000 to 4,300,000,000 miles (4,000,000,000 to 7,000,000,000 km). During each 248-year orbit, Pluto orbits closer to the Sun than Neptune for nearly 20 years. Although Pluto appears to cross paths with Neptune, it is impossible for them to collide.

NEW HORIZONS MISSION
The first space probe to be sent to Pluto was launched on January 19, 2006. It is to reach the dwarf planet in July 2015 and achieve the first flyby of Pluto and Charon.

The Earth and the Moon

In the beginning, the Earth was an incandescent mass that slowly began to cool, allowing the continents to emerge and acquire their current form. Although many drastic changes took place during these early eras, our blue planet has still not stopped changing. It must be recognized that life on Earth would be impossible without the

AERIAL VIEW OF THE EARTH
In this partial image of the Earth,
we can see Bora-Bora, an island
that forms part of the Leeward
Islands, located in French Polynesia.

presence of the atmosphere—the colorless, odorless, invisible layer of gases that surrounds us, giving us air to breathe and protecting us from the Sun's harmful radiation. Although the atmosphere is approximately 435 miles (700 km) thick, it has no clear boundary and fades into space until it finally disappears.

The Blue Planet

The Earth is known as the blue planet because of the color of the oceans that cover two thirds of its surface. This planet, the third planet from the Sun, is the only one where the right conditions exist to sustain life, something that makes the Earth special. It has liquid water in abundance, a mild temperature, and an atmosphere that protects it from objects that fall from outer space. The atmosphere also filters solar radiation thanks to its ozone layer. Slightly flattened at its poles and wider at its equator, the Earth takes 24 hours to revolve once on its axis.

The Phenomenon of Life

Water, in liquid form, makes it possible for life to exist on the Earth, the only planet where temperatures vary from 32°F to 212°F (0°C to 100°C), allowing water to exist as a liquid. The Earth's average distance from the Sun, along with certain other factors, allowed life to develop 3.8 billion years ago.

70%
of the Earth's surface is water. From space, the planet looks blue.

-76°F
(-60°C)

ONLY ICE
Mars is so far from the Sun that all its water is frozen.

32° to 212°F
(0° to 100°C)

3 STATES
On the Earth, water is found in all three of its possible states.

Above 212°F
(100°C)

ONLY STEAM
On Mercury or Venus, which are very close to the Sun, water would evaporate.

1 EVAPORATION
Because of the Sun's energy, the water evaporates, entering the atmosphere from oceans and, to a lesser extent, from lakes, rivers, and other sources on the continents.

EARTH MOVEMENTS

The Earth moves, orbiting the Sun and rotating on its own axis.

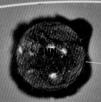

93,500,000 miles
(150,474,000 km)

ROTATION: The Earth revolves on its axis in 23 hours and 56 minutes.

REVOLUTION: It takes the Earth 365 days, 5 hours, and 57 minutes to travel once around the Sun.

The Moon, our only natural satellite, is four times smaller than the Earth and takes 27.32 days to orbit the Earth.

SOUTH POLE

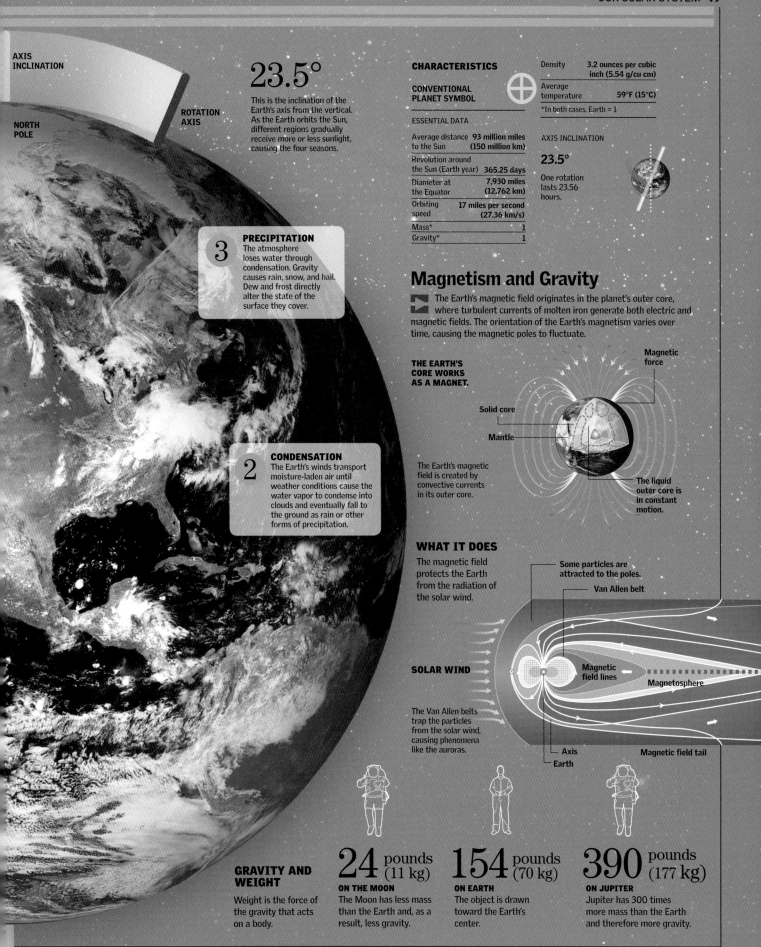

AXIS INCLINATION

ROTATION AXIS

NORTH POLE

23.5°

This is the inclination of the Earth's axis from the vertical. As the Earth orbits the Sun, different regions gradually receive more or less sunlight, causing the four seasons.

3 PRECIPITATION
The atmosphere loses water through condensation. Gravity causes rain, snow, and hail. Dew and frost directly alter the state of the surface they cover.

2 CONDENSATION
The Earth's winds transport moisture-laden air until weather conditions cause the water vapor to condense into clouds and eventually fall to the ground as rain or other forms of precipitation.

CHARACTERISTICS

CONVENTIONAL PLANET SYMBOL

ESSENTIAL DATA

Average distance to the Sun	93 million miles (150 million km)
Revolution around the Sun (Earth year)	365.25 days
Diameter at the Equator	7,930 miles (12,762 km)
Orbiting speed	17 miles per second (27.36 km/s)
Mass*	1
Gravity*	1

Density	3.2 ounces per cubic inch (5.54 g/cu cm)
Average temperature	59°F (15°C)

*In both cases, Earth = 1

AXIS INCLINATION

23.5°

One rotation lasts 23.56 hours.

Magnetism and Gravity

The Earth's magnetic field originates in the planet's outer core, where turbulent currents of molten iron generate both electric and magnetic fields. The orientation of the Earth's magnetism varies over time, causing the magnetic poles to fluctuate.

THE EARTH'S CORE WORKS AS A MAGNET.

Magnetic force

Solid core

Mantle

The Earth's magnetic field is created by convective currents in its outer core.

The liquid outer core is in constant motion.

WHAT IT DOES

The magnetic field protects the Earth from the radiation of the solar wind.

Some particles are attracted to the poles.

Van Allen belt

SOLAR WIND

The Van Allen belts trap the particles from the solar wind, causing phenomena like the auroras.

Magnetic field lines

Magnetosphere

Axis

Earth

Magnetic field tail

GRAVITY AND WEIGHT

Weight is the force of the gravity that acts on a body.

24 pounds (11 kg)
ON THE MOON
The Moon has less mass than the Earth and, as a result, less gravity.

154 pounds (70 kg)
ON EARTH
The object is drawn toward the Earth's center.

390 pounds (177 kg)
ON JUPITER
Jupiter has 300 times more mass than the Earth and therefore more gravity.

Movements and Coordinates

Yes, it moves. The Earth rotates on its axis while simultaneously orbiting the Sun. The natural phenomena of night and day, seasons, and years are caused by these movements. To track the passage of time, calendars, clocks, and time zones were invented. Time zones are divided by meridians and assigned a reference hour according to their location. When traveling east, an hour is added with each time zone. An hour is subtracted during westbound travel.

The Earth's Movements

Night and day, summer and winter, new year and old year result from the Earth's various movements during its orbit of the Sun. The most important motions are the Earth's daily rotation from west to east on its own axis and its revolution around the Sun. (The Earth follows an elliptical orbit that has the Sun at one of the foci of the ellipse, so the distance to the Sun varies slightly over the course of a year.)

ROTATION
1 DAY
The Earth revolves once on its axis in 23 hours and 56 minutes. We see this as day and night.

23.5°

REVOLUTION
1 YEAR
The Earth's orbit around the Sun lasts 365 days, 5 hours, and 57 minutes.

NUTATION
18.6 YEARS
is a sort of nod made by the Earth, causing the displacement of the geographic poles by nine arc seconds.

9°

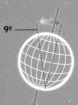

PRECESSION
25,800 YEARS
A slow turning of the direction of the Earth's axis (similar to that of a top), caused by the Earth's nonspherical shape and the gravitational forces of the Sun and the Moon

47°

Equinox and Solstice

Every year, around June 21, the Northern Hemisphere reaches its maximum inclination toward the Sun (a phenomenon referred to as the summer solstice in the Northern Hemisphere and the winter solstice in the Southern Hemisphere). The North Pole receives sunlight all day, while the South Pole is covered in darkness. Between one solstice and another the equinoxes appear, which is when the axis of the Earth points toward the Sun and the periods of daylight and darkness are the same all over our planet.

June 20 or 21

Summer solstice in the Northern Hemisphere and winter solstice in the Southern Hemisphere. Solstices exist because of the tilt of the Earth's axis. The length of the day and the height of the Sun in the sky are greatest in summer and least in winter.

MEASUREMENT OF TIME
Months and days are charted by calendars and clocks, but the measurement of these units of time is neither a cultural nor an arbitrary construct. Instead, it is derived from the natural movements of the Earth.

March 20 or 21

Spring equinox in the Northern Hemisphere and fall equinox in the Southern Hemisphere. The Sun passes directly above the Equator, and day and night have the same length.

SUN

September 21 or 22

FALL EQUINOX IN THE NORTHERN HEMISPHERE AND SPRING EQUINOX IN THE SOUTHERN HEMISPHERE.
The Sun passes directly above the Equator, and day and night have the same length.

PERIHELION
The point where the orbiting Earth most closely approaches the Sun (91 million miles [147 million km])

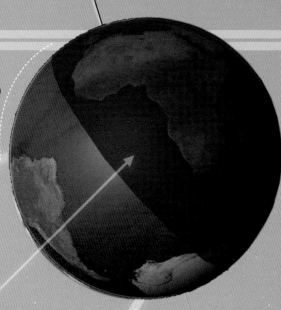

23.5°
TILT OF THE EARTH'S AXIS

93
MILLION MILES (150 MILLION KM)

December 21 or 22

Winter solstice in the Northern Hemisphere and summer solstice in the Southern Hemisphere. Solstices exist because of the tilt of the Earth's axis. The length of the day and the height of the Sun in the sky are greatest in summer and least in winter.

APHELION
The point in the Earth's orbit where it is farthest from the Sun (94 million miles [152 million km]). This occurs at the beginning of July.

Geographic Coordinates

Thanks to the grid formed by the lines of latitude and longitude, the position of any object on the Earth's surface can be easily located by using the intersection of the Earth's Equator and the Greenwich meridian (longitude 0°) as a reference point. This intersection marks the midpoint between the Earth's poles.

THE EARTH'S ORBIT
About 365 days

1 day **THE DAYS**
Period of time it takes the Earth to rotate on its axis

About 30 days **THE MONTHS**
Each period of time, between 28 and 31 days, into which a year is divided

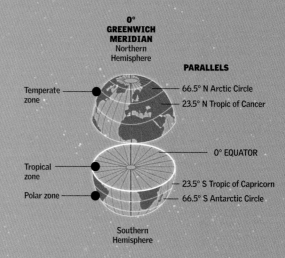

**0°
GREENWICH MERIDIAN**
Northern Hemisphere

PARALLELS

Temperate zone
66.5° N Arctic Circle
23.5° N Tropic of Cancer

0° EQUATOR

Tropical zone

Polar zone
23.5° S Tropic of Capricorn
66.5° S Antarctic Circle

Southern Hemisphere

Time Zones

The Earth is divided into 24 areas, or time zones, each one of which corresponds to an hour assigned according to the Coordinated Universal Time (UTC), using the Greenwich, England, meridian as the base meridian. One hour is added when crossing the meridian in an easterly direction, and one hour is subtracted when traveling west.

Jet Lag

The human body's biological clock responds to the rhythms of light and dark based on the passage of night and day. Long air flights east or west interrupt and disorient the body's clock, causing a disorder known as jet lag. It can cause fatigue, irritability, nausea, headaches, and difficulty sleeping at night.

12:00 A.M.
Departure time

Northern Hemisphere

12:00 P.M.
Arrival time

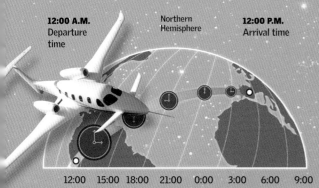

12:00 15:00 18:00 21:00 0:00 3:00 6:00 9:00

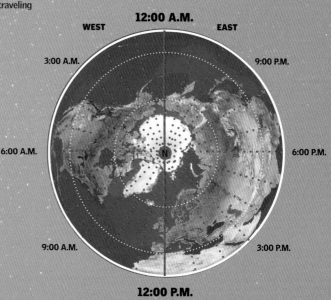

12:00 A.M.
WEST   EAST
3:00 A.M.   9:00 P.M.
6:00 A.M.   6:00 P.M.
N
9:00 A.M.   3:00 P.M.
12:00 P.M.

The Moon and Tides

Romance and terror, mystery and superstition—all these emotions are responses to the Moon, the Earth's one natural satellite, which always hides one of its two faces. However, whatever symbolic meanings are attributed to the Moon, its gravitational pull has a concrete effect on the Earth—it is a cause of the tides. Depending on the distance of the Moon from the Earth, the gravitational pull exerted by the Moon varies in strength and so can high tides and low tides. To reach full height, tides need large open areas of ocean. For this reason, tides in closed or small bodies of water are much lower.

ORIGIN OF THE MOON
The most widely accepted theory of the Moon's origin suggests that an object the size of Mars collided with the Earth during its formation.

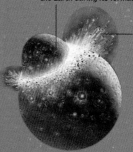

The ejected material scattered into space around the Earth, and over time, it coalesced into the Moon.

ARISTARCHUS
Brightest spot on the Moon

OCEANUS PROCELLARUM
The largest sea, it is not well preserved.

GRIMALDI

GASSENDI

THE MOON'S MOVEMENTS

As the Moon orbits the Earth, it revolves on its own axis in such a way that it always shows the Earth the same side.

LUNAR MONTH
It takes 29.53 days to complete its phases.

SIDEREAL MONTH
It takes 27.32 days to orbit the Earth.

Hidden face · Visible face · **MOON** · **EARTH** · Lunar orbit

HIDDEN FACE
Invisible from the Earth, this side of the Moon was a mystery until 1959, when the Russian probe *Luna 3* managed to photograph the hidden zone. Because of the greater thickness of the Moon's crust on this side, it has fewer seas.

The Tides

The water on the side of the Earth closest to the Moon feels the Moon's gravitational pull most intensely, and vice versa. Two tides are formed, and they track the Moon in its orbit around the Earth. However, they precede the Moon instead of being directly in line with it.

1 NEW MOON
SPRING TIDE
When the Sun and the Moon are aligned, the highest high tides and lowest low tides are produced.

2 FIRST QUARTER
NEAP TIDE
The Moon and the Sun are at right angles to the Earth, producing the lowest high tides and the highest low tides.

3 FULL MOON
SPRING TIDE
The Sun and the Moon align once again, and the Sun augments the Moon's gravitational pull, causing a second spring tide.

4 THIRD QUARTER
NEAP TIDE
The Moon and the Sun again form a right angle, causing a second neap tide.

KEY

↓ Gravitational pull of the Moon

↓ Gravitational pull of the Sun

● Influence on the tide by the gravitational pull of the Moon

● Influence on the tide by the gravitational pull of the Sun

Lunar orbit
Moon
Earth orbit
Sun

THE SUN'S GRAVITY ALSO INFLUENCES THE TIDES

INNER STRUCTURE

Various seismic analyses of the Moon suggest that its core is solid or semisolid.

2,160 miles (3,476 km)

The diameter of the Moon is one fourth of the Earth's.

MARE IMBRIUM is 3.85 billion years old.

VISIBLE FACE

Spotted with dark areas, it always faces the Earth.

ROCKY MANTLE Less than half the thickness of the Earth's mantle

OUTER CORE Partially melted

620 miles (1,000 km)

62 miles (100 km)

INNER CORE Central temperature of 2,730°F (1,500°C)

MARE CRISIUM Measures 280 miles by 370 miles (450 km by 595 km) and has large craters.

MARE TRANQUILLITATIS The seas are flatlands with few craters.

MARE NUBIUM

MARE HUMORUM

RUPES ALTAI Mountain chain 5,900 feet (1,800 m) high

HUMBOLDT Crater named in honor of the German naturalist

SCHICKARD

TYCHO 100 million years old

MAGINUS

COPERNICUS 60 miles (97 km) in diameter

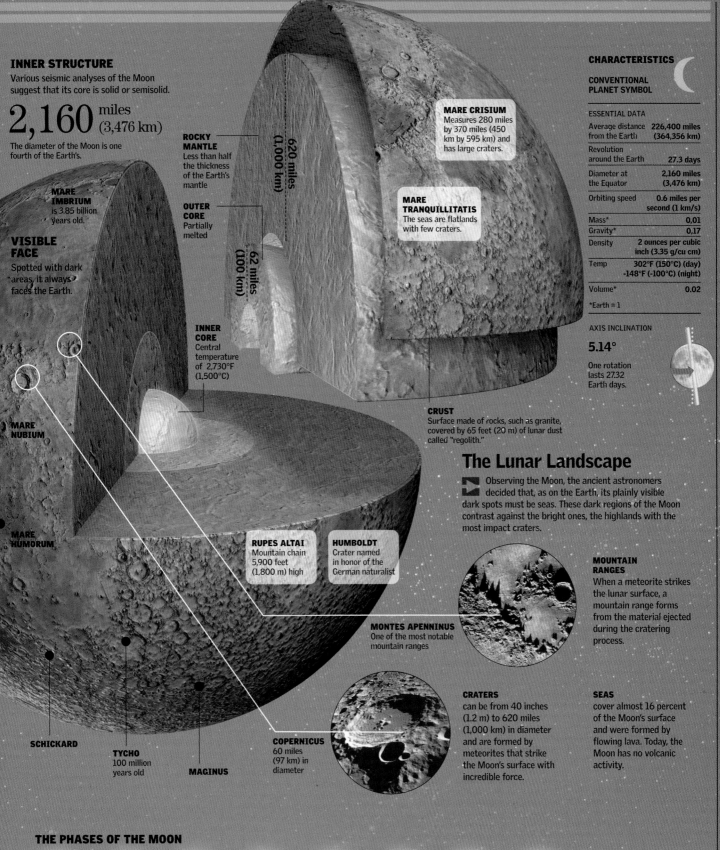

MONTES APENNINUS One of the most notable mountain ranges

CRUST Surface made of rocks, such as granite, covered by 65 feet (20 m) of lunar dust called "regolith."

CHARACTERISTICS

CONVENTIONAL PLANET SYMBOL

ESSENTIAL DATA

Average distance from the Earth	226,400 miles (364,356 km)
Revolution around the Earth	27.3 days
Diameter at the Equator	2,160 miles (3,476 km)
Orbiting speed	0.6 miles per second (1 km/s)
Mass*	0,01
Gravity*	0,17
Density	2 ounces per cubic inch (3.35 g/cu cm)
Temp	302°F (150°C) (day) -148°F (-100°C) (night)
Volume*	0.02

*Earth = 1

AXIS INCLINATION

5.14°

One rotation lasts 27.32 Earth days.

The Lunar Landscape

Observing the Moon, the ancient astronomers decided that, as on the Earth, its plainly visible dark spots must be seas. These dark regions of the Moon contrast against the bright ones, the highlands with the most impact craters.

MOUNTAIN RANGES When a meteorite strikes the lunar surface, a mountain range forms from the material ejected during the cratering process.

CRATERS can be from 40 inches (1.2 m) to 620 miles (1,000 km) in diameter and are formed by meteorites that strike the Moon's surface with incredible force.

SEAS cover almost 16 percent of the Moon's surface and were formed by flowing lava. Today, the Moon has no volcanic activity.

THE PHASES OF THE MOON

| NEW MOON | WAXING CRESCENT | FIRST QUARTER | WAXING GIBBOUS | FULL MOON | WANING GIBBOUS | THIRD QUARTER | WANING CRESCENT |

Unique

The Moon is the Earth's only natural satellite.

Eclipses

Typically four times a year, during the full or new moon, the centers of the Moon, the Sun, and the Earth become aligned, causing one of the most marvelous celestial phenomena: an eclipse. At these times, the Moon either passes in front of the Sun or passes through the Earth's shadow. The Sun—even during an eclipse—is not safe to look at directly, since it can cause irreparable damage to the eyes, such as burns on the retina. Special high-quality filters or indirect viewing by projecting the Sun's image on a sheet of paper are some of the ways in which this celestial wonder can be watched. Solar eclipses provide, in addition, a good opportunity for astronomers to conduct scientific research.

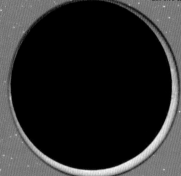

TOTAL LUNAR ECLIPSE, SEEN FROM THE EARTH

The orange color comes from sunlight that has been refracted and colored by the Earth's atmosphere.

ANNULAR ECLIPSE OF THE SUN, SEEN FROM THE EARTH

Solar Eclipse

Solar eclipses occur when the Moon passes directly between the Sun and the Earth, casting a shadow along a path on the Earth's surface. The central cone of the shadow is called the "umbra," and the area of partial shadow around it is called the "penumbra." Viewers in the regions where the umbra falls on the Earth's surface see the Moon's disk completely obscure the Sun—a total solar eclipse. Those watching from the surrounding areas that are located in the penumbra see the Moon's disk cover only part of the Sun—a partial solar eclipse.

ALIGNMENT

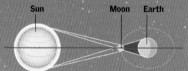

Sun   Moon   Earth

During a solar eclipse, astronomers take advantage of the blocked view of the Sun in order to use devices designed to study the Sun's atmosphere.

TYPES OF ECLIPSES

TOTAL
The Moon is between the Sun and the Earth and creates a cone-shaped shadow.

ANNULAR
The Sun appears larger than the Moon, and it remains visible around it.

PARTIAL
The Moon does not cover the Sun completely, so the Sun appears as a crescent.

SUN'S APPARENT SIZE

400 times larger than the Moon

SUNLIGHT

DISTANCE FROM THE SUN TO THE EARTH

400 times greater than the distance from the Earth to the Moon

Lunar Eclipse

When the Earth passes directly between the full Moon and the Sun, a lunar eclipse (which could be total, partial, or penumbral) occurs. Without the Earth's atmosphere, during each lunar eclipse, the Moon would become completely invisible (something that never happens). The totally eclipsed Moon's characteristic reddish color is caused by light refracted by the Earth's atmosphere. During a partial eclipse, on the other hand, part of the Moon falls in the shadow cone, while the rest is in the penumbra, the outermost, palest part. It is not dangerous to look at a lunar eclipse directly.

ALIGNMENT

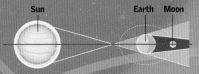

Sun   Earth   Moon

During an eclipse, the Moon is not completely black but appears reddish.

TYPES OF ECLIPSES

TOTAL
The Moon is completely in the shadow cone.

PARTIAL
The Moon is only partially inside the shadow cone.

PENUMBRAL
The Moon is in the penumbral cone.

Lunar orbit

Shadow cone

FULL MOON
TOTAL ECLIPSE

PARTIAL ECLIPSE

PENUMBRAL ECLIPSE

Penumbra cone

EARTH

NEW MOON
TOTAL ECLIPSE

Shadow cone

Earth orbit

THE ECLIPSE CYCLE

Eclipses repeat every 223 lunations—18 years and 11 days. These are called "Saros periods."

ECLIPSES IN A YEAR

2	7	4
Minimum	Maximum	Average

ECLIPSES IN A SAROS

41	29	70
of the Sun	of the Moon	Total

OBSERVATION FROM EARTH

A black, polymer filter, with an optical density of 5.0, produces a clear orange image of the Sun.

Prevents retinal burns

SOLAR ECLIPSES
are different for each local observer.

LUNAR ECLIPSES
are the same for all observers.

MAXIMUM DURATION
8 minutes

MAXIMUM DURATION
100 minutes

ECLIPSES IN 2006 AND BEYOND

OF THE SUN

3/29	9/22	3/19	9/11	2/07	1/26	7/22	1/15	7/11	1/4	11/25	5/20	11/13	5/10	11/3	4/29	10/23	3/20	9/13
Total	Total	Partial	Partial	Total	Total	Total	Total	Total	Partial	Partial	Annular	Annular	Annular	Hybrid	Annular	Partial	Total	Partial

2006	2007	2008	2009	2010	2011	2012	2013	2014	2015	2016

OF THE MOON

3/14	9/07	3/03	8/28	2/21	8/16	2/9	7/7	6/26	12/21	6/15	12/10	6/4	12/28	4/25	10/18	4/15	10/08	4/4	9/28
Partial	Partial	Total	Total	Total	Partial	Partial	Partial	Partial	Total	Total	Total	Partial	Partial	Partial	Partial	Total	Total	Total	Total

2 GEOLOGY AND FORMATION

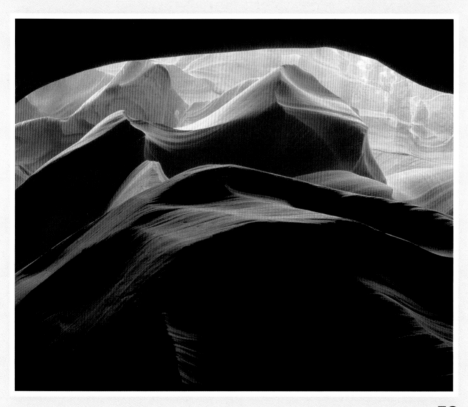

78

88

Dynamics of the Earth's Crust

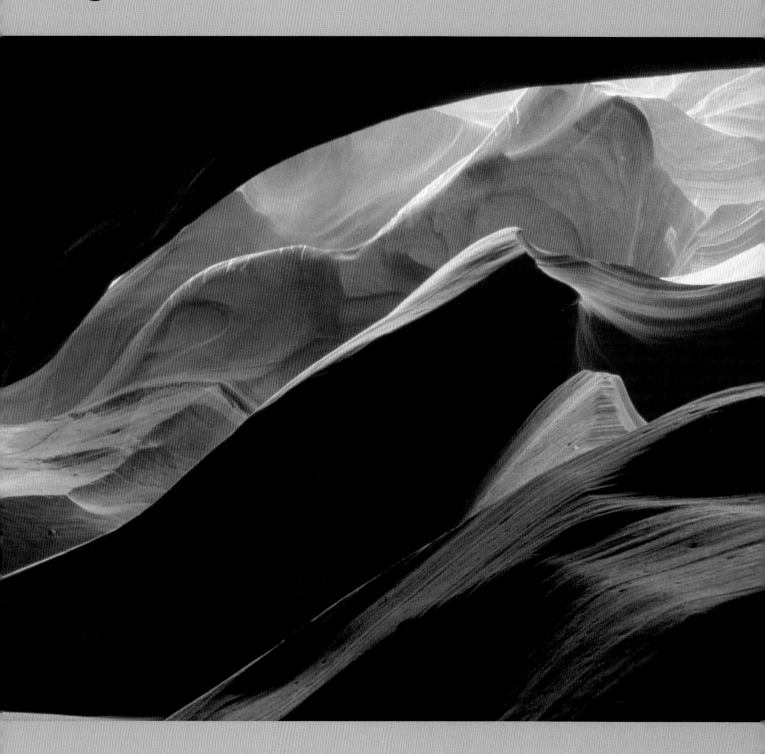

The Earth is like a blender in which rocks are moved around, broken, and crumbled. The fragments are deposited, forming different layers. Then weathering and erosion by wind and rain wear down and transform the rock. This produces mountains, cliffs, and sand dunes, among other features. These natural elements

MOUNTAINS OF SAND
Corkscrew Canyon in Arizona contains an
array of shapes, colors, and textures. The
sand varies from pink to yellow to red,
depending on the sunlight it receives.

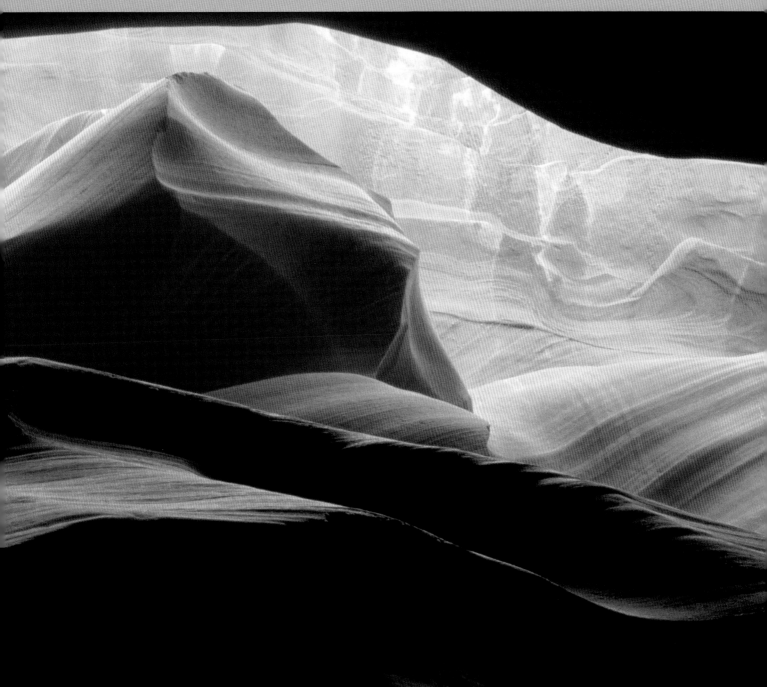

cause great changes in the Earth's landscape. Erosion and transportation are processes that produce and spread rock materials. Then, when these materials settle and become compacted, new rocks are created, which in turn will revert to sediment. This rock cycle never stops. In 50 million years, no single mountain we know will exist in the same condition as it does today.

Traversing Time

Geologists and paleontologists use many sources to reconstruct the Earth's history. The analysis of rocks, minerals, and fossils found on the Earth's surface provides data about the deepest layers of the planet's crust and reveals both climatic and atmospheric changes that are often associated with catastrophes. Craters caused by the impact of meteorites and other bodies on the surface of the Earth also reveal valuable information about the history of the planet.

2 COLLISION AND FUSION
Heavy elements migrate.

Complex Structure

The formation of the interior cosmic materials began to accumulate, forming a growing celestial body, the precursor of the Earth. High temperatures combined with gravity caused the heaviest elements to migrate to the center of the planet and the lighter ones to move toward the surface. Under a rain of meteors, the external layers began to consolidate and form the Earth's crust. In the center, metals such as iron concentrated into a red-hot nucleus.

1 Small bodies and dust accumulate to become the size of an asteroid.

The oldest minerals, such as zircon, form.

The oldest rocks metamorphose, forming gneiss.

1,100
Rodinia, an early supercontinent, forms.

A meteorite falls in Sudbury, Ontario, Canada.

Age in millions of years
4,600

2,500

ERA	Hadean	Proterozoic
PERIOD	Pregeologic	Precambrian
EPOCH		

Climate

Consolidation begins under a rain of meteors.

The Earth cools and the first ocean is formed.

2,500
Glaciations: White Earth
The Earth undergoes the first of its massive global cooling events (glaciations).

ELEMENTS PRESENT ACCORDING TO THE TABLE
Existing in different combinations, the crust of the Earth contains the same elements today as those that were present when the planet was formed. The most abundant element in the crust is oxygen, which bonds with metals and nonmetals to form different compounds.

800 Second glaciation
600 Last massive glaciation

O
46.6%

Si
27.7%

- Metals
- Transition metals
- Nonmetals
- Noble gases
- Lanthanide series
- Actinide series

Life

THE FIRST ANIMALS
Among the most mysterious fossils of the Precambrian Period are the remains of the Ediacaran fauna, the Earth's first-known animals. They lived at the bottom of the ocean. Many were round and reminiscent of jellyfish, while others were flat and sheetlike.

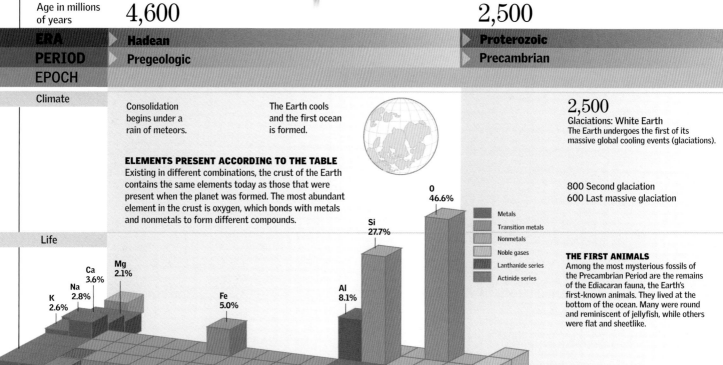

K
2.6%

Na
2.8%

Ca
3.6%

Mg
2.1%

Fe
5.0%

Al
8.1%

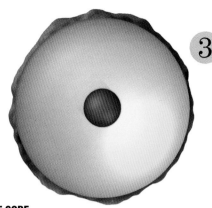

METALLIC CORE
3 The light elements form the mantle.

THE CORE
The Earth's core is extremely hot and is made mostly of iron and nickel.

Mountains

ARE EXTERNAL FOLDS OF THE CRUST PRODUCED BY EXTREMELY POWERFUL FORCES OCCURRING INSIDE THE EARTH.

542
The supercontinent Panotia forms, containing portions of present-day continents. North America separates from Panotia.

OROGENIES
Geological history recognizes long periods (lasting millions of years) of intense mountain formation called orogenies. Each orogeny is characterized by its own particular materials and location.

The first major orogeny (Caledonian folding) begins. Gondwana moves toward the South Pole.

Laurentia and Baltica converge, creating the Caledonian range. Gneiss forms on the coast of Scotland.

The region that will become North America moves toward the Equator, thus initiating the development of the most important carboniferous formations. Gondwana moves slowly; the ocean floor spreads at a similar speed.

The fragments of continents combine to form a single continent called Pangea.

The Appalachian Mountains form. The formation of slate through sedimentation is at its peak.

Baltica and Siberia clash, forming the Ural Mountains.

Eruptions of basalt occur in Siberia.

| 542 | 488.3 | 443.7 | 416 | 359.2 | 299 |

Paleozoic THE ERA OF PRIMITIVE LIFE

| Cambrian | Ordovician | Silurian | Devonian | Carboniferous | Permian |

Temperatures fall. The level of carbon dioxide (CO_2) in the atmosphere is 16 times higher than it is today.

It is thought that the Earth's atmosphere contained far less carbon dioxide during the Ordovician than today. Temperatures fluctuate within a range similar to what we experience today.

By this period, vertebrates: with mandibles, such as the placoderms, osteichthyans (bony fish), and acanthodians (spiny-finned fish), have already emerged.

Temperatures were typically warmer than today, and oxygen (CO_2) levels attained their maximum.

Hot, humid climates produce exuberant forests in swamplands.

The largest carbon deposits we observe today form where forests previously existed.

THE CAMBRIAN EXPLOSION
Fossils from this time attest to the great diversity of marine animals and the emergence of different types of skeletal structures, such as those found in sponges and trilobites.

TRILOBITES
Marine arthropods with mineralized exoskeletons

SILURIAN
One of the first pisciform vertebrates: an armored fish without mandibles

The rocks of this period contain an abundance of fish fossils.

Areas of solid ground are populated by gigantic ferns.

Amphibians diversify and reptiles originate from one amphibian group to become the first amniotes. Winged insects, such as dragonflies, emerge.

Palm trees and conifers replace the vegetation from the Carboniferous Period.

MASS EXTINCTION
Near the end of the Permian Period, an estimated 95 percent of marine organisms and over two thirds of terrestrial ones perish in the greatest-known mass extinction.

IMPACT FROM THE OUTSIDE

It is believed that a large meteor fell on Chicxulub, on the Yucatán Peninsula (Mexico), about 65 million years ago. The impact caused an explosion that created a cloud of ash mixed with carbon rocks. When the debris fell back to Earth, some experts believe it caused a great global fire.

The heat caused by the expansion of fragments from the impact together with the greenhouse effect brought about by the spreading of ashes in the stratosphere provoked a series of climatic changes. It is believed that this process resulted in the extinction of the dinosaurs.

62 miles
(100 km)

THE DIAMETER OF THE CRATER PRODUCED BY THE IMPACT OF THE METEOR ON THE YUCATÁN PENINSULA. IT IS NOW BURIED UNDER ALMOST 2 MILES (3.2 KM) OF LIMESTONE.

Gondwana reappears.

Africa separates from South America, and the South Atlantic Ocean appears.

FORMATION OF MOUNTAIN CHAINS

60 Central Rocky Mountains
30 Alps
20 Himalayas

251   199.6   145.5   **65.5**

Mesozoic THE ERA OF REPTILES			Cenozoic THE AGE OF MAMMALS
Triassic	Jurassic	Cretaceous	Paleogene
			Paleocene · Eocene

Carbon dioxide levels increase. Average temperatures are higher than today.

The level of oxygen (O_2) in the atmosphere is much lower than today.

THE AGE OF FLOWERING PLANTS
At the end of the Cretaceous Period, the first angiosperms—plants with protected seeds, flowers, and fruits—appear.

The global average temperature is at least 62°F (17°C). The ice layer covering Antarctica later thickens.

Proliferation of insects

Appearance of dinosaurs

The first mammals evolve from a group or order of reptiles called Therapsida.

Birds emerge.

The dinosaurs undergo adaptive radiation.

ALLOSAURUS
This carnivore measured 39 feet (12 m) long.

ANOTHER MASS EXTINCTION
Toward the end of the Cretaceous Period, about 50 percent of existing species disappear. The dinosaurs, the large marine reptiles (such as the Plesiosaurs), the flying creatures of that period (such as the Pterosaurs), and the ammonites (cephalopod mollusks) disappear from the Earth. At the beginning of the Cenozoic Era, most of the habitats of these extinct species begin to be occupied by mammals.

Elements in Equilibrium

MINERALS, SUCH AS IRON AND SILICATES, ARE WIDELY SPREAD AMONG THE MAJOR CONSTITUENTS OF THE CRUST. ONLY THE MOVEMENTS OF THE CRUST ON THE MOLTEN MANTLE DISRUPT THEIR EQUILIBRIUM.

CRUST
The Earth's crust can reach a thickness of up to 6 miles (10 km) at the bottom of the ocean and up to 30 miles (50 km) on the continents.

North America and Europe drift apart. North and South America are joined at the end of this time period. The formation of Patagonia concludes, and an important overthrust raises the Andes mountain range.

The African Rift Zone and the Red Sea open up. The Indian protocontinent collides with Eurasia.

23

LITHOSPHERE
The solid rock coating of the Earth, which includes the exterior of the mantle

MANTLE
The mantle is 1,800 miles (2,900 km) thick and is composed mainly of solid rock. Its temperature increases with depth. A notable component of the upper mantle is the asthenosphere, which is semisolid. In the asthenosphere, superficial rock layers that will eventually form the Earth's crust are melted.

Neogene				
Oligocene	Miocene	Pliocene	Pleistocene	Holocene

Temperatures drop to levels similar to those of today. The lower temperatures cause forests to shrink and grasslands to expand.

THE LAST GLACIATION
The most recent period of glaciation begins three million years ago and intensifies at the beginning of the Quaternary Period. North Pole glaciers advance, and much of the Northern Hemisphere becomes covered in ice.

CORE

OUTER CORE
The outer core is 1,400 miles (2,253 km) thick and contains melted iron, nickel, and other minor chemical compounds.

INNER CORE
The inner core has a diameter of 756 miles (1,216 km). It is made of iron and nickel, which are solidified due to their exposure to high pressure and temperature conditions.

Vast development of feathered bird species and mammals covered with long fur

MAMMOTHS
Mammoths lived in Siberia. The cause of their extinction is still under debate.

HUMAN BEINGS APPEAR ON EARTH.
Although the oldest hominid fossils (*Sahelanthropus*) date back to seven million years ago, it is believed that modern humans emerged in Africa at the end of the Pleistocene Epoch. Humans migrated to Europe 100,000 years ago, although settling there was difficult because of the glacial climate. According to one hypothesis, our ancestors reached the American continent about 10,000 years ago by traveling across the area now known as the Bering Strait.

A Changing Surface

The molding of the Earth's crust is the product of two great destructive forces: weathering and erosion. Through the combination of these processes, rocks merge, disintegrate, and join again. Living organisms, especially plant roots and digging animals, cooperate with these geologic processes. Once the structure of the minerals that make up a rock is disrupted, the minerals disintegrate and fall to the mercy of the rain and wind, which erode them.

Erosion

External agents, such as water, wind, air, and living beings, either acting separately or together, wear down, and their loose fragments may be transported. This process is known as "erosion." In dry regions, the wind transports grains of sand that strike and polish exposed rocks. On the coast, wave action slowly eats away at the rocks.

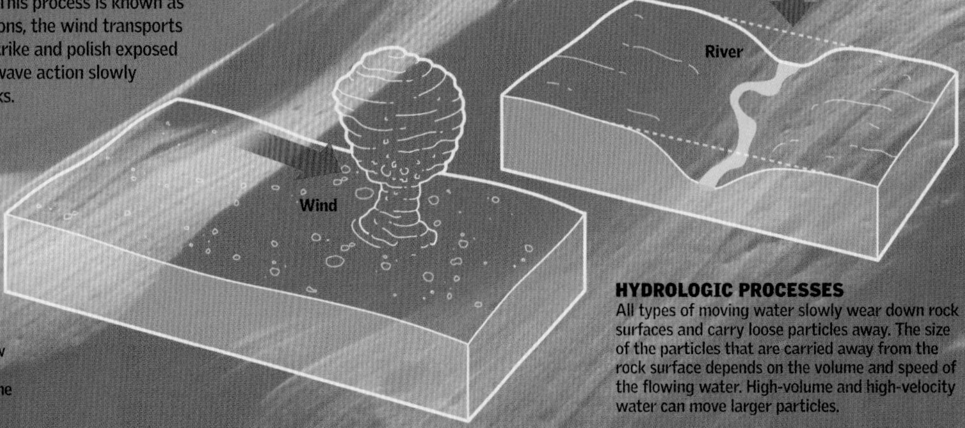

Wind

River

EOLIAN PROCESSES
The wind drags small particles against the rocks. This wears them down and produces new deposits of either loess or sand depending on the size of the particle.

HYDROLOGIC PROCESSES
All types of moving water slowly wear down rock surfaces and carry loose particles away. The size of the particles that are carried away from the rock surface depends on the volume and speed of the flowing water. High-volume and high-velocity water can move larger particles.

**CORKSCREW CANYON,
ARIZONA**
Latitude 36° 30´ N
Longitude 111° 24´ W

Weathering

Mechanical agents can disintegrate rocks, and chemical agents can decompose them. Disintegration and decomposition can result from the actions of plant roots, heat, cold, wind, and acid rain. The breaking down of rock is a slow but inexorable process.

CHEMICAL PROCESSES

The mineral components of rocks are altered. They either become new minerals or are released in solution.

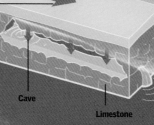

Water current

Cave

Limestone

MECHANICAL PROCESSES

A variety of forces can cause rock fragments to break into smaller pieces, either by acting on the rocks directly or by transporting rock fragments that chip away at the rock surface.

TEMPERATURE

When the temperature of the air changes significantly over a few hours, it causes rocks to expand and contract abruptly. The daily repetition of this phenomenon can cause rocks to rupture.

TRANSPORTATION AND SEDIMENTATION

In this process, materials eroded by the wind or water are carried away and deposited at lower elevations, and these new deposits can later turn into other rocks.

WATER

In a liquid or frozen state, water penetrates into the rock fissures, causing them to expand and shatter.

Everything Changes

Wind, ice, and water. These natural elements cause great changes in the Earth's landscape. Erosion and transportation are processes that produce and spread rock materials. Then, when these materials settle and become compacted, new rocks are created, which in turn will revert to sediment. These are sedimentary rocks: the most widely known rocks, they cover 70 percent of the Earth's surface. By observing sedimentary rocks of different ages, scientists can estimate how the climate and the environment have changed.

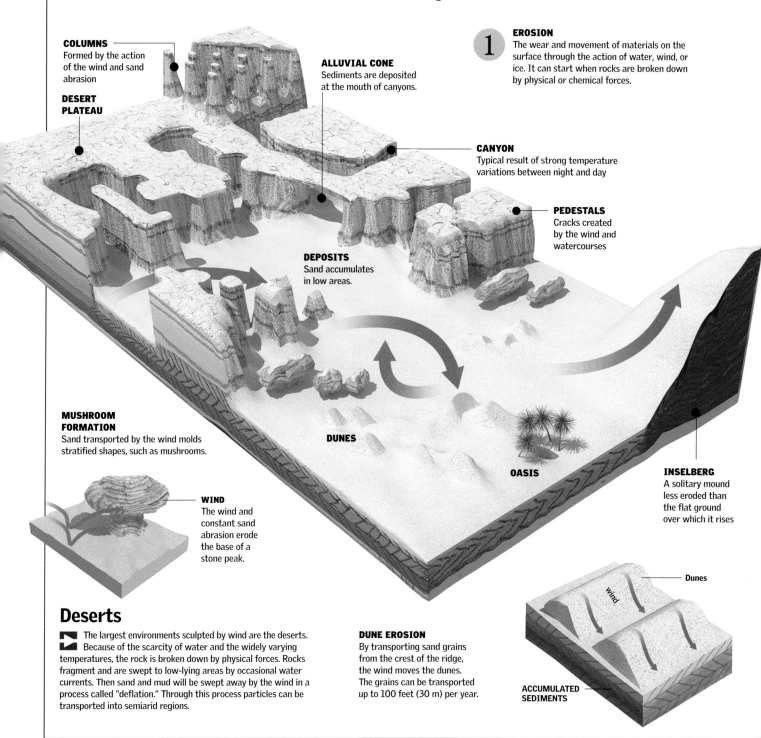

COLUMNS
Formed by the action of the wind and sand abrasion

DESERT PLATEAU

ALLUVIAL CONE
Sediments are deposited at the mouth of canyons.

1 EROSION
The wear and movement of materials on the surface through the action of water, wind, or ice. It can start when rocks are broken down by physical or chemical forces.

CANYON
Typical result of strong temperature variations between night and day

PEDESTALS
Cracks created by the wind and watercourses

DEPOSITS
Sand accumulates in low areas.

MUSHROOM FORMATION
Sand transported by the wind molds stratified shapes, such as mushrooms.

DUNES

OASIS

INSELBERG
A solitary mound less eroded than the flat ground over which it rises

WIND
The wind and constant sand abrasion erode the base of a stone peak.

Dunes

wind

Deserts

The largest environments sculpted by wind are the deserts. Because of the scarcity of water and the widely varying temperatures, the rock is broken down by physical forces. Rocks fragment and are swept to low-lying areas by occasional water currents. Then sand and mud will be swept away by the wind in a process called "deflation." Through this process particles can be transported into semiarid regions.

DUNE EROSION
By transporting sand grains from the crest of the ridge, the wind moves the dunes. The grains can be transported up to 100 feet (30 m) per year.

ACCUMULATED SEDIMENTS

TRANSPORT OF SEDIMENTS

**DESERT
TINY GRAINS**
In the desert, the wind moves particles in three ways: suspension (very fine grains and dust), transport (the most basic way), and sliding along the surface.

SAND

WIND

**3 INCHES
(7.6 CM)**

**GLACIER
FINE AND HETEROGENEOUS**
Glaciers transport rock fragments, which accumulate in moraines. They are made up of a heterogeneous material called "till," which, together with rocks, is carried along by the glacier.

ICE

**160 FEET
(50 M)**

TILL

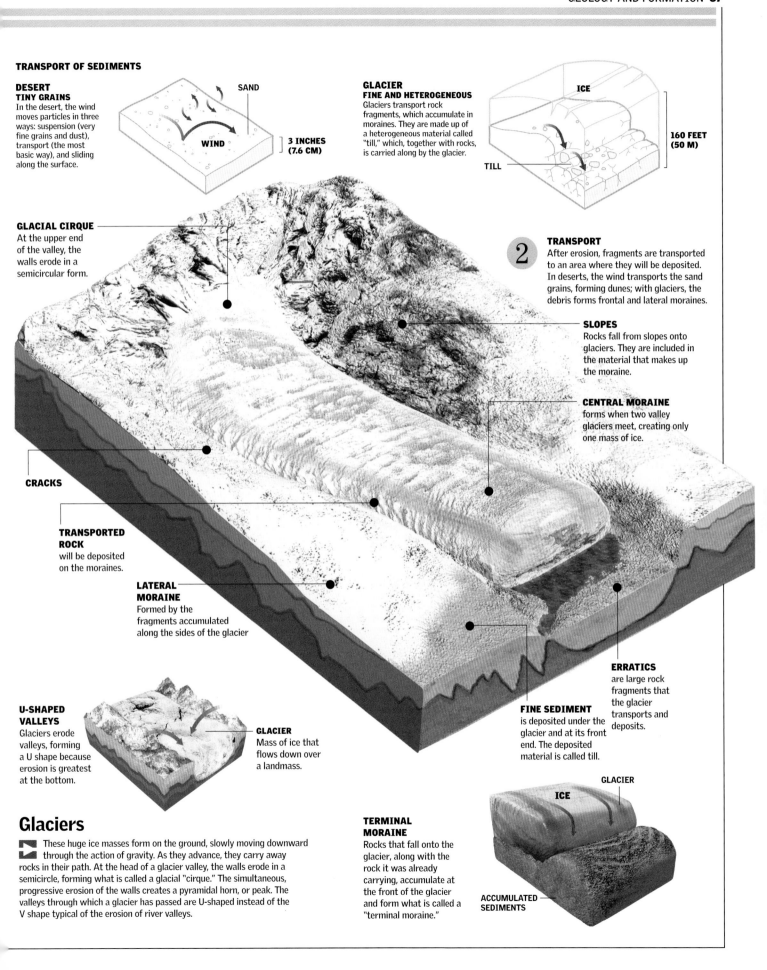

GLACIAL CIRQUE
At the upper end of the valley, the walls erode in a semicircular form.

2 TRANSPORT
After erosion, fragments are transported to an area where they will be deposited. In deserts, the wind transports the sand grains, forming dunes; with glaciers, the debris forms frontal and lateral moraines.

SLOPES
Rocks fall from slopes onto glaciers. They are included in the material that makes up the moraine.

CENTRAL MORAINE
forms when two valley glaciers meet, creating only one mass of ice.

CRACKS

**TRANSPORTED
ROCK**
will be deposited on the moraines.

**LATERAL
MORAINE**
Formed by the fragments accumulated along the sides of the glacier

**U-SHAPED
VALLEYS**
Glaciers erode valleys, forming a U shape because erosion is greatest at the bottom.

GLACIER
Mass of ice that flows down over a landmass.

ERRATICS
are large rock fragments that the glacier transports and deposits.

FINE SEDIMENT
is deposited under the glacier and at its front end. The deposited material is called till.

GLACIER

ICE

**ACCUMULATED
SEDIMENTS**

Glaciers

These huge ice masses form on the ground, slowly moving downward through the action of gravity. As they advance, they carry away rocks in their path. At the head of a glacier valley, the walls erode in a semicircle, forming what is called a glacial "cirque." The simultaneous, progressive erosion of the walls creates a pyramidal horn, or peak. The valleys through which a glacier has passed are U-shaped instead of the V shape typical of the erosion of river valleys.

**TERMINAL
MORAINE**
Rocks that fall onto the glacier, along with the rock it was already carrying, accumulate at the front of the glacier and form what is called a "terminal moraine."

TRANSPORT OF SEDIMENTS

RIVER
GREAT DISTANCES
A river can transport sediments over great distances. Rivers originate in elevated areas, from which they flow to lower areas and then to the sea. When the current gathers speed, it transports big boulders. When the energy is less, the current carries only smaller rocks.

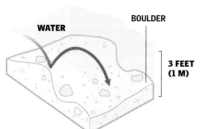

WATER

BOULDER

3 FEET (1 M)

COAST
LOCAL DEPOSITS
After each wave breaks, the undertow descends the beach slope, creating an accumulation of sand that has been transported by the waves in a process called a "coastal current." Sand is also transported by rivers, which deposit sediments in their deltas.

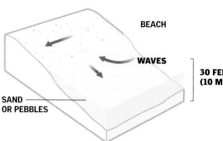

BEACH

WAVES

30 FEET (10 M)

SAND OR PEBBLES

WATERFALLS
Softer rock erodes, forming a cave with a rocky ceiling that will finally crumble and fall.

3 SEDIMENTATION
When the currents that transport sediment lose energy, the sediment is deposited in layers and distributed over extensive areas.

SLOPE
River valleys are steep because they are composed of layers of hard rock.

RAPIDS
In these geographic features, a high volume of matter is transported by river erosion.

CLIFF
A product of lateral undermining

MEANDERS
The outside of the curve is where the most sediment is deposited.

FORMATION OF V-SHAPED VALLEYS
Unlike glacial valleys, which are eroded in the shape of a U, river valleys are V-shaped.

ALLUVIAL PLAIN
Composed of sediments

RIVER
Close to the river's source, the current is very strong, and it erodes and digs into the riverbed to form V-shaped valleys.

SEDIMENTARY DEPOSITS

INITIAL PHASE

FINAL PHASE

Rivers

Close to their source, rivers flow through areas of high elevation. The water descends there with great force and energy, which enables the current to transport large boulders. At low elevations, rivers flow more smoothly over sediments, forming meanders and eroding laterally. On reaching the coast, rivers deposit sediments and form estuaries or deltas.

DELTA FORMATION
The sediment deposited at the river's mouth creates a "delta," an area with sandbars through which the river flows in various directions.

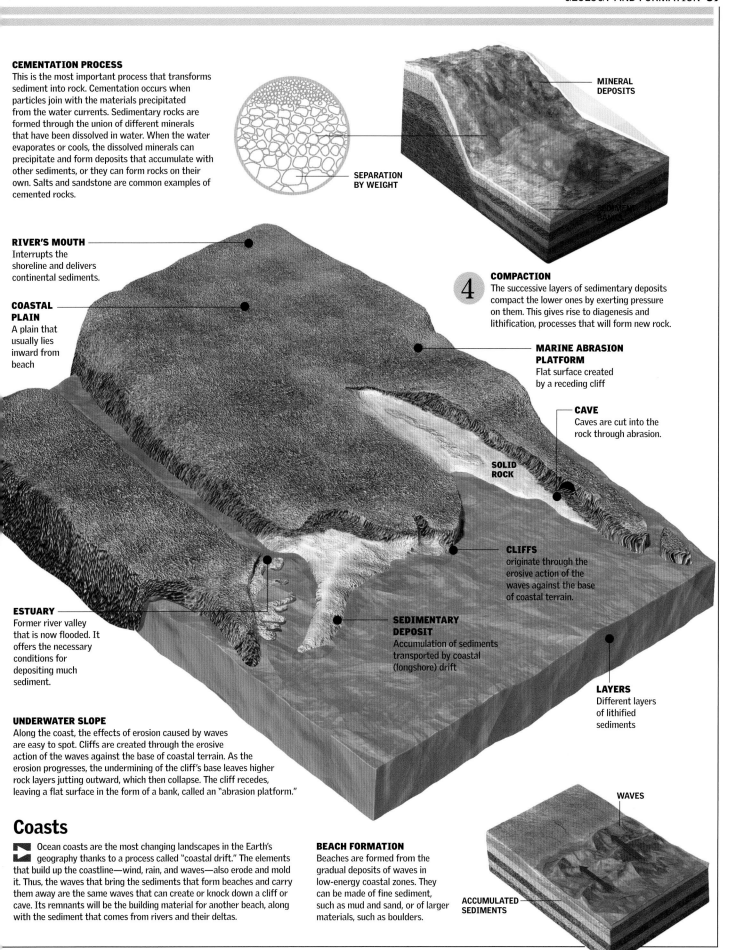

CEMENTATION PROCESS
This is the most important process that transforms sediment into rock. Cementation occurs when particles join with the materials precipitated from the water currents. Sedimentary rocks are formed through the union of different minerals that have been dissolved in water. When the water evaporates or cools, the dissolved minerals can precipitate and form deposits that accumulate with other sediments, or they can form rocks on their own. Salts and sandstone are common examples of cemented rocks.

SEPARATION BY WEIGHT

MINERAL DEPOSITS

RIVER'S MOUTH
Interrupts the shoreline and delivers continental sediments.

COASTAL PLAIN
A plain that usually lies inward from beach

4 COMPACTION
The successive layers of sedimentary deposits compact the lower ones by exerting pressure on them. This gives rise to diagenesis and lithification, processes that will form new rock.

MARINE ABRASION PLATFORM
Flat surface created by a receding cliff

CAVE
Caves are cut into the rock through abrasion.

SOLID ROCK

CLIFFS
originate through the erosive action of the waves against the base of coastal terrain.

ESTUARY
Former river valley that is now flooded. It offers the necessary conditions for depositing much sediment.

SEDIMENTARY DEPOSIT
Accumulation of sediments transported by coastal (longshore) drift

LAYERS
Different layers of lithified sediments

UNDERWATER SLOPE
Along the coast, the effects of erosion caused by waves are easy to spot. Cliffs are created through the erosive action of the waves against the base of coastal terrain. As the erosion progresses, the undermining of the cliff's base leaves higher rock layers jutting outward, which then collapse. The cliff recedes, leaving a flat surface in the form of a bank, called an "abrasion platform."

Coasts
Ocean coasts are the most changing landscapes in the Earth's geography thanks to a process called "coastal drift." The elements that build up the coastline—wind, rain, and waves—also erode and mold it. Thus, the waves that bring the sediments that form beaches and carry them away are the same waves that can create or knock down a cliff or cave. Its remnants will be the building material for another beach, along with the sediment that comes from rivers and their deltas.

BEACH FORMATION
Beaches are formed from the gradual deposits of waves in low-energy coastal zones. They can be made of fine sediment, such as mud and sand, or of larger materials, such as boulders.

WAVES

ACCUMULATED SEDIMENTS

If Stones Could Speak

Rock strata form from sediments deposited over time in successive layers. Sometimes these sediments bury remains of organisms that can later become fossils, which provide key data about the environment and prehistoric life on Earth. The geologic age of rocks and the processes they have undergone can be discovered through different methods that combine analyses of successive layers and the fossils they contain.

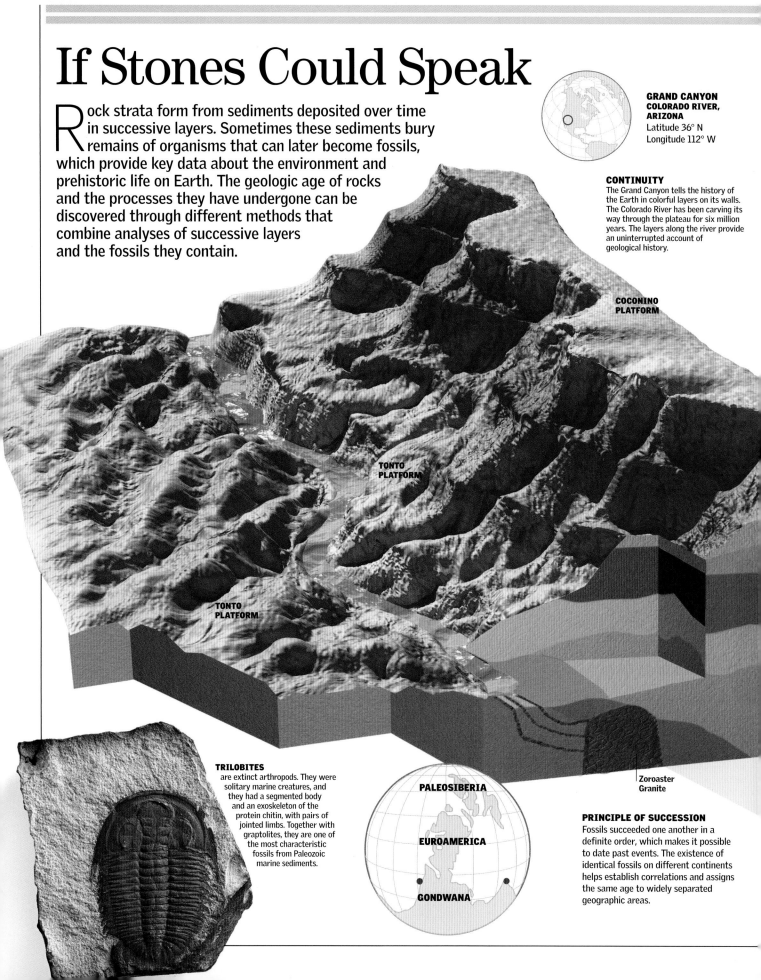

GRAND CANYON
COLORADO RIVER,
ARIZONA
Latitude 36° N
Longitude 112° W

CONTINUITY
The Grand Canyon tells the history of the Earth in colorful layers on its walls. The Colorado River has been carving its way through the plateau for six million years. The layers along the river provide an uninterrupted account of geological history.

COCONINO PLATFORM

TONTO PLATFORM

TONTO PLATFORM

Zoroaster Granite

TRILOBITES
are extinct arthropods. They were solitary marine creatures, and they had a segmented body and an exoskeleton of the protein chitin, with pairs of jointed limbs. Together with graptolites, they are one of the most characteristic fossils from Paleozoic marine sediments.

PALEOSIBERIA

EUROAMERICA

GONDWANA

PRINCIPLE OF SUCCESSION
Fossils succeeded one another in a definite order, which makes it possible to date past events. The existence of identical fossils on different continents helps establish correlations and assigns the same age to widely separated geographic areas.

1 When it dies, an animal can be submerged on a riverbed, protected from oxygen. The body begins to decompose.

2 The skeleton is completely covered with sediments. Over the years, new layers are added, burying the earlier layers.

A Fossil's Age

Fossils are remains of organisms that lived in the past. Today, scientists use several procedures, including carbon-14 dating, to estimate their age. This method makes it possible to date organic remains with precision from as long ago as 60,000 years. If organisms are older, there are other methods for absolute dating. However, within a known area, a fossil's location in a given sedimentary layer enables scientists to place it on an efficient, relative time scale. Following principles of original horizontality and of succession, it is possible to find out when an organism lived.

3 Once the water disappears, the fossil is already formed and crystallized. The crust's movements raise the layers, bringing the fossil to the surface.

4 Erosion exposes the fossil to full view. With carbon-14 dating, scientists can determine if it is less than 60,000 years old.

During fossilization, molecules of the original tissue are replaced precisely with minerals that petrify it.

Rock Layers and the Passage of Time

Rock layers are essential for time measurement because they retain information not only about the geologic past but also about past life-forms, climate, and more. The principle of original horizontality establishes that the layers of sediment are deposited horizontally and parallel to the surface and that they are defined by two planes that show lateral continuity. If layers are folded or bent, they must have been altered by some geologic process. These ruptures are called "unconformities." If the continuity between layers is interrupted, it means that there was an interval of time and, consequently, erosion in the layer below. This also is called unconformity, since it interrupts the horizontality principle.

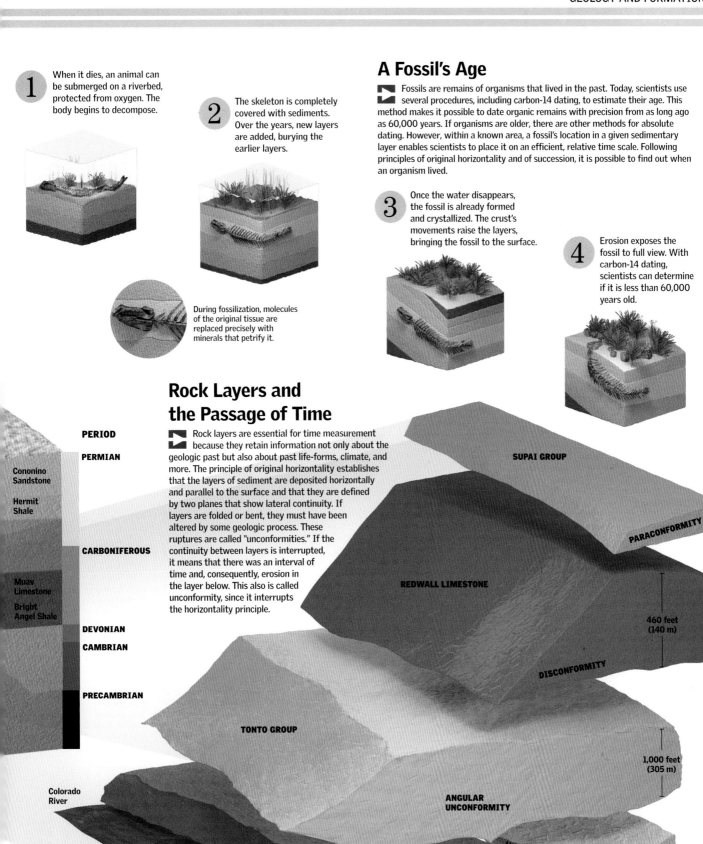

PERIOD

PERMIAN

Cononino Sandstone

Hermit Shale

CARBONIFEROUS

Muav Limestone

Bright Angel Shale

DEVONIAN

CAMBRIAN

PRECAMBRIAN

Colorado River

SUPAI GROUP

PARACONFORMITY

REDWALL LIMESTONE

460 feet (140 m)

DISCONFORMITY

TONTO GROUP

1,000 feet (305 m)

ANGULAR UNCONFORMITY

UNCONFORMITY

UNKAR GROUP

VISHNU SCHIST

TEMPORAL HIATUS
Unconformity between the Tonto Group and the Redwall Limestone indicates a temporal hiatus. Between the Redwall Limestone and the Supai Group, there is temporal continuity.

Metamorphic Processes

When rocks are subjected to certain conditions (high pressure and temperature or exposure to fluids with dissolved chemicals), they can undergo remarkable changes in both their mineral composition and their structure. This very slow process, called "metamorphism," is a veritable transformation of the rock. This phenomenon originates inside the Earth's crust as well as on the surface. The type of metamorphism depends on the nature of the energy that triggers the change. This energy can be heat or pressure.

SCOTLAND,
UNITED KINGDOM
Latitude   57° N
Longitude   04° W

Scotland was raised in the Caledonian orogeny 400 million years ago. This pressure produced the gneiss shown in the photo.

Dynamic Metamorphism

The least common type of metamorphism, dynamic metamorphism happens when the large-scale movement of the crust along fault systems causes the rocks to be compressed. Great rock masses thrust over others. Where they come in contact new metamorphic rocks, called "cataclasites" and "mylonites," are formed.

2

• Schist

SLATE
In environments with high temperature and pressure, slates will become phyllites.

570°F
(300°C)

SLATE
Metamorphic rock of low grade that forms through pressure at about 390°F (200°C). It becomes more compact and dense.

930°F
(500°C)

SCHIST
Very flaky rock produced by metamorphism at intermediate temperatures and depths greater than 6 miles (10 km). The minerals recrystallize.

1,200°F
(650°C)

GNEISS
Produced through highly metamorphic processes more than 12 miles (20 km) beneath the surface, it involves extremely powerful tectonic forces and temperatures near the melting point of rock.

1,470°F
(800°C)

FUSION
At this temperature, most rocks start to melt until they become liquid.

Regional Metamorphism

As mountains form, a large amount of rock is deformed and transformed. Rocks buried close to the surface descend to greater depths and are modified by higher temperatures and pressures. This metamorphism covers thousands of square miles and is classified according to the temperature and pressure reached. Slate is an example of rock affected by this type of process.

Contact Metamorphism

Magmatic rocks transmit heat, so a body of magma can heat rocks on contact. The affected area, located around an igneous intrusion or lava flow, is called an "aureole." Its size depends on the intrusion and on the magma's temperature. The minerals of the surrounding rock turn into other minerals, and the rock metamorphoses.

1

Intermediate Crust

Lower Crust

1

Sandstone

Schist

Limestone — Magma

2

Quarzite

Hornfels

Marble — Magma

PRESSURE
As the pressure increases on the rocks, the mineralogical structure of rocks is reorganized, which reduces their size.

TEMPERATURE
The closer the rock is to the heat source and the greater the temperature, the higher the degree of metamorphism that takes place.

The Basis of Life

Organisms are born, live, reproduce, and die on a natural layer of soil. From this layer, crops are harvested, livestock are raised, and construction materials are obtained. It establishes the link between life and the mineral part of the planet. Through the action of climate and biological agents, soil forms where rocks are broken down.

300 years

The time needed for the natural formation of soil with its three basic layers, or horizons.

Types of Soil

In the soil we find bedrock materials that have been greatly altered by air and water, living organisms, and decomposed organic materials. The many physical and chemical transformations that it undergoes produce different types of soil, some richer in humus, others with more clay, and so on. The soil's basic texture depends to a great extent on the type of bedrock from which the soil is formed.

RANKER

develops on top of slightly altered bedrock. It is typical in high mountains, especially if it forms on granite or other acidic rocks.

0.2%
of the world's land surface

PERMAFROST

Areas near the poles. The soil is saturated with frozen water. In the parts that thaw, big puddles are formed. Because of its characteristics, many animals cannot live there.

20%
of the world's land surface

DESERTIC

Arid soil. Containing very little humus, it rests directly on mineral deposits and rock fragments.

14%
of the world's land surface

LATERITE

Typical tropical soil. With abundant rains and humidity in these zones, the soil is well drained. The rain leaves a mix of oxides and hydroxides of aluminum, iron, manganese, nickel, and other minerals in the soil. This represents 70 percent of the world's iron reserves.

10%
of the world's land surface

HOW IT FORMS

Much of the Earth's crust is covered with a layer of sediment and decomposing organic matter. This layer, called "soil," covers everything except very steep slopes. Although it is created from decomposing plant and animal remains, the soil is a living and changing system. Its tiniest cavities, home to thousands of bacteria, algae, and fungi, are filled with water or air. These microorganisms speed up the decomposition process, turning the soil into a habitat favorable to plant roots as well as small animals and insects.

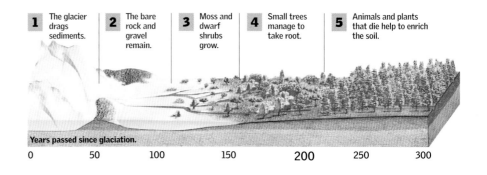

1 The glacier drags sediments.

2 The bare rock and gravel remain.

3 Moss and dwarf shrubs grow.

4 Small trees manage to take root.

5 Animals and plants that die help to enrich the soil.

Years passed since glaciation.

0   50   100   150   200   250   300

Different Characteristics

Observing the soil profile makes it possible to distinguish layers called "horizons." Each layer has different characteristics and properties, hence the importance of identifying the layers to study and describe them. The surface layer is rich in organic matter. Beneath is the subsoil, where nutrients accumulate and some roots penetrate. Deeper down is a layer of rocks and pebbles.

Living Organisms in the Soil

Many bacteria and fungi live in the soil; their biomass usually surpasses that of all animals living on the surface. Algae (mainly diatoms) also live closest to the surface, where there is most light. Mites, springtails, cochineal insects, insect larvae, earthworms, and others are also found there. Earthworms build tunnels that make the growth of roots easier. Their droppings retain water and contain important nutrients.

EARTHWORMS
It takes approximately 6,000 earthworms to produce 3,000 pounds (1,350 kg) of humus.

HUMUS
is the substance composed of organic materials, usually found in the upper layers of soil. It is produced by microorganisms, mainly acting on fallen branches and animal droppings. The dark color of this highly fertile layer comes from its high carbon content.

UPPER LAYER
This layer is dark and rich in nutrients. It contains a network of plant roots along with humus, which is formed from plant and animal residues.

SUBSOIL
contains many mineral particles from the bedrock. It is formed by complex humus.

BEDROCK
The continuous breakdown and erosion of the bedrock helps increase the thickness of the soil. Soil texture also depends to a great extent on the type of bedrock on which it forms.

0

3 ft
(1 m)

7 ft
(2 m)

10 ft
(3 m)

Rock Cycle

Some rocks go through the rock cycle to form soil. Under the action of erosive agents, rocks from the Earth's crust take on characteristic shapes. These shapes are a consequence partly of the rock's own composition and partly of several effects caused by erosive agents (meteorological and biological) responsible for breaking down rocky material.

Clouds of dust and ash are released to the atmosphere.

A volcano expels lava and pyroclastic material.

Igneous rock cools down and erodes.

Ash and other pyroclastic materials are deposited in layers.

EROSION

Some sedimentary and metamorphic rocks erode, forming new strata.

These layers compress and harden.

IGNEOUS ROCK
Extrusive rocks form as the lava cools.

Magma rises to the surface and comes out as lava through the volcano.

Igneous and plutonic rocks form as magma cools and solidifies below the Earth's surface.

SEDIMENTARY ROCK

Heat and pressure can recrystallize the rock without melting it, turning it into another type of rock.

METAMORPHIC ROCK
The rock melts to form magma.

If it is hot enough, the rock can turn into magma again.

IGNEOUS ROCK

Before Rock, Mineral

The planet on which we live can be seen as a large rock or, more precisely, as a large sphere composed of many types of rocks. These rocks are composed of tiny fragments of one or more materials. These materials are minerals, which result from the interaction of different chemical elements, each of which is stable only under specific conditions of pressure and temperature. Both rocks and minerals are studied in the branches of geology called "petrology" and "mineralogy."

TORRES DEL PAINE
CHILEAN PATAGONIA
Latitude 52° 20´ S
Longitude 71° 55´ W

Composition	Granite
Highest summit	**Paine Grande (10,000 feet [3,050 m])**
Surface	**598 acres (242 ha)**

Torres del Paine National Park is located in Chile between the massif of the Andes and the Patagonian steppes.

From Minerals to Rocks

From a chemical perspective, a mineral is a homogeneous substance. A rock, on the other hand, is composed of different chemical substances, which, in turn, are components of minerals. The mineral components of rocks are also those of mountains. Thus, according to this perspective, it is possible to distinguish between rocks and minerals.

12 million years ago

rock batholiths formed during a period of great volcanic activity and created the Torres del Paine and its high mountains.

QUARTZ
Composed of silica, quartz gives rock a white color.

MICA
Composed of thin, shiny sheets of silicon, aluminum, potassium, and other minerals, mica can be black or colorless.

GRANITE
Rock composed of feldspar, quartz, and mica

FELDSPAR
A light-colored silicate, feldspar makes up a large part of the crust.

CHANGE OF STATE
Temperature and pressure play a prominent part in rock transformation. Inside the Earth, liquid magma is produced. When it reaches the surface, it solidifies. A similar process happens to water when it freezes upon reaching 32° F (0° C).

Minerals

Dallol is basically a desert of minerals whose ivory-colored crust is scattered with green ponds and towers of sulfur salts in shades of orange. Some minerals belong to a very special class. Known as "gems," they are sought and hoarded for their great beauty. The most valuable gems are diamonds. Did you know

DALLOL VOLCANO
Located in Ethiopia, Dallol is the only nonoceanic volcano on Earth below sea level, making it one of the hottest places on the planet. Sulfur and other minerals that spring from this volcano create very vivid colors.

it took human beings thousands of years to separate metal from rock? Did you also know that certain nonmetallic minerals are valued for their usefulness? Graphite, for instance, is used to make pencils; gypsum is used in construction; and halite, also known as salt, is used in cooking.

How to Recognize Minerals

A mineral's physical properties are very important for recognizing it at first glance. One physical property is hardness. One mineral is harder than another when the former can scratch the latter. A mineral's degree of hardness is based on a scale, ranging from 1 to 10, that was created by German mineralogist Friedrich Mohs. Another physical property of a mineral is its tenacity, or cohesion—that is, its degree of resistance to rupture, deformation, or crushing. Yet another is magnetism, the ability of a mineral to be attracted by a magnet.

Exfoliation and Fracture

When a mineral tends to break along the planes of weak bonds in its crystalline structure, it separates into flat sheets parallel to its surface. This is called "exfoliation." Minerals that do not exfoliate when they break are said to exhibit fracture, which typically occurs in irregular patterns

TYPES OF EXFOLIATION

Cubic

Octahedral

Dodecahedral

Rhombohedral

Prismatic and Pinacoidal

Pinacoidal (Basal)

MOHS SCALE
ranks 10 minerals, from the softest to the hardest. Each mineral can be scratched by the one that ranks above it.

1 TALC
is the softest mineral.

2 GYPSUM
can be scratched by a fingernail.

3 CALCITE
is as hard as a bronze coin.

4 FLUORITE
can be scratched by a knife.

5 APATITE
can be scratched by a piece of glass.

Electricity Generation

Piezoelectricity and pyroelectricity are phenomena exhibited by certain crystals, such as quartz, which acquire a polarized charge because exposure to temperature change or mechanical tension creates a difference in electrical potential at their ends.

PIEZOELECTRICITY
The generation of electric currents that can occur when mechanical tension redistributes the negative and positive charges in a crystal. Tourmaline is an example.

Positive charge

PRESSURE

Negative charge

PYROELECTRICITY
The generation of electric currents that can occur when a crystal is subjected to changes in temperature and, consequently, changes in volume.

Positive charge

HEAT

Negative charge

DENSITY
reflects the structure and chemical composition of a mineral. Gold and platinum are among the most dense minerals.

FRACTURE
can be irregular, conchoidal, smooth, splintery, or earthy.

IRREGULAR FRACTURE
An uneven, splintery mineral surface

7 to 7.5
IS THE HARDNESS OF THE TOURMALINE ON THE MOHS SCALE.

6 ORTHOCLASE
can be scratched by a drill bit.

7 QUARTZ
can be scratched by tempered steel.

8 TOPAZ
can be scratched with a steel file.

9 CORUNDUM
can be scratched only by diamond.

10 DIAMOND
is the hardest mineral.

You Are What You Have

Minerals are the "bricks" of materials that make up the Earth and all other solid bodies in the universe. They are usually defined both by their chemical composition and by their orderly internal structure. Most are solid crystalline substances. However, some minerals have a disordered internal structure and are simply amorphous solids similar to glass. Studying minerals helps us to understand the origin of the Earth. Minerals are classified according to their composition and internal structure, as well as by the properties of hardness, weight, color, luster, and transparency. Although more than 4,000 minerals have been discovered, only about 30 are common on the Earth's surface.

Components

The basic components of minerals are the chemical elements listed on the periodic table. Minerals are classified as "native" if they are found in isolation, contain only one element, and occur in their purest state. On the other hand, they are classified as "compound" if they are composed of two or more elements. Most minerals fall into the compound category.

MINERALS COME FROM

112
elements

LISTED IN THE PERIODIC TABLE.

1 NATIVE MINERALS
These minerals are classified into:

A- METALS AND INTERMETALS
Native minerals have high thermal and electrical conductivity, a typically metallic luster, low hardness, ductility, and malleability. They are easy to identify and include gold, copper, and lead.

GOLD
An excellent thermal and electrical conductor. Acids have little or no effect on it.

SILVER
The close-up image shows the dendrites formed by the stacking of octahedrons, sometimes in an elongated form.

MICROPHOTOGRAPH OF SILVER CRYSTAL DENDRITES

2 COMPOUND MINERALS
Compound minerals are created when chemical bonds form between atoms of more than one element. The properties of a compound mineral differ from those of its constituent elements.

HALITE
is composed of chlorine and sodium.

B- SEMIMETALS
Native minerals that are more fragile than metals and have a lower conductivity. Examples are arsenic, antimony, and bismuth.

C- NONMETALS
An important group of minerals, which includes sulfur.

BISMUTH

SULFUR

Polymorphism

A phenomenon in which the same chemical composition can create multiple structures and, consequently, result in the creation of several different minerals. The transition of one polymorphous variant into another, facilitated by temperature or pressure conditions, can be fast or slow and either reversible or irreversible.

Chemical Composition	Crystallization System		Mineral
$CaCO_3$		Trigonal	Calcite
$CaCO_3$		Rhombic	Aragonite
FeS_2		Cubic	Pyrite
FeS_2		Rhombic	Marcasite
C		Cubic	Diamond
C		Hexagonal	Graphite

DIAMOND AND GRAPHITE

A mineral's internal structure influences its hardness. Both graphite and diamond are composed only of carbon; however, they have different degrees of hardness.

DIAMOND

GRAPHITE

CARBON ATOM

Model demonstrating how one atom bonds to the other four

Each atom is joined to four other atoms of the same type. The carbon network extends in three dimensions by means of strong covalent bonds. This provides the mineral with an almost unbreakable hardness.

HARDNESS OF 10 ON THE MOHS SCALE

Atoms form hexagons that are strongly interconnected in parallel sheets. This structure allows the sheets to slide over one another.

HARDNESS OF 1 ON THE MOHS SCALE

MORE THAN

4,000 types of minerals

HAVE BEEN RECOGNIZED BY THE INTERNATIONAL ASSOCIATION OF MINERALOGY.

Isotypic Minerals

Isomorphism happens when minerals with the same structure, such as halite and galena, exchange cations. The structure remains the same, but the resulting substance is different, because one ion has been exchanged for another. An example of this process is siderite (rhombic $FeCO_3$), which gradually changes to magnesite ($MgCO_3$) when it trades its iron (Fe) for similarly sized magnesium (Mg). Because the ions are the same size, the structure remains unchanged.

HALITE AND GALENA

HALITE NaCl
Cl   Na

GALENA PbS
S   Pb

Cubic Internal Structure

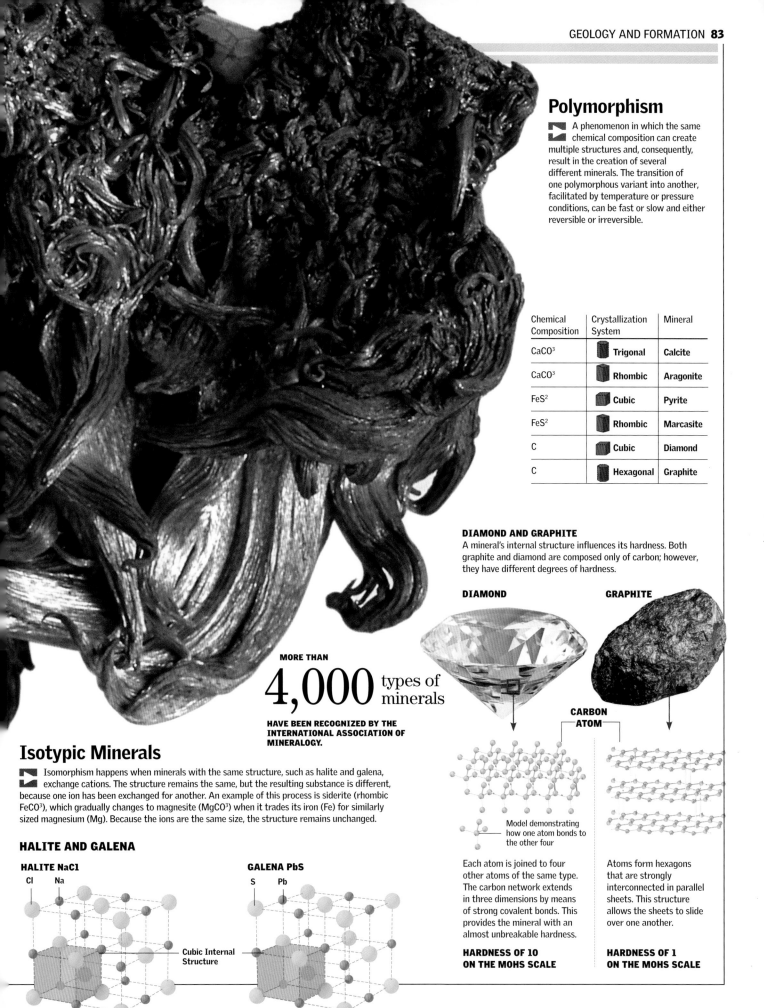

The Most Common Minerals

Silicates, which form 95 percent of the Earth's crust, are the most abundant type of mineral. Units of their tetrahedral structure, formed by the bonding of one silicon and four oxygen ions, combine to create several types of configurations, from isolated simple tetrahedrons to simple and double chains to sheets and three-dimensional complex networks. They can be light or dark; the latter have iron and magnesium in their chemical structures.

AUGITE

Structures

The basic unit of silicates consists of four oxygen ions located at the vertices of a tetrahedron, surrounding a silicon ion. Tetrahedrons can form by sharing oxygen ions, forming simple chains, laminar structures, or complex three-dimensional structures. The structural configuration also determines the type of exfoliation or fracture the silicate will exhibit: mica, which is composed of layers, exfoliates into flat sheets, whereas quartz fractures.

Complex Structure

This structure occurs when the tetrahedrons share three of their four oxygen ions with neighboring tetrahedrons, spreading out to form a wide sheet. Because the strongest bonds are formed between silicon and oxygen, exfoliation runs in the direction of the other bonds, parallel to the sheets. There are several examples of this type of structure, but the most common ones are micas and clays. The latter can retain water within its sheets, which makes its size vary with hydration.

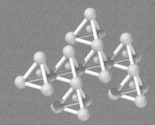

CHAINS
Clays are complex minerals with a very fine grain and a sheetlike structure.

Simple Structure

All silicates have the same basic component: a silicon-oxygen tetrahedron. This structure consists of four oxygen ions that surround a much smaller silicon ion. Because this tetrahedron does not share oxygen ions with other tetrahedrons, it keeps its simple structure.

UNCOMBINED SILICATES
This group includes all silicates composed of independent tetrahedrons of silicon and oxygen. Example: olivine.

Oxygen

Silicon

Compacted

KAOLINITE

OLIVINE

SILICATE MOLECULES

WATER MOLECULES

SILICATE MOLECULES

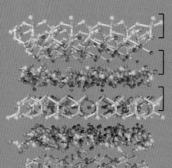

Three-dimensional Structure

Three fourths of the Earth's crust is composed of silicates with complex structures. Silicas, feldspars, feldspathoids, scapolites, and zeolites all have this type of structure. Their main characteristic is that their tetrahedrons share all their oxygen ions, forming a three-dimensional network with the same unitary composition. Quartz is part of the silica group.

LATERAL VIEW

THREE-DIMENSIONAL STRUCTURE

Quartz has a complex three-dimensional structure composed only of silicon and oxygen.

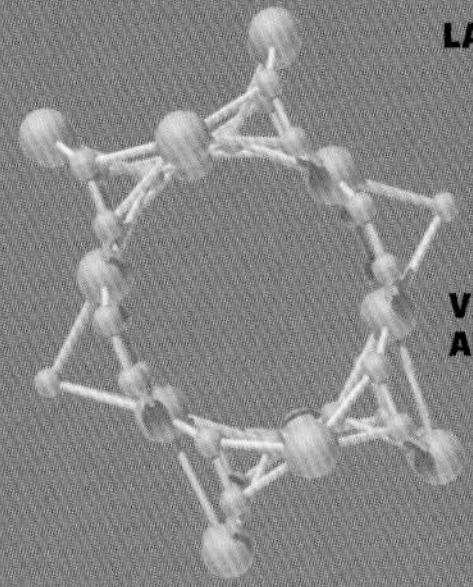

VIEW FROM ABOVE

MINERAL COMBINATIONS

DARK SILICATES

IRON AND MAGNESIUM

EXAMPLE: BIOTITE
The color and heaviness of this mineral are caused by the presence of iron and magnesium ions. Known as a "ferromagnesian mineral," biotite's specific gravity varies between 3.2 and 3.6.

LIGHT SILICATES

MAGNESIUM

EXAMPLE: MINERAL TALC
This mineral contains variable amounts of calcium, aluminum, sodium, and potassium. Its specific gravity is, on average, 2.7—much lower than that of ferromagnesian minerals.

Iron is added to its composition.

Calcium is added to its composition.

RESULTING SHAPE
The quartz crystal maintains a hexagonal shape with its six sides converging to a tip (pyramid).

A CRYSTAL OF GREAT VOLUME
For a quartz crystal to acquire large dimensions, it needs a great deal of silicon and oxygen, much time, and ample space.

Precious Crystals

Precious stones are characterized by their beauty, color, transparency, and rarity. Examples are diamonds, emeralds, rubies, and sapphires. Compared to other gems, semiprecious stones are composed of minerals of lesser value. Today, diamonds are the most prized gem for their "fire," luster, and extreme hardness. The origin of diamonds goes back millions of years, but people began to cut them only in the 14th century. Most diamond deposits are located in South Africa, Namibia, and Australia.

Diamond

Mineral composed of crystallized carbon in a cubic system. The beauty of its glow is due to a very high refraction index and the great dispersion of light in its interior, which creates an array of colors. It is the hardest of all minerals, and it originates underground at great depths.

1 EXTRACTION
Diamonds are obtained from kimberlite pipes left over from old volcanic eruptions, which brought the diamonds up from great depths.

KIMBERLEY MINE

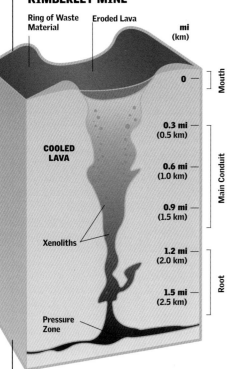

Ring of Waste Material

Eroded Lava

mi (km)

0 — Mouth

COOLED LAVA

0.3 mi (0.5 km)

0.6 mi (1.0 km) — Main Conduit

0.9 mi (1.5 km)

Xenoliths

1.2 mi (2.0 km) — Root

1.5 mi (2.5 km)

Pressure Zone

2 CUTTING AND CARVING
The diamond will be cut by another diamond to reach final perfection. This task is carried out by expert cutters.

B CUTTING:
Using a fine steel blade, the diamond is hit with a sharp blow to split it.

A INSPECTION:
Exfoliation is determined in order to cut the diamond.

C CARVING:
With a chisel, hammer, and circular saws, the diamond is shaped.

27.6 tons
(25 metric tons)

of mineral must be removed to obtain a 1-carat diamond.

1 carat = 0.007 ounce (0.2 grams)

8 CARATS

0.5 INCH (13 MM)

6.5 CARATS

0.3 INCH (7.6 MM)

0.03 CARAT

0.08 INCH (2 MM)

PRECIOUS STONES

DIAMOND
The presence of any color is due to chemical impurities.

EMERALD
Chromium gives it its characteristic green color.

OPAL
This amorphous silica substance has many colors.

RUBY
Its red color comes from chromium.

Gems

Mineral, rock, or petrified material that, after being cut and polished, is used in making jewelry. The cut and number of pieces that can be obtained is determined, based on the particular mineral and its crystalline structure.

③ POLISHING
The shaping of the facets of the finished gem

100
55.1
13.53
1.9
34.3°
40.9°
43.3

CROWN
GIRDLE
PAVILION

IDEAL DIAMOND STRUCTURE

BEZEL
STAR
TABLE

BRILLIANCE
The internal faces of the diamond act as mirrors because they are cut at exact angles and proportions.

FIRE
Flashes of color from a well-cut diamond. Each ray of light is refracted into the colors of the rainbow.

LIGHT

- Light enters the diamond.
- The facets of the pavilion reflect the light among themselves.
- The light is reflected back to the crown in the opposite direction.

LIGHT

- The rays divide into their components.
- Each color reflects separately in the crown.

320 microns
(0.32 mm)
MEASURED VERTICALLY

THE CHEMISTRY OF DIAMONDS
Strongly bonded carbon atoms crystallize in a cubic structure. Impurities or structural flaws can cause diamonds to show a hint of various colors, such as yellow, pink, green, and bluish white.

COMMON CUTS
A diamond can have many shapes, as long as its facets are carefully calculated to maximize its brilliance.

BRILLIANT   EMERALD   PRINCESS   TRILLION

PEAR   HEART   OVAL   MARQUISE

SEMIPRECIOUS STONES

SAPPHIRE
Blue to colorless corundum. They can also be yellow.

TOPAZ
A gem of variable color, composed of silicon, aluminum, and fluorine

AMETHYST
Quartz whose color is determined by manganese and iron

GARNET
A mix of iron, aluminum, magnesium, and vanadium

TURQUOISE
Aluminum phosphate and greenish blue copper

Rocks

Natural forces create an incredible variety of landscapes, such as deserts, beaches, elevated peaks, ravines, canyons, and underground caves. Rocks subjected to high pressure and temperatures can undergo remarkable changes. An initially igneous rock can become sedimentary and later metamorphic. Different types of rocks

YOSEMITE NATIONAL PARK, CALIFORNIA
The geology of the area is mostly composed of a
granitic batholith, but five percent of the park is
composed of formations from the metamorphism
of volcanic and sedimentary rocks.

can be distinguished based on their luster, density, and hardness, among other properties. A geode looks like a common rock on the outside, but when it is cut in half, a fantastic range of colors and shapes can be revealed. The several classes of rocks can also be grouped according to how they formed, giving us the categories of igneous, metamorphic, and sedimentary rocks.

How to Identify Rocks

Rocks can be classified as igneous, metamorphic, or sedimentary according to the manner in which they were formed. Their specific characteristics depend on the minerals that constitute them. Based on this information, it is possible to know how rocks gained their color, texture, and crystalline structure. With a little experience and knowledge, people can learn to recognize and identify some of the rocks that they often see.

Shapes

The final shape that a rock acquires depends to a great extent on its resistance to outside forces. The cooling process and subsequent erosion also influence the formation of rocks. Despite the changes caused by these processes, it is possible to infer information about a rock's history from its shape.

ANGULAR
Rocks have this shape when they have not been worn down.

ROUNDED
The wear caused by erosion and transport gives rocks a smooth shape.

Age

Being able to accurately determine the age of a rock is very useful in the study of geology.

Mineral Composition

Rocks are natural combinations of two or more minerals. The properties of rocks will change in accordance with their mineralogical composition. For instance, granite contains quartz, feldspar, and mica; the absence of any of these elements would result in a different rock.

Color

The color of a rock is determined by the color of the minerals that compose it. Some colors are generated by the purity of the rock, whereas others are produced by the impurities present in it. Marble, for instance, can have different shades if it contains impurities.

WHITE
If the rock is a marble composed of pure calcite or dolomite, it is usually white.

BLACK
Various impurities give rise to different shades in the marble.

**0.4 INCH
(1 CM)**

Fracture

When a rock breaks, its surface displays fractures. If the fracture results in a flat surface breaking off, it is called "exfoliation." Rocks usually break in locations where their mineral structure changes.

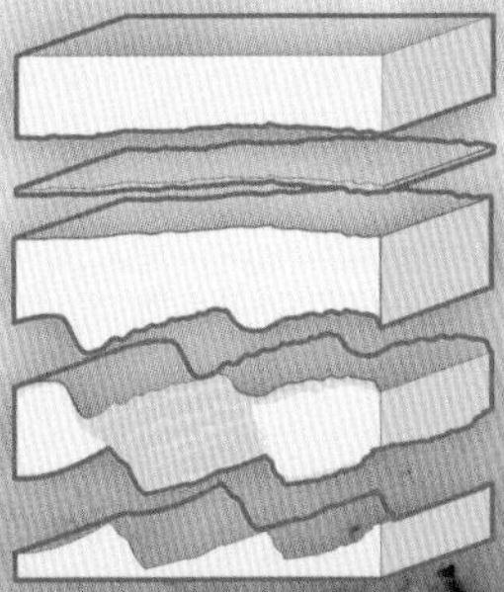

WHITE MARBLE

IMPURITY

WHITE MARBLE

PEGMATITE

WHITE MARBLE

Texture

refers to the size and arrangement of grains that form a rock. The grains can be thick, fine, or even imperceptible. There are also rocks, such as conglomerates, whose grains are formed by the fragments of other rocks. If the fragments are rounded, there is less compaction, and the rock is therefore more porous. In the case of sedimentary rocks in which the sedimentary cement prevails, the grain is finer.

GRAIN
is the size of the individual parts of a rock, be they crystals and/or fragments of other rocks. A rock's grain can be thick or fine.

**0.4 INCH
(1 CM)**

CRYSTALS
form when a melted rock cools and its chemical elements organize themselves. Minerals then take the shape of crystals.

Igneous Rocks

Formed from magma or lava, igneous rocks can be classified according to their composition. This classification specially takes into account: the relative proportion of silica, magnesium, and iron minerals found in these types of rocks; their grain size (which reveals how fast they cooled); and their color. Rocks that contain silica, along with much quartz and feldspar, tend to have pale colors; those with low silica content have dark colors created by iron and magnesium-containing minerals, such as olivine, pyroxene, and amphiboles. A rock's texture is determined by the configuration of its crystal grains.

Underground: Plutonic or Intrusive Rocks

Rocks of this type formed through the solidification of magma masses deep within other rocks. In general, they have undergone a slow cooling process in the Earth's crust, which has permitted the formation of pure mineral crystals large enough to be seen with the unaided eye. Usually, they display a compact structure and have low porosity. Depending on the composition of the magma, there are acidic plutonic rocks (rich in silicon) or basic rocks (with low silicon content). Granite is the most common type of intrusive rock.

GABBRO
This rock contains ferromagnesian minerals, such as olivine, pyroxene, and augite, which form dark-colored crystallizations, and feldspars, which give a white coloring to some of its parts. Gabbro generally solidifies slowly, leaving it with thick grains.

MACROPHOTOGRAPH OF PINK GRANITE

GRANITE
This rock is formed by big grains of feldspar, quartz, and mica. Its light-colored components indicate an abundance of silicon and that the rock is acidic. Because of its great resistance to wear, granite is often used as a construction material.

1 mile
(1.6 km)

THE MINIMUM DEPTH AT WHICH GRANITE FORMS

PERIDOTITE
This rock is mainly composed of olivine (which gives it a greenish color) and pyroxene. It is less than 45 percent silicon and is rich in magnesium, a very light metal. It is abundant in the upper layers of the mantle (at a depth of about 40 miles [60 km]) as a residue of old crust.

MACROPHOTOGRAPH OF GRANODIORITE

GRANODIORITE
This rock is often confused with granite, but it is grayer since it contains larger numbers of quartz and sodic plagioclase crystals than it does feldspar. It has thick grains and contains dark crystals called "nodules."

Dikes and Sills: Rocks Formed in Seams

Some types of igneous rocks are formed from ascending magma that solidifies in seams or fissures. The resulting sheetlike body of rock is called a "dike" if it has a vertical orientation or a "sill" if it has a horizontal orientation. The composition of these rocks is similar to those of intrusive and extrusive rocks. In fact, like dikes and sills, intrusive and extrusive rocks can also form in cracks. However, the manner in which the materials in a sill or dike solidify causes them to form crystalline structures different from those of their volcanic and plutonic relatives.

CRYSTAL JOINED BY VITREOUS MASS

PORPHYRITICS
These rocks solidify in two phases. In the first, slower phase, thick phenocrystals form. Then in the second phase, the phenocrystals are dragged along by magma, which causes the formation of smaller, vitreous crystals. The name "porphyritic" alludes to the color purple.

PEGMATITE IS NATURALLY SMOOTH.

PEGMATITE
This very abundant, acidic rock has a mineral composition identical to that of granite. However, its solidification process was very slow, thus enabling its crystals to grow to a size of several feet.

Index

PEGMATITE IS ASSOCIATED WITH THE PRESENCE OF GEMS AND RARE METALS.

Extrusive Rocks, Products of Volcanoes

Extrusive rocks form through the fast cooling of magma on or near the Earth's surface. Their structure and composition are closely related to the volcanic activity in the areas where they emerge. Because they are typically products of a fast solidification process, they usually have a very fine grain. When they are expelled from a volcano, they do not have a chance to crystallize before they cool, so they acquire a vitreous (glasslike) texture.

BASALT
This rock forms most of the oceanic crust. Its low silicon content gives it its characteristic dark color (between blue and black). Its rapid cooling and solidification gives it a very fine grain. Because of its hardness, it is used to build roads; it is not, however, used to make paving stones because it is too slippery.

PUMICE
This rock is produced from lava with a high silicon and gas content, which gives it a foamy texture. This explains its porous consistency—acquired during rapid solidification—which enables it to float in water.

GEOMETRIC PRISMS
These prisms were formed in the Giant's Causeway (Northern Ireland) through contraction, expansion, and rupture of basaltic lava flows that crystallized gradually.

OBSIDIAN
This rock is black; its shades vary in accordance with its impurities. Because it undergoes rapid cooling, its structure is vitreous, not crystalline; thus, it is commonly called "volcanic glass." Strictly speaking, obsidian is a mineraloid. It was often used to make arrowheads.

Hexagon
THE MOST COMMON SHAPE INTO WHICH BASALT CRYSTALLIZES

Common Metamorphic Rocks

The classification of metamorphic rocks is not simple because the same conditions of temperature and pressure do not always produce the same final rock. In the face of this difficulty, these rocks are divided into two large groups, taking into account that some exhibit foliation and others do not. During the transformation process, the density of rock increases, and recrystallization can induce the formation of bigger crystals. This process reorganizes the mineral grains, resulting in laminar or banded textures. Most rocks derive their color from the minerals of which they are composed, but their texture depends on more than just their composition.

GARNETIFEROUS SCHIST
This rock's name comes from its components. Schist determines its texture and garnet its color and distinctive features.

SLATE
Its black color comes from the carbon in organic matter present in sediments.

SLATE MICROGRAPHY
Composed of foliated or laminated clay minerals

MICACEOUS SCHIST
Its characteristic coloring is determined by colorless or white muscovite crystals.

HORNBLENDE SCHIST
It contains some sodium as well as considerable amounts of iron and aluminum.

Slates and Phyllites

▟ These foliated rocks recrystallized under moderate pressure and temperature conditions. Slate has very fine grains made of small mica crystals. It is very useful in the production of roof tiles, floor tiles, blackboards, and billiard tables. It almost always is formed through low-grade metamorphism in sediments and, less often, from volcanic ash. Phyllite represents a gradation in metamorphism between slate and schist; it is composed of very fine mica crystals, such as muscovite or chlorite.

PHYLLITE
Similar to slate, it is notable for its silky luster.

Gneiss

▟ Striped rock that usually contains long and granular minerals. The most common types are quartz, potash feldspar, and plagioclase. It can also have smaller amounts of muscovite, biotite, and hornblende. Its characteristic stripes are due to a segregation of light and dark silicates. Gneiss rock, which has a mineral composition similar to that of granite, is formed through sedimentary processes or derived from igneous rocks. However, it can also form through high-grade metamorphism of schists. It is the last rock of the metamorphic sequence.

SLATE
Because of exfoliation, it tends to break into flat sheets.

Foliation

LAMINATED OR STRIPED TEXTURE, RESULTING FROM THE PRESSURE TO WHICH THE ROCK WAS SUBJECTED

Stripes

MAKE IT POSSIBLE TO DETERMINE THE DIRECTION IN WHICH PRESSURE WAS EXERTED ON THE ROCK.

GARNETIFEROUS SCHIST
The dark red crystals of garnet formed during metamorphism.

Marble and Quartzite

These rocks are compacted and nonfoliated. Marble is a thick-grained crystalline rock, derived from limestone or dolostone. Because of its color and toughness, marble is used in the construction of large buildings. Quartzite is a very hard rock, usually made of sandstone rich in quartz, which, under elevated metamorphic conditions, melts like pieces of glass. Quartzite is normally white, but iron oxide can give it a reddish or pinkish tone.

Schist

This rock is more prone to foliation, and it can break off in small sheets. It is more than 20 percent composed of flat, elongated minerals, which normally include mica and amphiboles. For schist to be formed, a more intense metamorphism is needed. The different schistose rocks' names and characteristics depend on the predominant mineral that composes them or on the one that produces exfoliation. Among the most important schistose rocks are mica, hornblende, and talc. Because this type of rock has different layers, it has been used in sculpture.

QUARTZITE
It is hard and tough; it is compacted because the quartz grains entwine.

7 IS THE LEVEL OF HARDNESS OF QUARTZITE.

0.04 inch (1 mm)

OR MORE. THE SIZE OF MICA GRAINS IN SCHIST—LARGE ENOUGH TO SEE WITH THE UNAIDED EYE.

MARBLE
It is highly valued for its texture and color. It is used in sculpture and architecture.

MARBLE MICROGRAPH
Impurities and accessory minerals color the marble.

GNEISS
Heat and pressure can change granite into gneiss.

Collection of Detrital Rocks

Among the sedimentary rocks, detrital rocks are the most abundant. They form through the agglomeration of rounded fragments (clasts) of older rocks. Depending on the size of the clasts, they are classified as (from smallest to largest) pelite, lutite and limestone, sandstone, and conglomerates. The analysis of their components, cementation matrix, and arrangement in layers makes it possible to reconstruct the geologic history both of the rocks and of the areas in which they are found. Some break off easily and are used in industrial processes and construction as rock granules, whereas others are appreciated for their toughness and hardness.

Clay, Lime, and Ash

These materials form the less porous, fine-grained detritic rocks. Lutites are rocks of clay, composed of particles whose diameter does not exceed 0.0002 inch (0.005 mm). In general, they are compacted and cemented through chemical precipitation. Limestone rocks are also called "limolites," named after lime, a sedimentary material with a somewhat thicker grain (up to 0.0025 inch [0.06 mm]). Some rocks composed of volcanic ash have a similar granulation. These rocks are very important in construction.

COMPACTED ASH
It is possible to find one or more layers of fine-grained pyroclastic material (volcanic ash) in many sedimentary rocks. Rocks formed from larger pyroclasts, which solidified in the air during an eruption before they touched the ground, are rarer. Their origin is igneous, but their formation is sedimentary.

TUFF
is rock that is formed from deposits of volcanic ash that have been cemented together. There are several types: crystalline tuff, which is largely composed of igneous glass; lithic tuff, which contains rock fragments; and hybrid tuff, which is formed from fragmented volcanic material combined with some clay.

40%
THE REDUCTION IN THE VOLUME OF CLAY AS IT IS COMPACTED

**CLAY
(KAOLINITE)**
When hydrated, it increases in size.

CLAY
The substance commonly known as clay is an unconsolidated rock, made of hydrated aluminum silicates and typically full of impurities. Kaolin is the name for pure granular clay; it is soft and white and keeps its color even after it has been fired in a kiln. It has scale-shaped microcrystals and generally contains impurities.

CHALK
Composed of calcite debris of biochemical origin, this mineral originates in the sea near the coast. After being eroded and transported, it accumulates on slopes where it becomes compacted. The chalk we use on blackboards is, in reality, gypsum.

COMPACTED
Very fine sediment

A Variety of Sandstones

Sandstone is rock composed of grains that are mostly between 0.003 and 0.08 inch (0.08 and 2 mm) in size. Sandstones are classified according to their mineral composition, their level of complexity (or geologic history), and the proportion of cementation material they contain. Quartzarenite (which is more than 95 percent quartz), arkose (which is mostly feldspar), red sandstone (which is cemented by iron compounds), and graywacke belong to this class of rocks.

ARKOSE

possesses a varied composition, although it contains up to 25 percent quartz and feldspar. Generally, it has a porous consistency, and less than one percent of its interstices are empty. In this specimen, the pinkish section is composed of feldspar, and the white portion is quartz.

SANDSTONE

is made up of small grains of sand that are here stratified by color and texture. This type of sandstone indicates that an alternating process of sedimentation involving two types of particles has occurred.

GRAYWACKE

has a defined proportion of calcium carbonate, quartz, feldspar, and mica. It differs from common sandstone because it contains a higher amount of cementation materials (more than 15 percent), which form its grain matrix. This makes it more compacted.

20%
OF SEDIMENTARY ROCKS ARE SANDSTONES.

Conglomerates

Most of the grains that compose these rocks are larger than 0.08 inch (2 mm). In some cases, it is possible to identify with the unaided eye the primary rocks from which a conglomerate is formed. As a result, it is possible to determine the areas where the sediments originated. Accumulations of gravel and cementation material can indicate either slopes in the rocks where the conglomerates formed or the action of fluvial currents. All this information makes it possible to reconstruct the geologic history of a rock.

MICROPHOTOGRAPH OF BRECCIA

CONGLOMERATE

Formed by large fragments, they are good examples of sediments that have been compacted after landslides. The irregularity of this specimen's clasts points to a chaotic origin, which could be alluvial in nature or associated with a glacial moraine.

85%
PERCENTAGE OF CLASTS LARGER THAN 0.08 INCH (2 MM)

BRECCIA

Its grains are thick but with straight angles and edges. This shows that the sediments have not traveled far and that cementation has taken place near the area from which the materials originated.

Organic Rocks

Organic rocks are composed of the remains of living organisms that have undergone processes of decomposition and compaction millions of years ago. In these processes, the greater the depth and heat, the greater the caloric power and thermal transformation of the rock. The change experienced by these substances is called "carbonization."

PETROLEUM TRAPS

FAULT TRAP

Caprock   Storage Rock

ANTICLINE

SALINE DOME

STRATIGRAPHIC TRAP

FORMATION OF PETROLEUM
In an anaerobic environment at a depth of about 1 mile (1.6 km), organic sediments that developed in environments with little oxygen turn into rocks that produce crude oil.

KEY
Gas
Petroleum (Oil)
Water

The movements of the Earth's crust subjected the strata rich in organic remains to great pressure and transformed them into hard coal over the course of 300 million years.

LOCATION INSIDE THE EARTH

Vegetation that will form peat after dying

Peat is compacted and transformed.

DEPTH
up to 1,000 feet (300 m)

TEMPERATURE
up to 77°F (25°C)

26%
OF THE PRIMARY ENERGY CONSUMED IN THE WORLD COMES FROM COAL.

Coal Formation

Plant materials, such as leaves, woods, barks, and spores, accumulated in marine or continental basins 285 million years ago. Submerged in water and protected from oxygen in the air, this material slowly became enriched with carbon through the action of anaerobic bacteria.

Transformation of Vegetation into Hard Coal

1 VEGETATION
Organic compounds on the surface became covered by oxygen-poor water found in a peat bog, which effectively shielded them from oxidation.

2 PEAT
Through partial putrefaction and carbonization in the acidic water of the peat bog, the organic matter changes into coal.

Contains 60% carbon

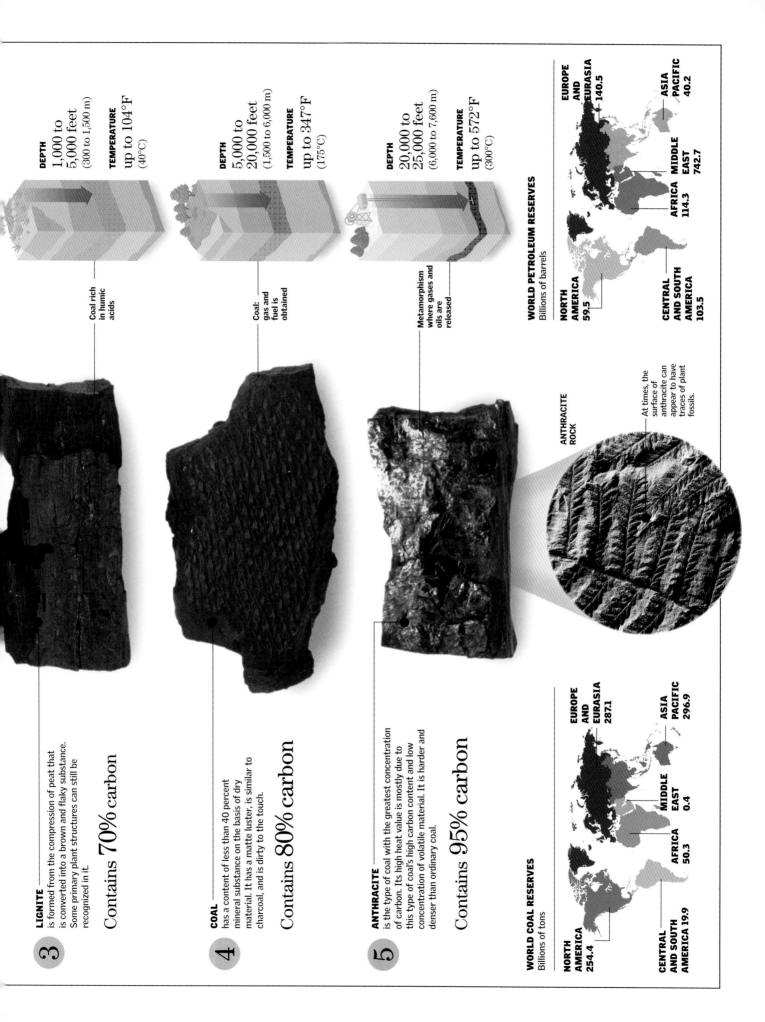

3

LIGNITE
is formed from the compression of peat that is converted into a brown and flaky substance. Some primary plant structures can still be recognized in it.

Contains 70% carbon

DEPTH
1,000 to 5,000 feet
(300 to 1,500 m)

TEMPERATURE
up to 104°F
(40°C)

Coal rich in humic acids

4

COAL
has a content of less than 40 percent mineral substance on the basis of dry material. It has a matte luster, is similar to charcoal, and is dirty to the touch.

Contains 80% carbon

DEPTH
5,000 to 20,000 feet
(1,500 to 6,000 m)

TEMPERATURE
up to 347°F
(175°C)

Coal: gas and fuel is obtained

5

ANTHRACITE
is the type of coal with the greatest concentration of carbon. Its high heat value is mostly due to this type of coal's high carbon content and low concentration of volatile material. It is harder and denser than ordinary coal.

Contains 95% carbon

DEPTH
20,000 to 25,000 feet
(6,000 to 7,600 m)

TEMPERATURE
up to 572°F
(300°C)

Metamorphism where gases and oils are released

ANTHRACITE ROCK

At times, the surface of anthracite can appear to have traces of plant fossils.

WORLD PETROLEUM RESERVES
Billions of barrels

EUROPE AND EURASIA 140.5

ASIA PACIFIC 40.2

MIDDLE EAST 742.7

AFRICA 114.3

NORTH AMERICA 59.5

CENTRAL AND SOUTH AMERICA 103.5

WORLD COAL RESERVES
Billions of tons

EUROPE AND EURASIA 287.1

ASIA PACIFIC 296.9

MIDDLE EAST 0.4

AFRICA 50.3

NORTH AMERICA 254.4

CENTRAL AND SOUTH AMERICA 19.9

3 THE POWER OF NATURE

102

114

130

Continuous Movement

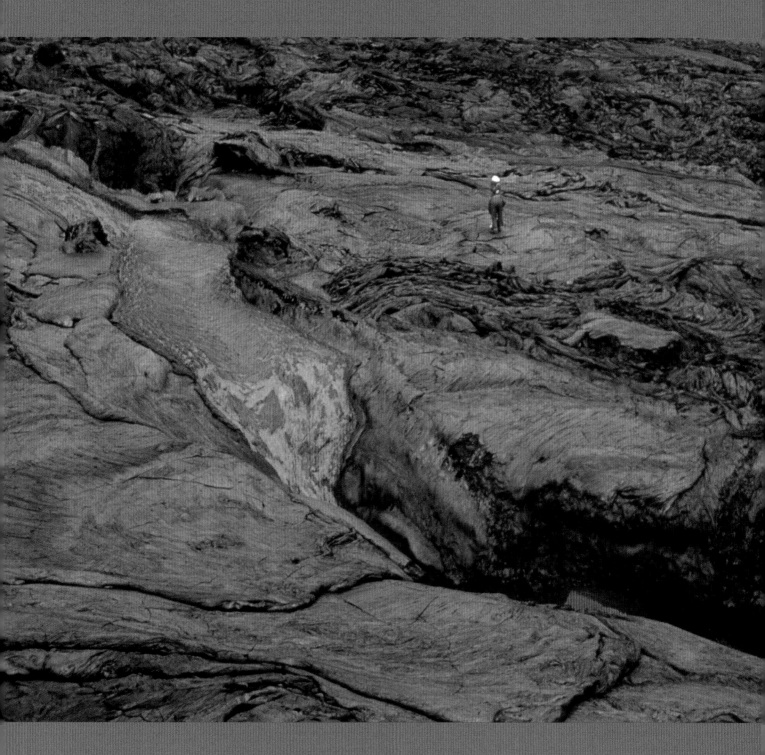

Our planet is not a dead body, complete and unchanging. It is an ever-changing system whose activity we experience all the time: volcanoes erupt, earthquakes occur, and new rocks emerge on the Earth's surface. These phenomena, which originate in the interior of the planet are studied in a branch of geology called internal geodynamics. This science analyzes

processes, such as continental drift and isostatic movement, which originates with the movement of the Earth's crust and result in the raising and sinking of large areas. The movement of the crust also generates the conditions that form new rocks. This movement affects magmatism, the melting of materials that solidify to become igneous rock, and metamorphism, giving rise to metamorphic rock.

The Long History of the Earth

The nebular hypothesis developed by astronomers suggests that the Earth was formed in the same way and at the same time as the rest of the planets and the Sun. It all began with an immense cloud of helium and hydrogen and a small portion of heavier materials 4.6 billion years ago. Earth emerged from one of these "small" revolving clouds, where the particles constantly collided with one another, producing very high temperatures. Later, a series of processes took place that gave the planet its present shape.

From Chaos to Today's Earth

Earth was formed 4.6 billion years ago. In the beginning it was a body of incandescent rock in the solar system. The first clear signs of life appeared in the oceans 3.6 billion years ago, and since then life has expanded and diversified. The changes have been unceasing, and, according to experts, there will be many more changes in the future.

4.5
BILLION YEARS AGO

COOLING
The first crust formed as it was exposed to space and cooled. Earth's layers became differentiated by their density.

4.6 BILLION YEARS AGO

FORMATION
The accumulation of matter into solid bodies, a process called "accretion," ended, and the Earth stopped increasing in volume.

60
MILLION YEARS AGO

FOLDING IN THE TERTIARY PERIOD
The folding began that would produce the highest mountains that we now have (the Alps, the Andes, and the Himalayas) and that continues to generate earthquakes even today.

540
MILLION YEARS AGO
PALEOZOIC ERA

FRAGMENTATION
The great landmass formed that would later fragment to provide the origin of the continents we have today. The oceans reached their greatest rate of expansion.

1.0
MILLION YEARS AGO

SUPERCONTINENTS
Rodinia, the first supercontinent, formed, but it completely disappeared about 650 million years ago.

4
BILLION YEARS AGO
METEORITE COLLISION
Meteorite collisions, at a rate 150 times as great as that of today, evaporated the primitive ocean and resulted in the rise of all known forms of life.

3.8
BILLION YEARS AGO
ARCHEAN EON
STABILIZATION
The processes that formed the atmosphere, the oceans, and protolife intensified. At the same time, the crust stabilized, and the first plates of Earth's crust appeared. Because of their weight, they sank into Earth's mantle, making way for new plates, a process that continues today.

When the first crust cooled, intense volcanic activity freed gases from the interior of the planet, and those gases formed the atmosphere and the oceans.

THE AGE OF THE SUPER VOLCANOES
Indications of komatiite, a type of igneous rock that no longer exists.

The oldest rocks appeared.

1.8
MILLION YEARS AGO
PROTEROZOIC EON
CONTINENTS
The first continents, made of light rocks, appeared. In Laurentia (now North America) and in the Baltic, there are large rocky areas that date back to that time.

2.2
MILLION YEARS AGO
WARMING
Earth warmed again, and the glaciers retreated, giving way to the oceans, in which new organisms would be born. The ozone layer began to form.

2.3
MILLION YEARS AGO
"SNOWBALL" EARTH
Hypothesis of a first, great glaciation.

Stacked Layers

Every 110 feet (33 m) below the Earth's surface, the temperature increases by 1.8 degrees Fahrenheit (1 degree Celsius). To reach the Earth's center—which, in spite of temperatures above 12,000°F (6,700°C), is assumed to be solid because of the enormous pressure exerted on it—a person would have to burrow through four well-defined layers. The gases that cover the Earth's surface are also divided into layers with different compositions. Forces act on the Earth's crust from above and below to sculpt and permanently alter it.

Earth's crust

Earth's crust is its solid outer layer, with a thickness of 3 to 9 miles (5 to 15 km) under the oceans and up to 44 miles (70 km) under mountain ranges. Volcanoes on land and volcanic activity in the mid-ocean ridges generate new rock, which becomes part of the crust. The rocks at the bottom of the crust tend to melt back into the rocky mantle.

KEY ● Sedimentary Rock ● Igneous Rock ● Metamorphic Rock

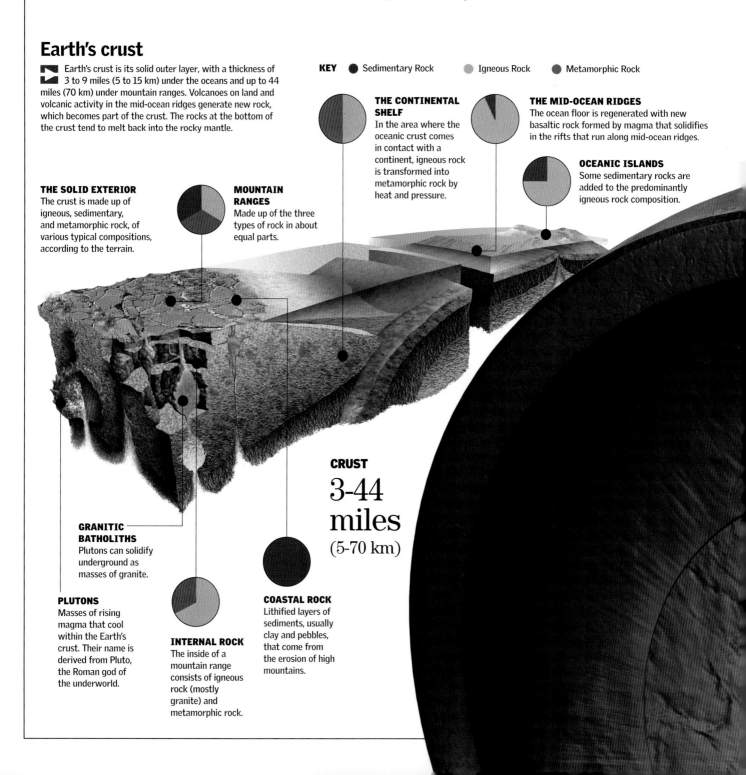

THE CONTINENTAL SHELF
In the area where the oceanic crust comes in contact with a continent, igneous rock is transformed into metamorphic rock by heat and pressure.

THE MID-OCEAN RIDGES
The ocean floor is regenerated with new basaltic rock formed by magma that solidifies in the rifts that run along mid-ocean ridges.

OCEANIC ISLANDS
Some sedimentary rocks are added to the predominantly igneous rock composition.

THE SOLID EXTERIOR
The crust is made up of igneous, sedimentary, and metamorphic rock, of various typical compositions, according to the terrain.

MOUNTAIN RANGES
Made up of the three types of rock in about equal parts.

GRANITIC BATHOLITHS
Plutons can solidify underground as masses of granite.

PLUTONS
Masses of rising magma that cool within the Earth's crust. Their name is derived from Pluto, the Roman god of the underworld.

INTERNAL ROCK
The inside of a mountain range consists of igneous rock (mostly granite) and metamorphic rock.

COASTAL ROCK
Lithified layers of sediments, usually clay and pebbles, that come from the erosion of high mountains.

CRUST
3-44 miles
(5-70 km)

The Gaseous Envelope

The air and most of the weather events that affect our lives occur only in the lower layer of the Earth's atmosphere. This relatively thin layer, called the "troposphere," is up to 11 miles (18 km) thick at the equator but only 5 miles (8 km) thick at the poles. Each layer of the atmosphere has a distinct composition.

Less than
11 miles
(18 km)

TROPOSPHERE
Contains 75 percent of the gas and almost all of the water vapor in the atmosphere.

Less than
31 miles
(50 km)

STRATOSPHERE
Very dry; water vapor freezes and falls out of this layer, which contains the ozone layer.

Less than
50 miles
(80 km)

MESOSPHERE
The temperature is -130°F (-90°C), but it increases gradually above this layer.

Less than
280 miles
(450 km)

THERMOSPHERE
Very low density. Below 155 miles (250 km) it is made up mostly of nitrogen; above that level it is mostly oxygen.

Less than
300 miles
(480 km)

EXOSPHERE
No fixed outer limit. It contains lighter gases such as hydrogen and helium, mostly ionized.

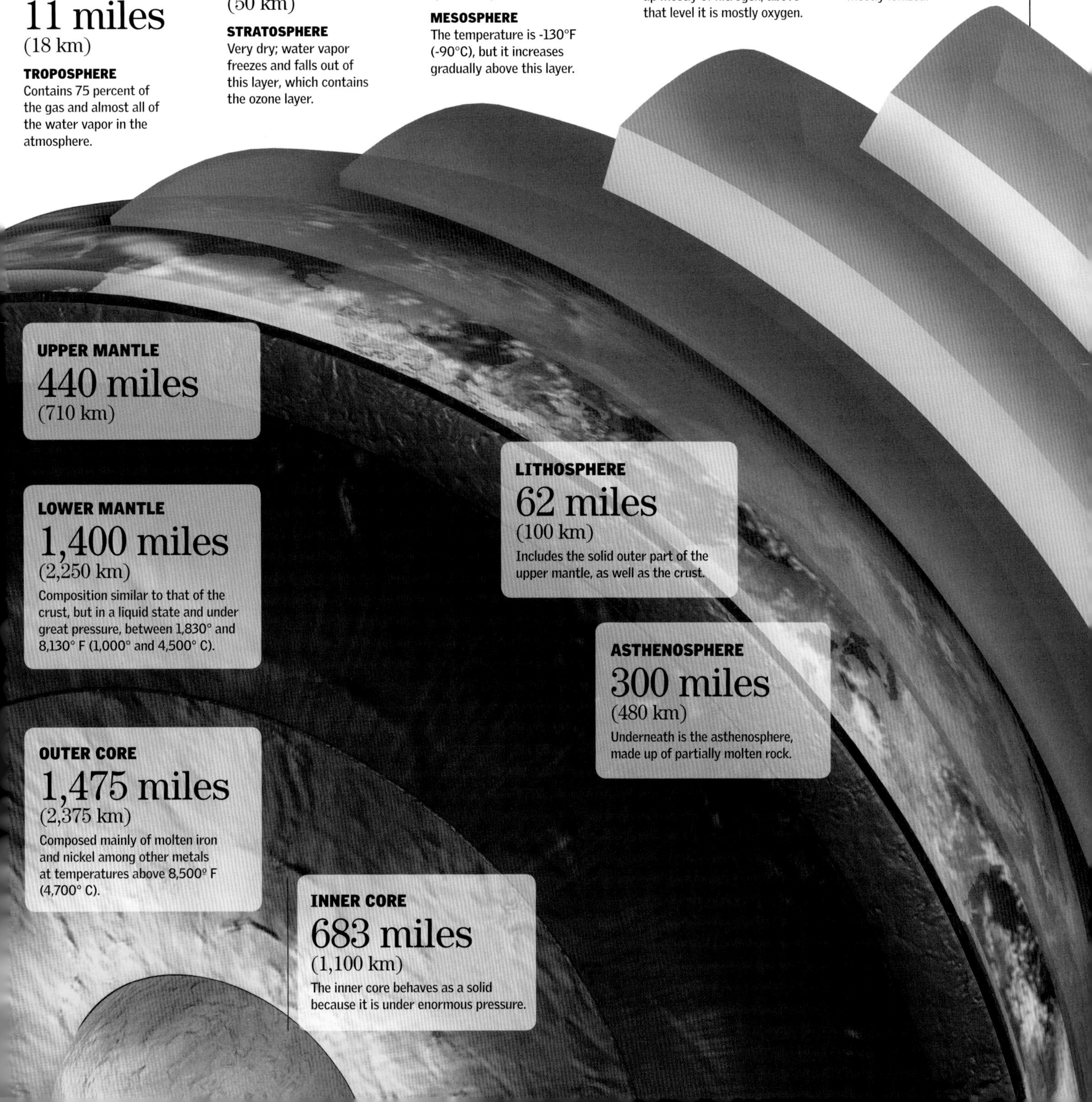

UPPER MANTLE
440 miles
(710 km)

LOWER MANTLE
1,400 miles
(2,250 km)
Composition similar to that of the crust, but in a liquid state and under great pressure, between 1,830° and 8,130° F (1,000° and 4,500° C).

OUTER CORE
1,475 miles
(2,375 km)
Composed mainly of molten iron and nickel among other metals at temperatures above 8,500° F (4,700° C).

INNER CORE
683 miles
(1,100 km)
The inner core behaves as a solid because it is under enormous pressure.

LITHOSPHERE
62 miles
(100 km)
Includes the solid outer part of the upper mantle, as well as the crust.

ASTHENOSPHERE
300 miles
(480 km)
Underneath is the asthenosphere, made up of partially molten rock.

The Journey of the Plates

When geophysicist Alfred Wegener suggested in 1910 that the continents were moving, the idea seemed fantastic. There was no way to explain the idea. Only a half-century later, plate tectonic theory was able to offer an explanation of the phenomenon. Volcanic activity on the ocean floor, convection currents, and the melting of rock in the mantle power the continental drift that is still molding the planet's surface today.

Continental Drift

The first ideas on continental drift proposed that the continents floated on the ocean. That idea proved inaccurate. The seven tectonic plates contain portions of ocean beds and continents. They drift atop the molten mantle like sections of a giant shell. Depending on the direction in which they move, their boundaries can converge (when they tend to come together), diverge (when they tend to separate), or slide horizontally past each other (along a transform fault).

The Hidden Motor

Convection currents of molten rock propel the crust. Rising magma forms new sections of crust at divergent boundaries. At convergent boundaries, the crust melts into the mantle. Thus, the tectonic plates act like a conveyor belt on which the continents travel.

...180 MILLION YEARS AGO
The North American Plate has separated, as has the Antarctic Plate. The supercontinent Gondwana (South America and Africa) has started to divide and form the South Atlantic. India is separating from Africa.

250 MILLION YEARS AGO
The landmass today's continents come from was a single block (Pangea) surrounded by the ocean.

LAURASIA

GONDWANA

ANTARCTICA

PANGEA

2 inches (5 cm)
Typical distance the plates travel in a year.

INDO-AUSTRALIAN PLATE

CONVERGENT BOUNDARY
When two plates collide, one sinks below the other, forming a subduction zone. This causes folding in the crust and volcanic activity.

TONGA TRENCH

NAZCA PLATE

EASTERN PACIFIC RIDGE

PERU-CHILE TRENCH

CONVECTION CURRENTS
The hottest molten rock rises; once it rises, it cools and sinks again. This process causes continuous currents in the mantle.

OUTWARD MOVEMENT
The action of the magma causes the tectonic plate to move toward a subduction zone at its far end.

...100 MILLION YEARS AGO

The Atlantic Ocean has formed. India is headed toward Asia, and when the two masses collide, the Himalayas will rise. Australia is separating from Antarctica.

... 60 MILLION YEARS AGO

The continents are near their current location. India is beginning to collide with Asia. The Mediterranean is opening, and the folding is already taking place that will give rise to the highest mountain ranges of today.

250 MILLION YEARS

The number of years it will take for the continents to drift together again.

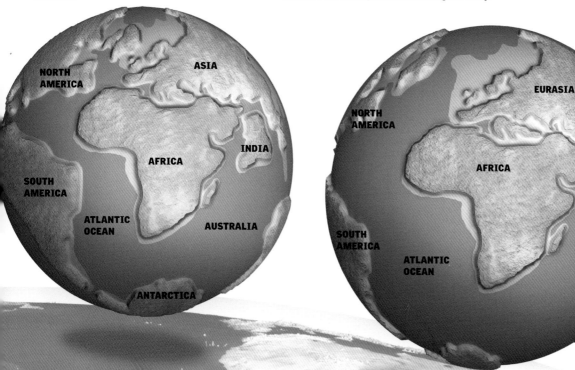

NORTH AMERICA

ASIA

AFRICA

INDIA

SOUTH AMERICA

ATLANTIC OCEAN

AUSTRALIA

ANTARCTICA

NORTH AMERICA

EURASIA

AFRICA

SOUTH AMERICA

ATLANTIC OCEAN

MID-ATLANTIC RIDGE

SOUTH AMERICAN PLATE

Continental granite

DIVERGENT BOUNDARY

When two plates separate, a rift is formed between them. Magma exerts great pressure, and it renews the ocean floor as it solidifies. The Atlantic Ocean was formed in this way.

AFRICAN PLATE

EAST AFRICAN RIFT VALLEY

SOMALIAN SUBPLATE

SUBDUCTION ZONE

CONTINENTAL CRUST

WIDENING

At divergent plate boundaries the magma rises, forming new oceanic crust. Folding occurs where plates converge.

Folding in the Earth's Crust

The movement of tectonic plates causes distortions and breaks in the Earth's crust, especially in convergent plate boundaries. Over millions of years, these distortions produce larger features called "folds," which become mountain ranges. Certain characteristic types of terrain give clues about the great folding processes in Earth's geological history.

Distortions of the Crust

The crust is composed of layers of solid rock. Tectonic forces, resulting from the differences in speed and direction between plates, make these layers stretch elastically, flow, or break. Mountains are formed in processes requiring millions of years. Then external forces, such as erosion from wind, ice, and water, come into play. If slippage releases rock from the pressure that is deforming it elastically, the rock tends to return to its former state and can cause earthquakes.

1 A portion of the crust subjected to a sustained horizontal tectonic force is met by resistance, and the rock layers become deformed.

2 The outer rock layers, which are often more rigid, fracture and form a fault. If one rock boundary slips underneath another, a thrust fault is formed.

3 The composition of rock layers shows the origin of the folding, despite the effects of erosion.

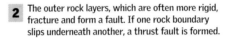

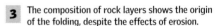

The Three Greatest Folding Events

The Earth's geological history has included three major mountain-building processes, called "orogenies." The mountains created during the first two orogenies (the Caledonian and the Hercynian) are much lower today because they have undergone millions of years of erosion.

MATERIALS
Mostly granite, slate, amphibolite, gneiss, quartzite, and schist.

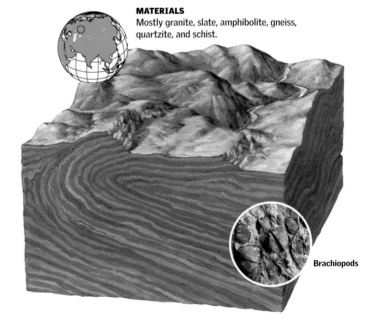

MATERIALS
Mudstone, slate, and sandstone, in lithified layers.

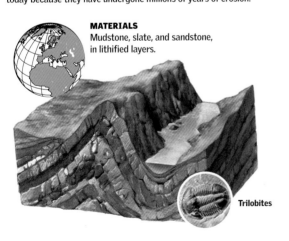

Trilobites

Brachiopods

430 Million Years

CALEDONIAN OROGENY
Formed the Caledonian range. Remnants can be seen in Scotland, the Scandinavian Peninsula, and Canada (which all collided at that time).

300 Million Years

HERCYNIAN OROGENY
Took place between the late Devonic and the early Permian Periods. It was more important than the Caledonian Orogeny. It shaped central and western Europe and produced large veins of iron ore and coal. This orogeny gave rise to the Ural Mountains, the Appalachian range in North America, part of the Andes, and Tasmania.

Formation of the Himalayas

The highest mountains on Earth were formed following the collision of India and Eurasia. The Indian Plate is sliding horizontally underneath the Asiatic Plate. A sedimentary block trapped between the plates is cutting the upper part of the Asiatic Plate into segments that are piling on top of each other. This folding process gave rise to the Himalayan range, which includes the highest mountain on the planet, Mount Everest (29,035 feet [8,850 m]). This deeply fractured section of the old plate is called an "accretion prism." At that time, the Asian landmass bent, and the plate doubled in thickness, forming the Tibetan plateau.

SOUTHEAST ASIA

INDIA TODAY

10 MILLION YEARS AGO

20 MILLION YEARS AGO

30 MILLION YEARS AGO

60 MILLION YEARS

ALPINE OROGENY
Began in the Cenozoic Era and continues today. This orogeny raised the entire system of mountain ranges that includes the Pyrenees, the Alps, the Caucasus, and even the Himalayas. It also gave the American Rockies and the Andes Mountains their current shape.

MATERIALS
High proportions of sediment in Nepal, batholiths in the Asiatic Plate, and intrusions of new granite: iron, tin, and tungsten.

Ammonites

A COLLISION OF CONTINENTS

Lighter sediments | Tethys Sea | Heavy sediments

INDIAN PLATE   **ASIATIC PLATE**

60 MILLION YEARS AGO
The Tethys Sea gives way as the plates approach. Layers of sediment begin to rise.

Heavy sediments | Tethys Sea | Tibet

40 MILLION YEARS AGO
As the two plates approach each other, a subduction zone begins to form.

Heavy sediments | Tibet

20 MILLION YEARS AGO
The Tibetan plateau is pushed up by pressure from settling layers of sediment.

India | Nepal | Tibet

THE HIMALAYAS TODAY
The movement of the plates continues to fold the crust, and the land of Nepal is slowly disappearing.

When the Faults Resound

Faults are small breaks that are produced along the Earth's crust. Many, such as the San Andreas Fault, which runs through the state of California, can be seen readily. Others, however, are hidden within the crust. When a fault fractures suddenly, an earthquake results. Sometimes fault lines can allow magma from lower layers to break through to the surface at certain points, forming a volcano.

Relative Movement along Fault Lines

 Fault borders do not usually form straight lines or right angles; their direction along the surface changes. The angle of vertical inclination is called "dip." The classification of a fault depends on how the fault was formed and on the relative movement of the two plates that form it. When tectonic forces compress the crust horizontally, a break causes one section of the ground to push above the other. In contrast, when the two sides of the fault are under tension (pulled apart), one side of the fault will slip down the slope formed by the other side of the fault.

350 miles
(563 km)

The distance that the opposite sides of the fault have slipped past each other, throughout their history.

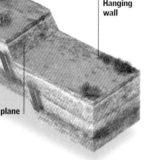

Footwall

Hanging wall

Fault plane

1
Normal Fault

This fault is the product of horizontal tension. The movement is mostly vertical, with an overlying block (the hanging wall) moving downward relative to an underlying block (the footwall). The fault plane typically has an angle of 60 degrees from the horizontal.

Footwall

Hanging wall

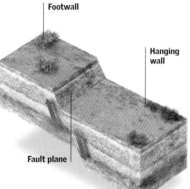

2
Reverse Fault

This fault is caused by a horizontal force that compresses the ground. A fracture causes one portion of the crust (the hanging wall) to slide over the other (the footwall). Thrust faults (*see* pages 110–111), are a common form of reverse fault that can extend up to hundreds of miles. However, reverse faults with a dip greater than 45° are usually only a few yards long.

Dip angle

OPPOSITE DIRECTIONS
The northwestward movement of the Pacific Plate and the southeastward movement of the North American Plate cause folds and fissures throughout the region.

PACIFIC OCEAN

Rodgers Creek
Concord-Green Valley
Mt. Diablo
OAKLAND
Greenville
SAN FRANCISCO
Hayward
Calaveras
San Gregorio

3
Oblique-Slip Fault

This fault has horizontal as well as vertical movements. Thus, the relative displacement between the edges of the fault can be diagonal. In the oldest faults, erosion usually smoothes the differences in the surrounding terrain, but in more recent faults, cliffs are formed. Transform faults that displace mid-ocean ridges are a specific example of oblique-slip faults.

Elevated block

4
Strike-Slip Fault

In this fault the relative movement of the plates is mainly horizontal, along the Earth's surface, parallel to the direction of the fracture but not parallel to the fault plane. Transform faults between plates are usually of this type. Rather than a single fracture, they are generally made up of a system of smaller fractures, slanted from a centerline and more or less parallel to each other. The system can be several miles wide.

Streambeds Diverted by Tectonic Movement

Through friction and surface cracking, a transform fault creates transverse faults and, at the same time, alters them with its movement. Rivers and streams distorted by the San Andreas Fault have three characteristic forms: streambeds with tectonic displacement, diverted streambeds, and streambeds with an orientation that is nearly oblique to the Fault.

1

DIVERTED STREAMBED
The stream changes course as a result of the break.

2

DISPLACED STREAMBED
The streambed looks "broken" along its fault line.

WEST COAST OF THE UNITED STATES

Length of California	770 miles (1,240 km)
Length of fault	800 miles (1,300 km)
Maximum width of fault	60 miles (100 km)
Greatest displacement (1906)	20 feet (6 m)

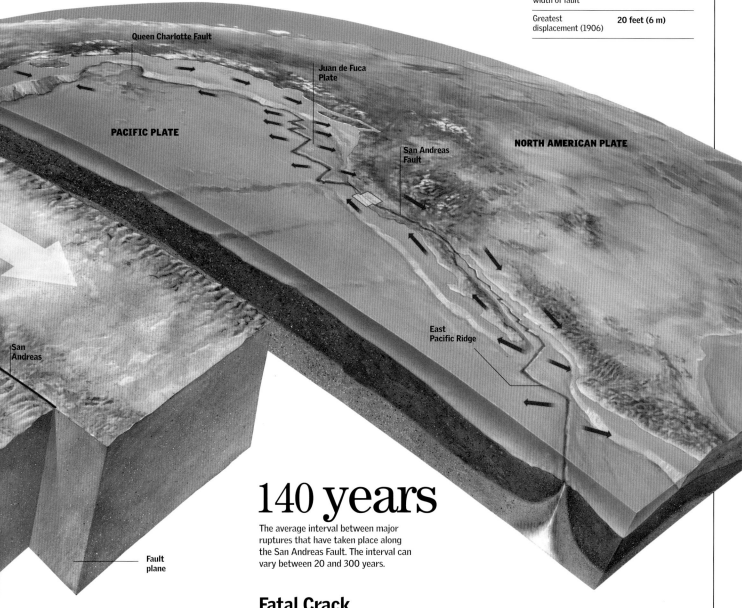

Queen Charlotte Fault

Juan de Fuca Plate

PACIFIC PLATE

San Andreas Fault

NORTH AMERICAN PLATE

San Andreas

East Pacific Ridge

Fault plane

140 years

The average interval between major ruptures that have taken place along the San Andreas Fault. The interval can vary between 20 and 300 years.

PAST AND FUTURE
Some 30 million years ago, the Peninsula of California was west of the present coast of Mexico. Thirty million years from now, it is possible that it may be some distance off the coast of Canada.

Fatal Crack

The great San Andreas Fault in the western United States is the backbone of a system of faults. Following the great earthquake that leveled San Francisco in 1906, this system has been studied more than any other on Earth. It is basically a horizontal transform fault that forms the boundary between the Pacific and North American tectonic plates. The system contains many complex lesser faults, and it has a total length of 800 miles (1,300 km). If both plates were able to slide past each other smoothly, no earthquakes would result. However, the borders of the plates are in contact with each other. When the solid rock cannot withstand the growing strain, it breaks and unleashes an earthquake.

Volcanoes

M ount Etna has always been an active volcano, as seen from the references to its activity that have been made throughout history. It could be said that the volcano has not given the beautiful island of Sicily a moment's rest. The Greek philosopher Plato was the first to study Mount Etna. He traveled to Italy especially to see it up close, and he

MOUNT ETNA
With a height of 10,810 feet (3,295 m),
Etna is the largest and most active
volcano in Europe.

subsequently described how the lava cooled. Today, Etna's periodic eruptions continue to draw hundreds of thousands of tourists, who enjoy the spectacular fireworks produced by its red-hot explosions. This phenomenon is visible from the entire east coast of Sicily because of the region's favorable weather conditions and the constant strong winds.

Flaming Furnace

Volcanoes are among the most powerful manifestations of our planet's dynamic interior. The magma they release at the Earth's surface can cause phenomena that devastate surrounding areas: explosions, enormous flows of molten rock, fire and ash that rain from the sky, floods, and mudslides. Since ancient times, human beings have feared volcanoes, even seeing their smoking craters as an entrance to the underworld. Every volcano has a life cycle, during which it can modify the topography and the climate and after which it becomes extinct.

MOUNTAIN-RANGE VOLCANOES

Many volcanoes are caused by phenomena occurring in subduction zones along convergent plate boundaries.

1 When two plates converge, one moves under the other (subduction).

2 The rock melts and forms new magma. Great pressure builds up between the plates.

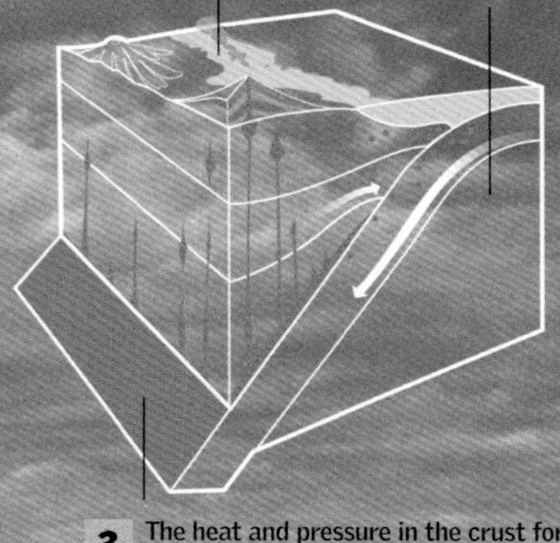

3 The heat and pressure in the crust force the magma to seep through cracks in the rock and rise to the surface, causing volcanic eruptions.

Life and Death of a Volcano: the Formation of a Caldera

1 Explosive eruptions can expel huge quantities of lava, gas, and rock.

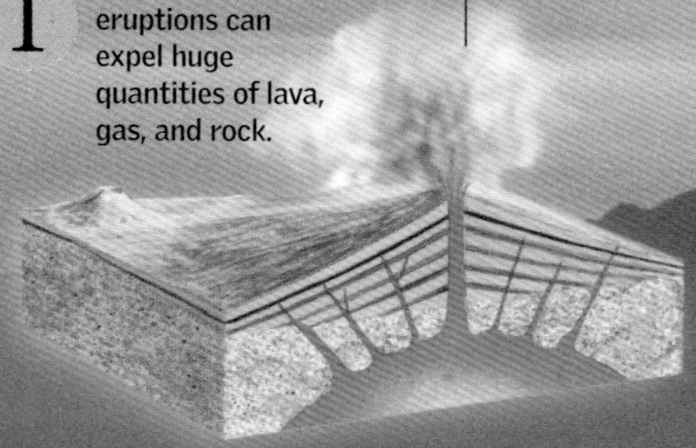

2 A void is left in the conduit and in the internal chamber.

ERUPTION OF LAVA

CRATER
Depression or hollow from which eruptions expel magmatic materials (lava, gas, steam, ash, etc.)

PARASITIC VOLCANO
Composite volcanic cones have more than one crater.

SECONDARY CONDUIT

CLOUD OF ASH

STREAMS OF LAVA
flow down the flanks of the volcano.

VOLCANIC CONE
Made of layers of igneous rock, formed from previous eruptions. Each lava flow adds a new layer.

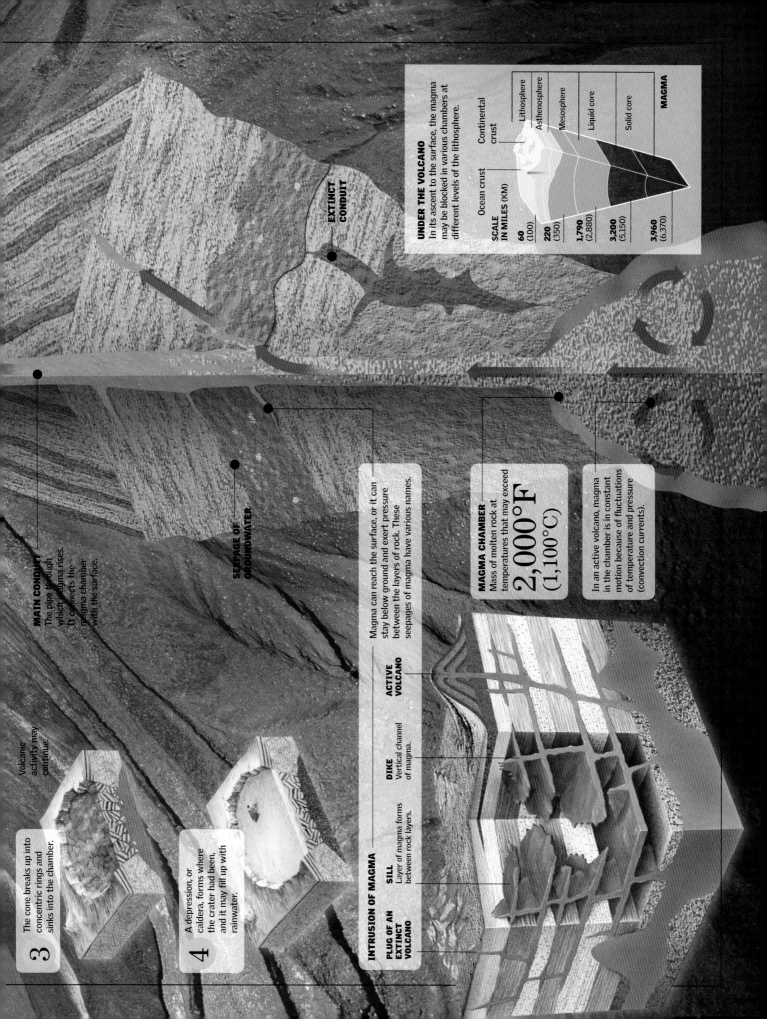

EXTINCT CONDUIT

MAIN CONDUIT
The pipe through which magma rises. It connects the magma chamber with the surface.

SEEPAGE OF GROUNDWATER

3 The cone breaks up into concentric rings and sinks into the chamber.

Volcanic activity may continue.

4 A depression, or caldera, forms where the crater had been, and it may fill up with rainwater.

INTRUSION OF MAGMA

PLUG OF AN EXTINCT VOLCANO

SILL
Layer of magma forms between rock layers.

DIKE
Vertical channel of magma.

ACTIVE VOLCANO

Magma can reach the surface, or it can stay below ground and exert pressure between the layers of rock. These seepages of magma have various names.

MAGMA CHAMBER
Mass of molten rock at temperatures that may exceed

2,000°F (1,100°C)

In an active volcano, magma in the chamber is in constant motion because of fluctuations of temperature and pressure (convection currents).

Classification

No two volcanoes on Earth are exactly alike, although they have characteristics that permit them to be studied according to six basic types: shield volcanoes, cinder cones, stratovolcanoes, lava cones, fissure volcanoes, and calderas. A volcano's shape depends on its origin, how the eruption began, and processes that accompany the volcanic activity. They are sometimes classified by the degree of danger they pose to life in surrounding areas.

The Most Common

Stratovolcanoes, or composite cones, are strung along the edges of the Pacific Plate in the region known as the "Ring of Fire."

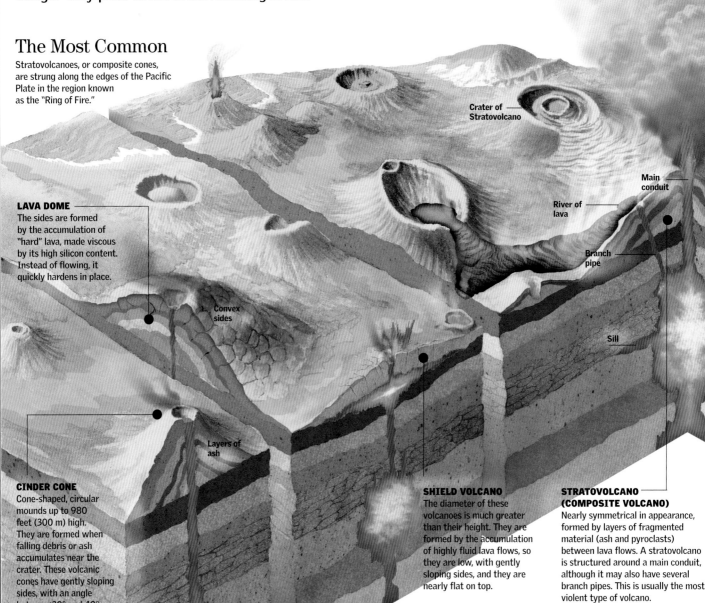

Crater of Stratovolcano

Main conduit

River of lava

Branch pipe

Sill

LAVA DOME
The sides are formed by the accumulation of "hard" lava, made viscous by its high silicon content. Instead of flowing, it quickly hardens in place.

Convex sides

Layers of ash

CINDER CONE
Cone-shaped, circular mounds up to 980 feet (300 m) high. They are formed when falling debris or ash accumulates near the crater. These volcanic cones have gently sloping sides, with an angle between 30° and 40°.

SHIELD VOLCANO
The diameter of these volcanoes is much greater than their height. They are formed by the accumulation of highly fluid lava flows, so they are low, with gently sloping sides, and they are nearly flat on top.

STRATOVOLCANO (COMPOSITE VOLCANO)
Nearly symmetrical in appearance, formed by layers of fragmented material (ash and pyroclasts) between lava flows. A stratovolcano is structured around a main conduit, although it may also have several branch pipes. This is usually the most violent type of volcano.

MOUNT ILAMATEPEC
Cinder cone located 45 miles (73 km) west of the capital of El Salvador. Its last recorded eruption was in October 2005.

MOUNT KILAUEA
Shield volcano in Hawaii. One of the most active shield volcanoes on Earth.

MOUNT FUJI
Composite volcano 12,400 feet (3,780 m) high, the highest in Japan. Its last eruption was in 1707.

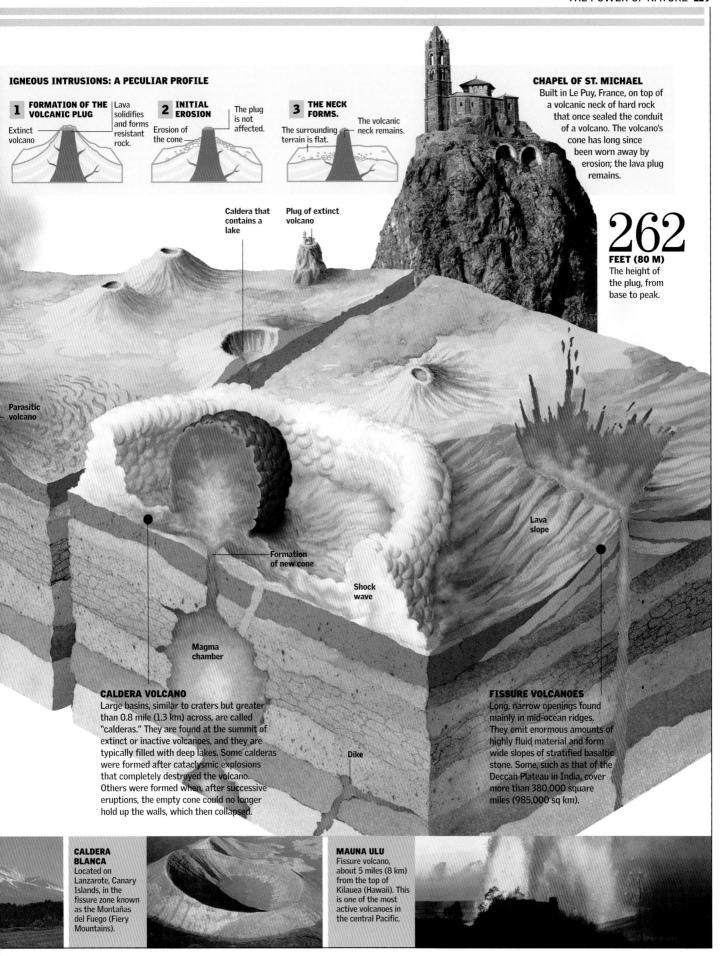

IGNEOUS INTRUSIONS: A PECULIAR PROFILE

1 FORMATION OF THE VOLCANIC PLUG

Lava solidifies and forms resistant rock.

Extinct volcano

2 INITIAL EROSION

The plug is not affected.

Erosion of the cone

3 THE NECK FORMS.

The volcanic neck remains.

The surrounding terrain is flat.

CHAPEL OF ST. MICHAEL

Built in Le Puy, France, on top of a volcanic neck of hard rock that once sealed the conduit of a volcano. The volcano's cone has long since been worn away by erosion; the lava plug remains.

262
FEET (80 M)
The height of the plug, from base to peak.

Caldera that contains a lake

Plug of extinct volcano

Parasitic volcano

Formation of new cone

Shock wave

Lava slope

Magma chamber

CALDERA VOLCANO

Large basins, similar to craters but greater than 0.8 mile (1.3 km) across, are called "calderas." They are found at the summit of extinct or inactive volcanoes, and they are typically filled with deep lakes. Some calderas were formed after cataclysmic explosions that completely destroyed the volcano. Others were formed when, after successive eruptions, the empty cone could no longer hold up the walls, which then collapsed.

Dike

FISSURE VOLCANOES

Long, narrow openings found mainly in mid-ocean ridges. They emit enormous amounts of highly fluid material and form wide slopes of stratified basaltic stone. Some, such as that of the Deccan Plateau in India, cover more than 380,000 square miles (985,000 sq km).

CALDERA BLANCA

Located on Lanzarote, Canary Islands, in the fissure zone known as the Montañas del Fuego (Fiery Mountains).

MAUNA ULU

Fissure volcano, about 5 miles (8 km) from the top of Kilauea (Hawaii). This is one of the most active volcanoes in the central Pacific.

Flash of Fire

A volcanic eruption is a process that can last from a few hours to several decades. Some are devastating, but others are mild. The severity of the eruption depends on the dynamics between the magma, dissolved gas, and rocks within the volcano. The most potent explosions often result from thousands of years of accumulation of magma and gas, as pressure builds up inside the chamber. Other volcanoes, such as Stromboli and Etna in Italy, reach an explosive point every few months and have frequent emissions.

How it Happens

3 THE ESCAPE
When the mounting pressure of the magma becomes greater than the materials between the magma and the floor of the volcano's crater can bear, these materials are ejected.

2 IN THE CONDUIT
A solid layer of fragmented materials blocks the magma that contains the volatile gases. As the magma rises and mixes with volatile gases and water vapor, the pockets of gases and steam that form give the magma its explosive power.

1 IN THE CHAMBER
There is a level at which liquefaction takes place and at which rising magma, under pressure, mixes with gases in the ground. The rising currents of magma increase the pressure, hastening the mixing.

ASH

LAPILLI

4 PYROCLASTIC PRODUCTS
In addition to lava, an eruption can eject solid materials called "pyroclasts." Volcanic ash consists of pyroclastic material less than 0.08 inch (2 mm) in size. An explosion can even expel granite blocks.

Bomb	2.5 inches (64 mm) and up
Lapilli	0.08 to 2.5 inches (2 mm to 64 mm)
Ash	Up to 0.08 inch (2 mm)

5 LAVA FLOWS
On the volcanic island of Hawaii, nonerupting flows of lava abound. Local terms for lava include "a'a," viscous lava flows that sweep away sediments, and "pahoehoe," more fluid lava that solidifies in soft waves.

Effusive Activity

Mild eruptions with a low frequency of explosions. The lava has a low gas content, and it flows out of openings and fissures.

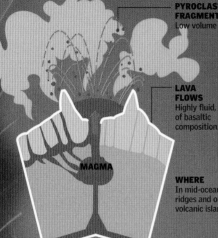

PYROCLASTIC FRAGMENTS
Low volume

LAVA FLOWS
Highly fluid, of basaltic composition.

MAGMA

WHERE
In mid-ocean ridges and on volcanic islands.

TYPES OF EFFUSIVE ERUPTION

Dome low, like a shield volcano, with a single opening

Large, Frequent Lava Flows

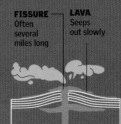

FISSURE Often several miles long

LAVA Seeps out slowly

HAWAIIAN
Volcanoes such as Mauna Loa and Kilauea expel large amounts of basaltic lava with a low gas content, so their eruptions are very mild. They sometimes emit vertical streams of bright lava ("fountains of fire") that can reach up to 330 feet (100 m) in height.

FISSURE
Typical in ocean rift zones, fissures are also found on the sides of composite cones such as Etna (Italy) or near shield volcanoes (Hawaii). The greatest eruption of this type was that of Laki, Iceland, in 1783: 2.9 cubic miles (12 cu km) of lava was expelled from a crack 16 miles (25 km) long.

FROM OUTER SPACE
A photo of the eruption of Mt. Augustine in Alaska, taken by the *Landsat 5* satellite hours after the March 27, 1986, eruption.

SMOKE COLUMN
7 Miles
(11.5 Km) HIGH

Volcanic ash

Snow and ice

Lava flow

Explosive Activity

Comes from the combination of high levels of gas with relatively viscous lava, which can produce pyroclasts and build up great pressure. Different types of explosions are distinguished based on their size and volume. The greatest explosions can raise ash into a column several miles high.

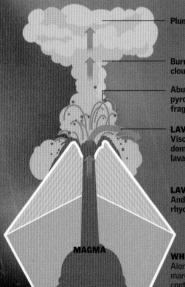

Plume of ash

Burning clouds

Abundant pyroclastic fragments

LAVA FLOWS Viscous and dome-shaped lava

LAVA Andesitic or rhyolitic

MAGMA

WHERE Along the margins of continents and island chains.

Types of Explosive Eruption

Cloud can reach above 82,000 feet (25 km).

The column can reach a height of 49,000 feet (15 km)

Cloud of burning material from about 330 to 3,300 feet (100–1,000 m) high

Lava flow

Burning cloud moving down the slope

Lava plug

STROMBOLIAN
The volcano Stromboli in Sicily, Italy, gave its name to these high-frequency eruptions. The relatively low volume of expelled pyroclasts allows these eruptions to occur approximately every five years.

VULCANIAN
Named after Vulcano in Sicily. As eruptions eject more material and become more explosive, they become less frequent. The 1985 eruption of Nevado del Ruiz in Colombia expelled tens of thousands of cubic yards of lava and ash.

VESUVIAN
Also called Plinian, the most violent explosions raise columns of smoke and ash that can reach into the stratosphere and last up to two years, as in the case of Krakatoa, Indonesia (1883).

PELEAN
A plug of lava blocks the crater and diverts the column to one side after a large explosion. As with Mt. Pelée on Martinique, in 1902, the pyroclastic flow and lava are violently expelled down the slope in a burning cloud that sweeps away everything in its path.

LAVA FLOW MT. KILAUEA, HAWAII

LAKE OF LAVA MAKA-O-PUHI, HAWAII   COOLED LAVA (PAHOEHOE) MT. KILAUEA, HAWAII

Aftermath of Fury

When a volcano becomes active and explodes, it sets in motion a chain of events beyond the mere danger of the burning lava that flows down its slopes. Gas and ash are expelled into the atmosphere and affect the local climate. At times they interfere with the global climate, with more devastating effects. The overflow of lakes can also cause mudslides called "lahars," which bury whole cities. In coastal areas, lahars can cause tsunamis.

SNOW

LAVA

VOLCANO

MUD

Lava flows

In volcanoes with calderas, low-viscosity lava can flow without erupting, as with the Laki Iceland, fissures in 1783. Low-viscosity lava drips with the consistency of clear honey. Viscous lava is thick and sticky, like crystallized honey.

LAVA IN VOLCANO NATIONAL PARK, HAWAII

CINDER CONE

Cone with walls of hardened lava.

As the lava flows upward, the cone explodes.

MOLDS OF TREES

Burned tree underneath cooled lava.

The petrified mold forms a minivolcano.

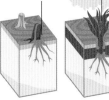

LAVA TUBES

Outer layer of hardened lava.

Inside, the lava stays hot and fluid.

RESCUE IN ARMERO, COLOMBIA
Mudslide after the eruption of the volcano Nevado del Ruiz. A rescue worker helps a boy trapped in a lahar.

MUDSLIDES
OR LAHARS

Rain mixed with snow and melted by the heat, along with tremors and overflowing lakes, can cause mudslides called "lahars." These can be even more destructive than the eruption itself, destroying everything in their path as they flow downhill. They occur frequently on high volcanoes that have glaciers on their summit.

ARMERO FROM ABOVE
On Nov. 13, 1985, the city of Armero, Colombia, was devastated by mudslides from the eruption of the volcano Nevado del Ruiz.

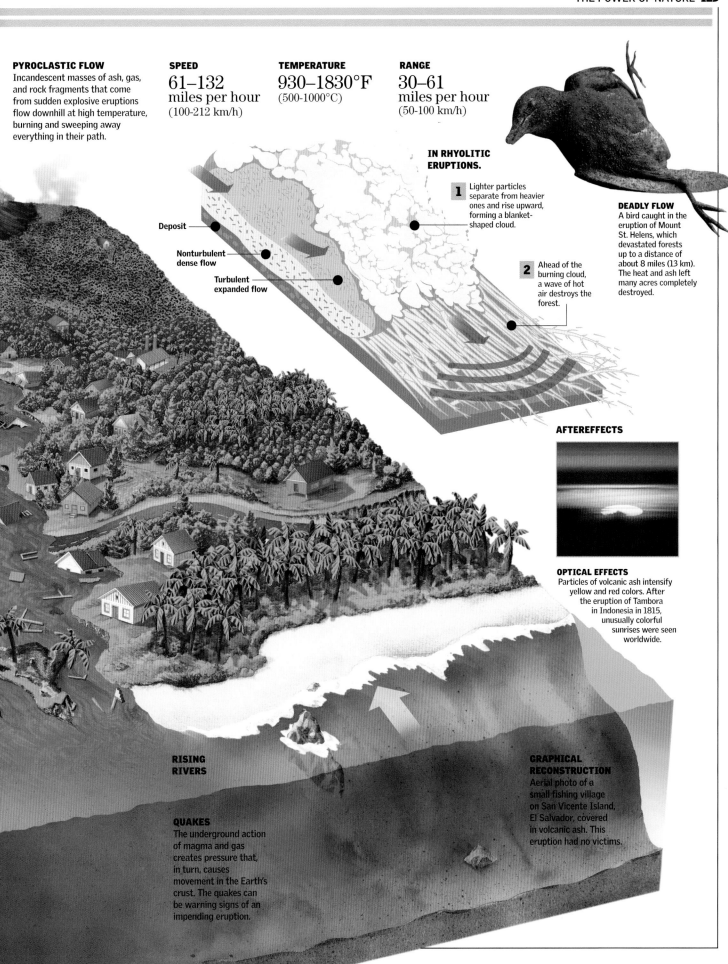

PYROCLASTIC FLOW
Incandescent masses of ash, gas, and rock fragments that come from sudden explosive eruptions flow downhill at high temperature, burning and sweeping away everything in their path.

SPEED
61–132 miles per hour
(100-212 km/h)

TEMPERATURE
930–1830°F
(500-1000°C)

RANGE
30–61 miles per hour
(50-100 km/h)

IN RHYOLITIC ERUPTIONS.

1 Lighter particles separate from heavier ones and rise upward, forming a blanket-shaped cloud.

2 Ahead of the burning cloud, a wave of hot air destroys the forest.

Deposit

Nonturbulent dense flow

Turbulent expanded flow

DEADLY FLOW
A bird caught in the eruption of Mount St. Helens, which devastated forests up to a distance of about 8 miles (13 km). The heat and ash left many acres completely destroyed.

AFTEREFFECTS

OPTICAL EFFECTS
Particles of volcanic ash intensify yellow and red colors. After the eruption of Tambora in Indonesia in 1815, unusually colorful sunrises were seen worldwide.

RISING RIVERS

QUAKES
The underground action of magma and gas creates pressure that, in turn, causes movement in the Earth's crust. The quakes can be warning signs of an impending eruption.

GRAPHICAL RECONSTRUCTION
Aerial photo of a small fishing village on San Vicente Island, El Salvador, covered in volcanic ash. This eruption had no victims.

Jets of Water

Geysers are intermittent spurts of hot water that can shoot up dozens of yards into the sky. Geysers form in the few regions of the planet with favorable hydrogeology, where the energy of past volcanic activity has left water trapped in subterranean rocks. Days or weeks may pass between eruptions. Most of these spectacular phenomena are found in Yellowstone National Park (U.S.) and in northern New Zealand.

The Eruptive Cycle

5

THE CYCLE REPEATS

When the water pressure in the chambers is relieved, the spurt of water abates, and the cycle repeats. Water builds up again in cracks of the rock and in permeable layers.

ON AVERAGE, A GEYSER CAN EXPEL UP TO

7,900 gallons

(30,000 l) OF WATER PER EVENT

Streams of water and steam

4

SPURTING SPRAY

The water spurts out of the cone at irregular intervals. The lapse between spurts depends on the time it takes for the chambers to fill up with water, come to a boil, and produce steam.

THE AVERAGE HEIGHT REACHED OF THE SPURT OF WATER IS ABOUT

148 feet

(45 m)

PRINCIPAL GEOTHERMAL FIELDS

There are some 1,000 geysers worldwide, and 50 percent are in Yellowstone National Park (U.S.).

Kamchatka (Russia)

Great Geysir (Iceland)

North Island (New Zealand)

Ummak Island (U.S.)

El Tatio (Chile)

Steamboat Springs/ Beowawe (U.S.)

YELLOWSTONE (U.S.)

GRAND PRISMATIC SPRING

This spring, in Yellowstone National Park, is the largest hot spring in the United States and the third largest in the world. It measures 246 by 377 feet (75 by 115 m), and it emits about 530 gallons (2,000 l) of water per minute. It has a unique color: red mixed with yellow and green.

In the middle of the spring, the mineral water is 200°F (93°C), and it cools gradually toward the edges.

Path

377 feet (115 m)

DISCHARGE

530 gallons (2,000 l)

OF WATER PER MINUTE

RECORD HEIGHT

In 1904, New Zealand's Waimangu Geyser (now inactive) emitted a record-setting spurt of water. In 1903, four tourists lost their lives when they unknowingly came too close to the geyser.

1,450 FT (442 M)

1,500 FT (457 M)

TALLEST U.S. BUILDING

RECORD HEIGHT

OTHER POSTVOLCANIC ACTIVITY

FUMAROLE

This is a place where there is a constant emission of water vapor because the temperature of the magma is above 212°F (100°C).

Water vapor

Hot water

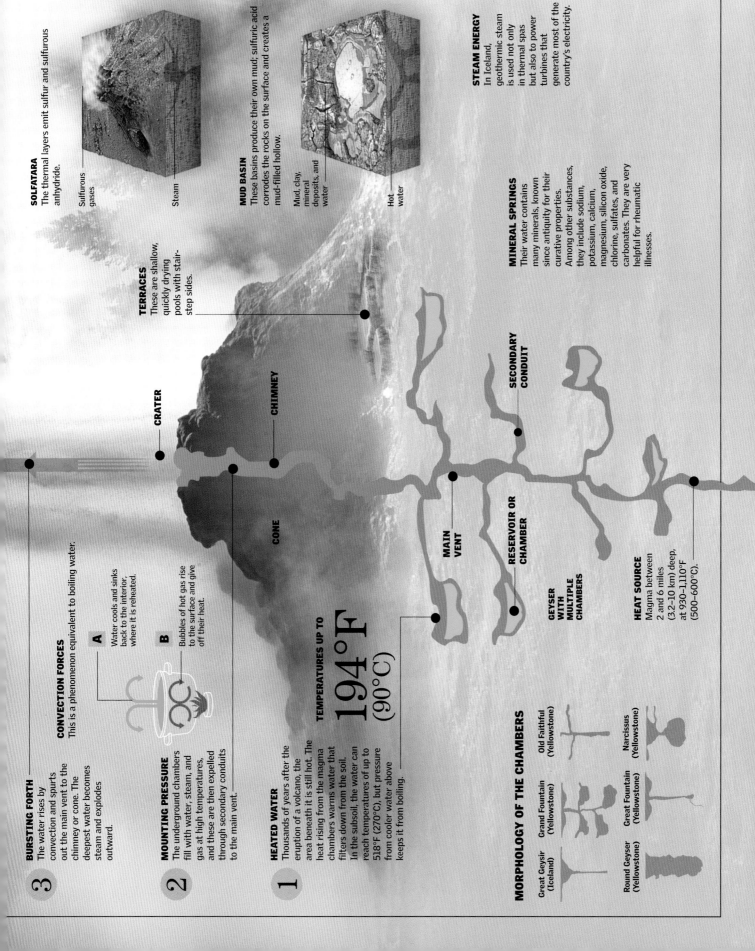

SOLFATARA
The thermal layers emit sulfur and sulfurous anhydride.

Sulfurous gases

Steam

MUD BASIN
These basins produce their own mud; sulfuric acid corrodes the rocks on the surface and creates a mud-filled hollow.

Mud, clay, mineral deposits, and water

Hot water

STEAM ENERGY
In Iceland, geothermic steam is used not only in thermal spas but also to power turbines that generate most of the country's electricity.

TERRACES
These are shallow, quickly drying pools with stair-step sides.

MINERAL SPRINGS
Their water contains many minerals, known since antiquity for their curative properties. Among other substances, they include sodium, potassium, calcium, magnesium, silicon oxide, chlorine, sulfates, and carbonates. They are very helpful for rheumatic illnesses.

CRATER

CHIMNEY

CONE

SECONDARY CONDUIT

MAIN VENT

RESERVOIR OR CHAMBER

GEYSER WITH MULTIPLE CHAMBERS

HEAT SOURCE
Magma between 2 and 6 miles (3.2–10 km) deep, at 930–1,110°F (500–600°C).

3 BURSTING FORTH
The water rises by convection and spurts out the main vent to the chimney or cone. The deepest water becomes steam and explodes outward.

CONVECTION FORCES
This is a phenomenon equivalent to boiling water.

A
Water cools and sinks back to the interior, where it is reheated.

B
Bubbles of hot gas rise to the surface and give off their heat.

2 MOUNTING PRESSURE
The underground chambers fill with water, steam, and gas at high temperatures, and these are then expelled through secondary conduits to the main vent.

TEMPERATURES UP TO
194°F (90°C)

1 HEATED WATER
Thousands of years after the eruption of a volcano, the area beneath it is still hot. The heat rising from the magma chambers warms water that filters down from the soil. In the subsoil, the water can reach temperatures of up to 518°F (270°C), but pressure from cooler water above keeps it from boiling.

MORPHOLOGY OF THE CHAMBERS

Great Geysir (Iceland)

Grand Fountain (Yellowstone)

Old Faithful (Yellowstone)

Narcissus (Yellowstone)

Round Geyser (Yellowstone)

Great Fountain (Yellowstone)

Latent Danger

Some locations have a greater propensity for volcanic activity. Most of these areas are found where tectonic plates meet, whether they are approaching or moving away from each other. The largest concentration of volcanoes is found in a region of the Pacific known as the "Ring of Fire." Volcanoes are also found in the Mediterranean Sea, in Africa, and in the Atlantic Ocean.

Arctic Ocean

The Pacific "Ring of Fire"

Formed by the edges of the Pacific tectonic plate, where most of the world's volcanoes are found.

AVACHINSKY
RUSSIA
This is a young, active cone inside an old caldera, on the Kamchatka peninsula.

NOVARUPTA
ALASKA, U.S.
It is in the Valley of Ten Thousand Smokes.

MOUNT ST. HELENS
WASHINGTON, U.S.
It had an unexpected, violent eruption in 1980.

ASIA

FUJIYAMA
JAPAN
This sacred mountain is the country's largest volcano.

PINATUBO
PHILIPPINES
In 1991, it had the second most violent eruption of the 20th century.

50 Volcanoes
Indonesia has the highest concentration of volcanoes in the world. Java alone has 50 active volcanoes.

MAUNA LOA
HAWAII, U.S.
The largest active volcano on Earth is rooted in the ocean floor and takes up nearly half of the island.

KILAUEA
HAWAII, U.S.
The most active shield volcano, its lava flows have covered more than 40 square miles (100 sq km) since 1983.

KRAKATOA
INDONESIA
Its 1883 eruption destroyed an entire island.

OCEANIA

Pacific Ocean

TAMBORA
INDONESIA
In 1815, it produced 35 cubic miles (150 cu km) of ash. It was the largest recorded eruption in human history.

EAST EPI
VANUATU
This is an undersea caldera with slow eruptions lasting for months.

Subduction
Most volcanoes in the western United States were formed by subduction of the Pacific Plate.

Indian Ocean

INDO-AUSTRALIAN PLATE

PACIFIC PLATE

The tallest

These are found in the middle of the Andes range, which forms part of the Pacific Ring of Fire. They were most active 10,000 years ago, and many are now extinct or dampened by fumarolic action.

OJOS DEL SALADO	LLULLAILLACO	TIPAS	INCAHUASI	SAJAMA	MAUNA LOA	
Chile/Argentina	Chile/Argentina	Argentina	Chile/Argentina	Bolivia	Hawaii	The "top five" list changes when the volcanoes are measured from the base rather than from their altitude above sea level.
22,595 ft (6,887 m)	22,110 ft (6,739 m)	21,850 ft (6,660 m)	21,720 ft (6,621 m)	21,460 ft (6,541 m)	Shield volcano 13,680 feet (4,170 m) above sea level.	

CALDERA

SEA LEVEL

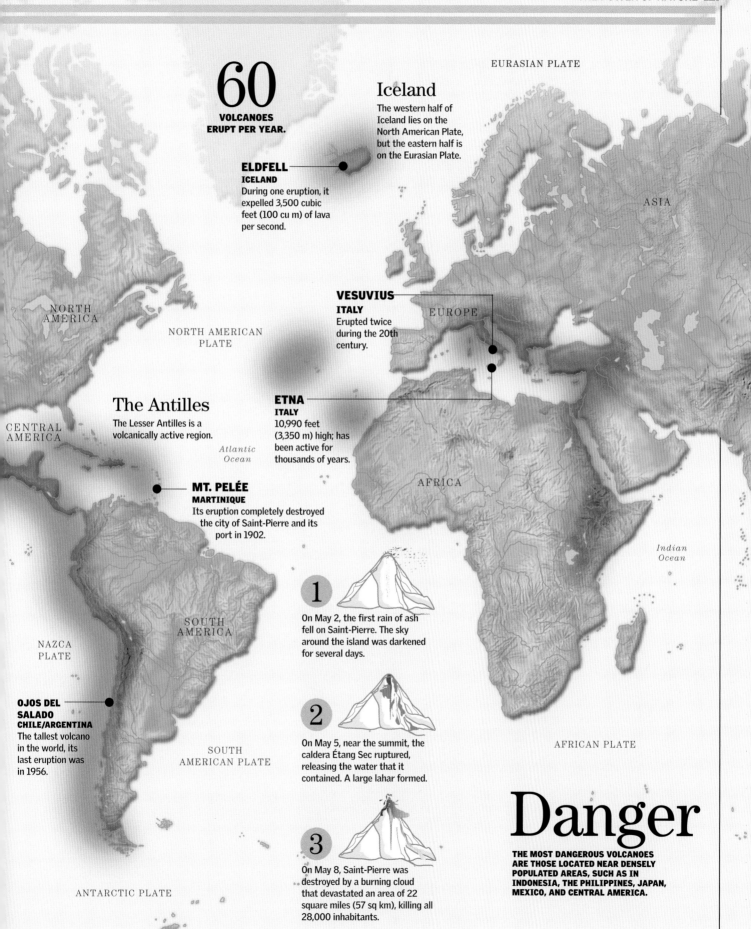

60
VOLCANOES ERUPT PER YEAR.

Iceland
The western half of Iceland lies on the North American Plate, but the eastern half is on the Eurasian Plate.

ELDFELL
ICELAND
During one eruption, it expelled 3,500 cubic feet (100 cu m) of lava per second.

EURASIAN PLATE

ASIA

NORTH AMERICA

NORTH AMERICAN PLATE

VESUVIUS
ITALY
Erupted twice during the 20th century.

EUROPE

The Antilles
The Lesser Antilles is a volcanically active region.

Atlantic Ocean

ETNA
ITALY
10,990 feet (3,350 m) high; has been active for thousands of years.

CENTRAL AMERICA

MT. PELÉE
MARTINIQUE
Its eruption completely destroyed the city of Saint-Pierre and its port in 1902.

AFRICA

Indian Ocean

1
On May 2, the first rain of ash fell on Saint-Pierre. The sky around the island was darkened for several days.

SOUTH AMERICA

NAZCA PLATE

OJOS DEL SALADO
CHILE/ARGENTINA
The tallest volcano in the world, its last eruption was in 1956.

2
On May 5, near the summit, the caldera Étang Sec ruptured, releasing the water that it contained. A large lahar formed.

AFRICAN PLATE

SOUTH AMERICAN PLATE

3
On May 8, Saint-Pierre was destroyed by a burning cloud that devastated an area of 22 square miles (57 sq km), killing all 28,000 inhabitants.

Danger

THE MOST DANGEROUS VOLCANOES ARE THOSE LOCATED NEAR DENSELY POPULATED AREAS, SUCH AS IN INDONESIA, THE PHILIPPINES, JAPAN, MEXICO, AND CENTRAL AMERICA.

ANTARCTIC PLATE

Historic Eruptions

The lava falls and flows, sweeping away everything in its path. This happens in a slow, uninterrupted way, and the lava destroys entire cities, towns, and forests and claims thousands of human lives. One of the most famous examples was the eruption of Mount Vesuvius in AD 79, which wiped out two cities, Pompeii and Herculaneum. In the 20th century, the eruption of Mount Pelée destroyed the city of Saint-Pierre in Martinique in a few minutes and instantly killed almost its entire population. Volcanic activity also seems to be closely related to changes in climate.

AD 79

MOUNT VESUVIUS
Naples, Italy

Volume of ejected ash in cubic feet (cu m)	No figures available
Victims	2,200
Characteristics	Active

The cities of Pompeii and Herculaneum were destroyed in 79 when Mount Vesuvius erupted. Until that day, it was not known that the mountain was a volcano because it had been inactive for over 300 years. This was one of the first eruptions to be recorded: Pliny the Younger stated in one of his manuscripts that he had seen how the mountain exploded. He described the gas and ash cloud rising above Vesuvius and how thick, hot lava fell. Many people died because they inhaled the poisonous gases.

Volcanoes and Climate

There is a strongly supported theory that relates climate changes to volcanic eruptions. The idea of linking the two phenomena is based on the fact that explosive eruptions spew huge amounts of gases and fine particles high into the stratosphere, where they spread around the Earth and remain for years. The volcanic material blocks a portion of solar radiation, reducing air temperatures around the world. Perhaps the most notable cold period related to volcanic activity was the one that followed the eruption of Tambora in 1815. Some areas of North America and Europe had an especially harsh winter.

KALAPANA
After the Kilauea volcano (Hawaii) erupted in 1991, a lava flow advanced on the city, covering everything in its path.

1783

LAKI VOLCANO
Iceland

Volume of ejected ash in cubic feet (cu m)	494 billion (14 billion)
Victims	10,000
Characteristics	Very active

In spite of the fact that the eruptions are related to conic forms, most of the volcanic material comes out through fractures in the crust, called "fissures." The fissure eruptions of Laki were the greatest in Iceland; they created more than 20 vents in a distance of 15 miles (25 km). The gases ruined grasslands and killed livestock. The subsequent famine took the lives of 10,000 people.

1815

TAMBORA VOLCANO
Indonesia

Volume of ejected ash in cubic feet (cu m)	35 billion (1 billion)
Victims	92,000
Characteristics	Stratovolcano

After giving off fumes for seven months, Tambora erupted, and the ensuing catastrophe was felt around the globe. The ash cloud expanded to more than 370 miles (600 km) away from the epicenter of the eruption, and it was so thick that it hid the Sun for two days. The ashfall covered an area of 193,051 square miles (500,000 sq km). It is considered to be the most destructive volcanic explosion that ever took place. More than 10,000 people died during the eruption, and 82,000 died of illness and starvation after the eruption.

1883
KRAKATOA VOLCANO
Java, Indonesia

Volume of ejected ash in cubic feet (cu m)	883 billion (25 billion)
Victims	36,000
Characteristics	Very active

Even though Krakatoa began to announce its forthcoming eruption with clouds of vapor and smoke, these signs, instead of preventing a disaster, became a tourist attraction. When the explosion took place, it destroyed two thirds of the island. Stones shot from the volcano reached a height of 34 miles (55 km) beyond the stratosphere. A crater 4 miles (6.4 km) in diameter opened a chasm 820 feet (250 m) deep. Land and islands were swept bare.

1902
MOUNT PELÉE
Martinique, Antilles

Volume of ejected ash in cubic feet (cu m)	No figures available
Victims	30,000
Characteristics	Stratovolcano

A burning cloud and a thick mass of ash and hot lava were shot from this small volcano that completely destroyed the port city of Saint-Pierre. Most striking is the fact that this destruction took place in only a few minutes. The energy released was so great that trees were uprooted. Almost the entire population died, and only three people survived, one of them because he was trapped in the city jail.

1973
ELDFELL VOLCANO
Heimaey Island, Iceland

Volume of ejected ash in cubic feet (cu m)	No figures available
Victims	0
Characteristics	656 feet (200 m)

The lava advanced, and it appeared that it would take everything in its path. Volcanologists decided that Heimaey Island, south of Iceland, should be evacuated. But a physics professor proposed watering the lava with seawater to solidify or harden it. Forty-seven pumps were used, and, after three months and 6.5 million tons (6 million metric tons) of water, the lava was stopped, and the port was saved. The eruption began on January 23 and ended on June 28.

1980
MOUNT ST. HELENS
Washington State, U.S.

Volume of ejected ash in cubic feet (cu m)	35 billion (1 billion)
Victims	57
Characteristics	Active

Also known as the Mount Fuji of the American continent. During the 1980 explosion, 1,315 feet (401 m) of the mountain's top gave way through a fault on its side. A few minutes after the volcano began its eruption, rivers of lava flowed down its sides, carrying away the trees, houses, and bridges in their path. The eruption destroyed whole forests, and the volcanic debris devastated entire communities.

1944
MOUNT VESUVIUS
Naples, Italy

Volume of ejected ash in cubic feet (cu m)	No figures available
Victims	2,000
Characteristics	End of a cycle

With this last activity, the Vesuvius volcano ended the cycle of eruptions it began in 1631. This explosion, along with the previous one in 1906, caused severe material damage. The eruptions were responsible for more than 2,000 deaths from avalanches and lava bombs. Additionally, the 1944 eruption took place during World War II and caused as much damage as the eruption at the beginning of the 20th century had, because it flooded Somma, Atrio del Cavallo, Massa, and San Sebastiano.

1982
EL CHICHÓN VOLCANO
Mexico

Volume of ejected ash in cubic feet (cu m)	No figures available
Victims	2,000
Characteristics	Active

On Sunday, March 28, after 100 years of inactivity, this volcano became active again and unleashed an eruption on April 4. The eruption caused the deaths of about 2,000 people who lived in the surrounding area, and it destroyed nine settlements. It was the worst volcanic disaster in Mexico's history.

Earthquakes

Earthquakes shake the ground in all directions, even though the effects of a quake depend on the magnitude, depth, and distance from its point of origin. Often the waves are so strong that the Earth buckles, causing the collapse of houses and buildings, as happened in Loma Prieta. In mountainous regions earthquakes can be followed by landslides and mudslides,

LOMA PRIETA
On Oct. 18, 1989, an earthquake measuring 7.0 on the Richter scale, with its epicenter in Loma Prieta, 52 miles (84 km) south of San Francisco, caused great damage, including the collapse of a section of the Bay Bridge.

whereas in the oceans, tsunamis may form; these walls of water strike the coast with enough force to destroy whole cities, as occurred in Indonesia in December 2004. Thailand recorded the highest number of tourist deaths, and 80 percent of tourist areas were destroyed.

Deep Rupture

Earthquakes take place because tectonic plates are in constant motion, and therefore they collide with, slide past, and, in some cases, even slip on top of each other. The Earth's crust does not give outward signs of all the movement within it. Rather energy builds up from these movements within its rocks until the tension is more than the rock can bear. At this point the energy is released at the weakest parts of the crust. This causes the ground to move suddenly, unleashing an earthquake.

1 FORESHOCK
Small tremor that can anticipate an earthquake by days or even years. It could be strong enough to move a parked car.

2 AFTERSHOCK
New seismic movement that can take place after an earthquake. At times it can be even more destructive than the earthquake itself.

EARTHQUAKES PER YEAR
30 Seconds: The time lapse between each tremor of the Earth's crust

MAGNITUDE	QUANTITY
8 or Greater	1
7 to 7.9	18
6 to 6.9	120
5 to 5.9	800
4 to 4.9	6,200
3 to 3.9	49,000

EPICENTER
Point on the Earth's surface located directly above the focus.

HYPOCENTER OR FOCUS
Point of rupture, where the disturbance originates. Can be up to 435 miles (700 km) below the surface.

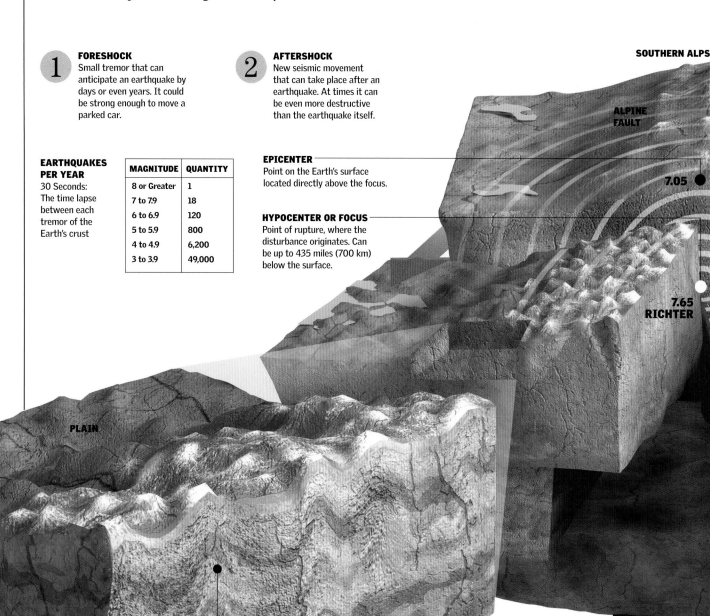

SOUTHERN ALPS

ALPINE FAULT

7.05

7.65 RICHTER

PLAIN

FOLDS
These result from tension that accumulates between tectonic plates. Earthquakes release part of the tension energy generated by orogenic folds.

Origin of an Earthquake

1

TENSION IS GENERATED
The plates move in opposite directions, sliding along the fault line. At a certain point along the fault, they catch on each other. Tension begins to increase between the plates.

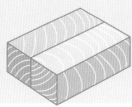

2

TENSION VERSUS RESISTANCE
Because the force of displacement is still active even when the plates are not moving, the tension grows. Rock layers near the boundary are distorted and crack.

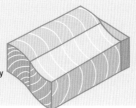

3

EARTHQUAKE
When the rock's resistance is overcome, it breaks and suddenly shifts, causing an earthquake typical of a transform-fault boundary.

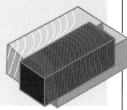

3 **EARTHQUAKE**
The main movement or tremor lasts a few seconds, after which some alterations become visible in the terrain near the epicenter.

NEW ZEALAND
Latitude 42° S
Longitude 174° E

Surface area	**103,737 square miles (268,680 sq km)**
Population	**4,137,000**
Population density	**35 people per square mile (13.63 people per sq km)**
Earthquakes per year (>4.0)	**60–100**
Total earthquakes per year	**14,000**

SOUTH ISLAND

Riverbeds follow a curved path because of movement along the fault line.

LAKE TEKAPO

6.10

SEISMIC WAVES
transmit the force of the earthquake over great distances in a characteristic back-and-forth movement. Their intensity decreases with distance.

FAULT PLANE
Usually curves rather than following a straight line. This irregularity causes the tectonic plates to collide, which leads to earthquakes as the plates move.

ALPINE FAULT IN NEW ZEALAND
As seen in the cross section, South Island is divided by a large fault that changes the direction of subduction, depending on the area. To the north the Pacific Plate is sinking under the Indo-Australian Plate at an average rate of 1.7 inches (4.3 cm) per year. To the south, the Indo-Australian Plate is sinking 1.4 inches (3.6 cm) per year under the Pacific Plate.

FUTURE DEFORMATION OF THE ISLAND

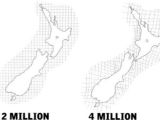

To the west there is a plain that has traveled nearly 310 miles (500 km) to the north in the past 20 million years.

2 MILLION YEARS

4 MILLION YEARS

Potential earthquake zone

NORTH ISLAND

Alpine fault

Australian Plate

SOUTH ISLAND

Pacific Plate

15 miles (25 km)
Average depth of the Earth's crust below the island.

Elastic Waves

S eismic energy is a wave phenomenon, similar to the effect of a stone dropped into a pool of water. Seismic waves radiate out in all directions from the earthquake's hypocenter, or focus. The waves travel faster through hard rock and more slowly through loose sediment and through water. The forces produced by these waves can be broken down into simpler wave types to study their effects.

FOCUS
Vibrations travel outward from the focus, shaking the rock.

2.2 MILES PER SECOND (3.6 KM/S)

S waves are 1.7 times as slow as P waves.

They travel only through solids. They cause splitting motions that do not affect liquids. Their direction of travel is perpendicular to the direction of travel.

Different Types of Waves

There are basically two types of waves: body waves and surface waves. The body waves travel inside the Earth and transmit foreshocks that have little destructive power. They are divided into primary (P) waves and secondary (S) waves. Surface waves travel only along the Earth's surface, but, because of the tremors they produce in all directions, they cause the most destruction.

Direction of seismic waves

Vibration of rock particles

3.7 MILES PER SECOND (6 KM/S)

Typical Speed of P Waves in the Crust.

P waves travel through all types of material, and the waves themselves move in the direction of travel.

Primary Waves

High-speed waves that travel in straight lines, compressing and stretching solids and liquids they pass through.

SPEED IN DIFFERENT MATERIALS

MATERIAL	Granite	Basalt	Limestone	Sandstone	Water
Wave speed in feet per second (m/s)	17,000 (5,200)	21,000 (6,400)	7,900 (2,400)	11,500 (3,500)	4,800 (1,450)

The ground is compressed and stretched by turns along the path of wave propagation.

Surface Waves

appear on the surface after the P and S waves reach the epicenter. Having a lower frequency, surface waves have a greater effect on solids, which makes them more destructive.

1.9 MILES PER SECOND (3.1 KM/S)

Speed of surface waves in the same medium.

These waves travel only along the surface, at 90 percent of the speed of S waves.

LOVE WAVES

These move like horizontal S waves, trapped at the surface, but they are somewhat slower and make cuts parallel to their direction.

RAYLEIGH WAVES

These waves spread with an up-and-down motion, similar to ocean waves, causing fractures perpendicular to their travel by stretching the ground.

The soil is moved to both sides.

The ground is moved in an elliptical pattern.

The soil is moved to both sides, perpendicular to the wave's path of motion.

Secondary Waves

Body waves that shake the rock up and down and side to side as they move.

SPEED IN DIFFERENT MATERIALS

MATERIAL	Granite	Basalt	Limestone	Sandstone
Wave speed in feet per second (m/s)	9,800 (3,000)	1,500 (460)	4,430 (1,350)	7,050 (2,150)

TRAJECTORY OF P AND S WAVES

The Earth's outer core acts as a barrier to S waves, blocking them from reaching any point that forms an angle between 105° and 140° from the epicenter. P waves are transmitted farther through the core, but they may be diverted later on.

↝ Primary (P) Waves

I Secondary (S) Waves

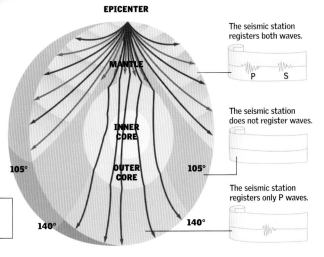

EPICENTER

MANTLE

INNER CORE

OUTER CORE

105°

105°

140°

140°

The seismic station registers both waves.

P   S

The seismic station does not register waves.

The seismic station registers only P waves.

Types of Earthquakes

Although earthquakes generally cause all types of waves, some kinds of waves may predominate. This fact leads to a classification that depends on whether vertical or horizontal vibration causes the most movement. The depth of the focus can also affect its destructiveness.

BASED ON TYPE OF MOVEMENT

TREPIDATORY

Located near the epicenter, where the vertical component of the movement is greater than the horizontal.

OSCILLATORY

When a wave reaches soft soil, the horizontal movement is amplified, and the movement is said to be oscillating.

BASED ON FOCUS DEPTH

Earthquakes originate at points between 3 and 430 miles (5 and 700 km) underground. Ninety percent originate in the first 62 miles (100 km). Those originating between 43 and 190 miles (70 and 300 km) are considered intermediate. Superficial earthquakes (often of higher magnitude) occur above that level, and deep-focus earthquakes occur below it.

0

Superficial · **43 MILES (70 KM)**

Intermediate · **190 MILES (300 KM)**

Deep focus · **430 MILES (700 KM)**

Measuring an Earthquake

Earthquakes can be measured in terms of force, duration, and location. Many scientific instruments and comparative scales have been developed to take these measurements. Seismographs measure all three parameters. The Richter scale describes the force or intensity of an earthquake. Naturally, the destruction caused by earthquakes can be measured in many other ways: numbers of people left injured, dead, or homeless, damage and reconstruction costs, government and business expenditures, insurance costs, school days lost, and in many more ways.

CHARLES RICHTER
American seismologist (1900–85) who developed the scale of magnitude that bears his name.

Intensity
Concept of the destruction caused by an earthquake.

Modified Mercalli Scale

Between 1883 and 1902, this Italian volcanologist developed a scale to measure the intensity of earthquakes. It originally had 10 points based on the observation of the effects of seismic activity; it was later modified to 12. The first few levels consist of barely perceptible sensations. The highest levels apply to the destruction of buildings. This scale is widely used to compare levels of damage among different regions and socioeconomic conditions.

Richter Scale

In 1935, seismologist Charles Richter designed a scale to measure the amplitude of the largest waves registered by seismographs. An important feature of this scale is that the levels increase exponentially. Each point on the scale represents 10 times the movement and 30 times the energy of the point below it. Temblors of magnitude 2 or less are not perceptible to humans. This scale is the most widely used in the world because it can be used to compare the strength of earthquakes apart from their effects.

Magnitude
The energy released in a seismic event.

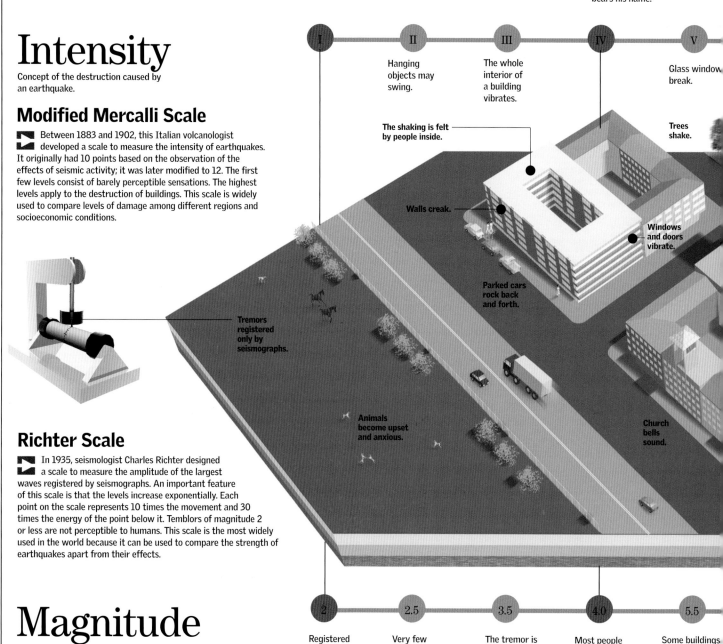

I

II
Hanging objects may swing.

III
The whole interior of a building vibrates.

IV

V
Glass windows break.

Trees shake.

The shaking is felt by people inside.

Walls creak.

Windows and doors vibrate.

Parked cars rock back and forth.

Church bells sound.

Tremors registered only by seismographs.

Animals become upset and anxious.

2	2.5	3.5	4.0	5.5
Registered only by seismographs.	Very few people feel the tremor.	The tremor is felt. Only minor damages.	Most people perceive the quake.	Some buildings are lightly damaged.

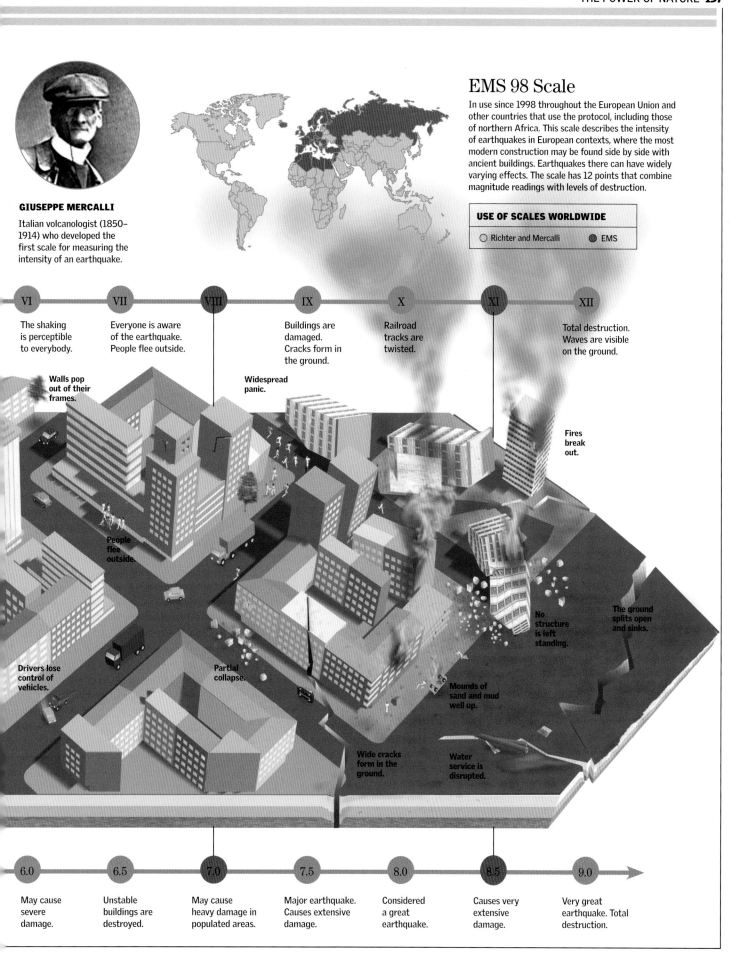

GIUSEPPE MERCALLI

Italian volcanologist (1850–1914) who developed the first scale for measuring the intensity of an earthquake.

EMS 98 Scale

In use since 1998 throughout the European Union and other countries that use the protocol, including those of northern Africa. This scale describes the intensity of earthquakes in European contexts, where the most modern construction may be found side by side with ancient buildings. Earthquakes there can have widely varying effects. The scale has 12 points that combine magnitude readings with levels of destruction.

USE OF SCALES WORLDWIDE

○ Richter and Mercalli   ● EMS

| VI | VII | VIII | IX | X | XI | XII |

VI The shaking is perceptible to everybody.

VII Everyone is aware of the earthquake. People flee outside.

IX Buildings are damaged. Cracks form in the ground.

X Railroad tracks are twisted.

XII Total destruction. Waves are visible on the ground.

Walls pop out of their frames.

Widespread panic.

Fires break out.

People flee outside.

No structure is left standing.

The ground splits open and sinks.

Drivers lose control of vehicles.

Partial collapse.

Mounds of sand and mud well up.

Wide cracks form in the ground.

Water service is disrupted.

| 6.0 | 6.5 | 7.0 | 7.5 | 8.0 | 8.5 | 9.0 |

6.0 May cause severe damage.

6.5 Unstable buildings are destroyed.

7.0 May cause heavy damage in populated areas.

7.5 Major earthquake. Causes extensive damage.

8.0 Considered a great earthquake.

8.5 Causes very extensive damage.

9.0 Very great earthquake. Total destruction.

Violent Seas

A large earthquake or volcanic eruption can cause a tsunami, which means "wave in the harbor" in Japanese. Tsunamis travel very fast, up to 500 miles per hour (800 km/h). On reaching shallow water, they decrease in speed but increase in height. A tsunami can become a wall of water more than 33 feet (10 m) high on approaching the shore. The height depends partly on the shape of the beach and the depth of coastal waters. If the wave reaches dry land, it can inundate vast areas and cause considerable damage. A 1960 earthquake off the coast of Chile caused a tsunami that swept away communities along 500 miles (800 km) of the coast of South America. Twenty-two hours later the waves reached the coast of Japan, where they damaged coastal towns.

The word **tsunami** comes from Japanese

TSU NAMI
Harbor Wave

1

THE EARTHQUAKE
A movement of the ocean floor displaces an enormous mass of water upward.

How It Happens

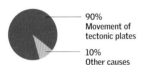 A tremor that generates vibrations on the ocean water's surface can be caused by seismic movement on the seafloor. Most of the time the tremor is caused by the upward or downward movement of a block of oceanic crust that moves a mass of ocean water. A volcanic eruption, meteorite impact, or nuclear explosion can also cause a tsunami.

90%
Movement of tectonic plates

10%
Other causes

RISING PLATE

Water level rises   Water level drops

SINKING PLATE

The displaced water tends to level out, generating the force that causes waves.

7.5

Only earthquakes above this magnitude on the Richter scale can produce a tsunami strong enough to cause damage.

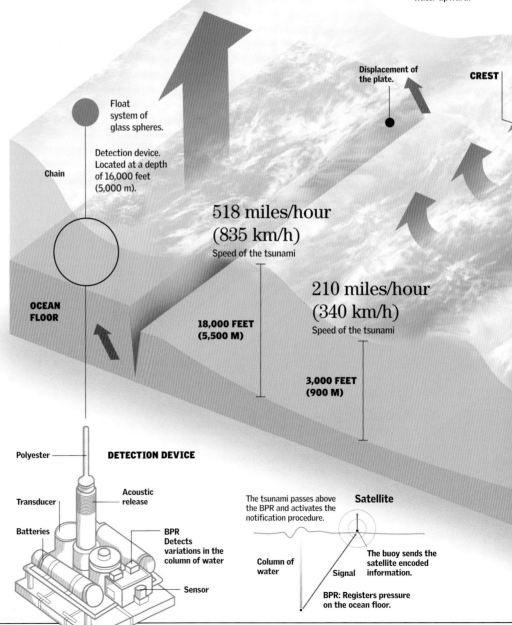

Float system of glass spheres.

Chain

Detection device. Located at a depth of 16,000 feet (5,000 m).

OCEAN FLOOR

Displacement of the plate.

CREST

518 miles/hour (835 km/h)
Speed of the tsunami

210 miles/hour (340 km/h)
Speed of the tsunami

18,000 FEET (5,500 M)

3,000 FEET (900 M)

Polyester

DETECTION DEVICE

Transducer

Acoustic release

Batteries

BPR Detects variations in the column of water

Sensor

The tsunami passes above the BPR and activates the notification procedure.

Satellite

Column of water

Signal

The buoy sends the satellite encoded information.

BPR: Registers pressure on the ocean floor.

WHEN THE WAVE HITS THE COAST

A Sea level drops abnormally low. Water is "sucked" away from the coast by the growing wave.

B The giant wave forms. At its highest, the wave may become nearly vertical.

COMPARISON OF THE SIZE OF THE WAVE

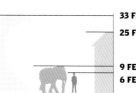

33 FEET (10 M)
25 FEET (7.6 M)
9 FEET (2.7 M)
6 FEET (1.8 M)

33 feet
(10 m)
TYPICAL HEIGHT A MAJOR TSUNAMI CAN REACH.

C The wave breaks along the coast. The force of the wave is released in the impact against the coast. There may be one wave or several waves.

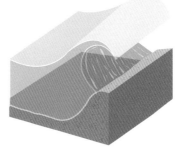

D The land is flooded. The water may take several hours or even days to return to its normal level.

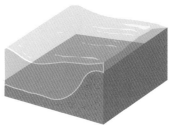

② THE WAVES ARE FORMED

As this mass of water drops, the water begins to vibrate. The waves, however, are barely 1.5 feet (0.5 m) high, and a boat may cross over them without the crew even noticing.

TROUGH

CREST

③ THE WAVES ADVANCE

Waves may travel thousands of miles without weakening. As the sea becomes shallower near the coast, the waves become closer together, but they grow higher.

LENGTH OF THE WAVE

From 62 to 430 miles (100 to 700 km) on the open sea, measured from crest to crest.

④ TSUNAMI

On reaching the coast, the waves find their path blocked. The coast, like a ramp, diverts all the force of the waves upward.

Buildings on the coast may be damaged or destroyed.

31 miles per hour (50 km/h)
Speed of the tsunami

65 FEET (20 M)

Between 5 and 30 minutes before the tsunami arrives, the sea level suddenly drops.

INDIAN OCEAN

Surface area	28.3 million square miles (73.3 million sq km)
Percentage of Earth's surface	14%
Percentage of total volume of the oceans	20%
Length of plate boundaries (in focus)	745 miles (1,200 km)
Countries affected in 2004	21

Cause and Effect

On Dec. 26, 2004, an earthquake occurred that measured 9.0 on the Richter scale, the third most powerful earthquake since 1900. The epicenter was 100 miles (160 km) off the west coast of Sumatra, Indonesia. This quake generated a tsunami that pummeled all the coasts of the Indian Ocean. The islands of Sumatra and Sri Lanka suffered the worst effects. India, Thailand, and the Maldives also suffered damage, and there were victims as far away as Kenya, Tanzania, and Somalia, in Africa.

7:58
Local time when the tsunami was unleashed (00:58 universal time)

230,507
ESTIMATED DEAD

30 percent were children

THE VICTIMS
On this map, the number of confirmed deaths and the number of missing persons in each country are added together, giving an estimated total death toll. In addition, 1,600,000 persons had to be evacuated.

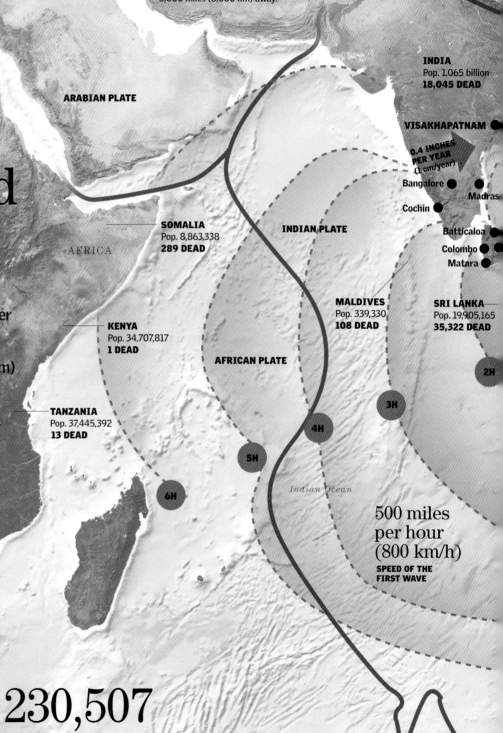

Duration
The tremor lasted between 8 and 10 minutes, one of the longest on record. The waves took six hours to reach Africa, over 5,000 miles (8,000 km) away.

ARABIAN PLATE

AFRICA

INDIA
Pop. 1.065 billion
18,045 DEAD

VISAKHAPATNAM

0.4 INCHES PER YEAR (1 cm/year)

Bangalore
Madras
Cochin

INDIAN PLATE

SOMALIA
Pop. 8,863,338
289 DEAD

Batticaloa
Colombo
Matara

KENYA
Pop. 34,707,817
1 DEAD

MALDIVES
Pop. 339,330
108 DEAD

SRI LANKA
Pop. 19,905,165
35,322 DEAD

AFRICAN PLATE

TANZANIA
Pop. 37,445,392
13 DEAD

2H

3H

4H

5H

6H

Indian Ocean

500 miles per hour (800 km/h)
SPEED OF THE FIRST WAVE

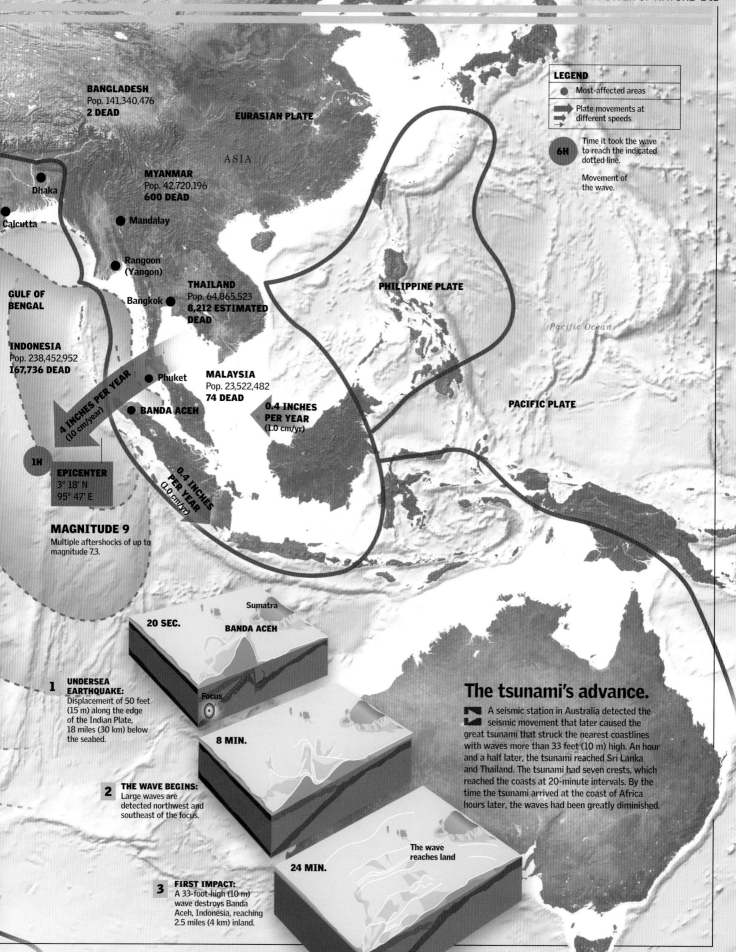

LEGEND
- Most-affected areas
- Plate movements at different speeds
- **6H** Time it took the wave to reach the indicated dotted line.
- Movement of the wave.

EURASIAN PLATE

ASIA

BANGLADESH
Pop. 141,340,476
2 DEAD

Dhaka

Calcutta

MYANMAR
Pop. 42,720,196
600 DEAD

Mandalay

Rangoon
(Yangon)

GULF OF BENGAL

Bangkok

THAILAND
Pop. 64,865,523
8,212 ESTIMATED DEAD

INDONESIA
Pop. 238,452,952
167,736 DEAD

Phuket

MALAYSIA
Pop. 23,522,482
74 DEAD

BANDA ACEH

PHILIPPINE PLATE

Pacific Ocean

PACIFIC PLATE

4 INCHES PER YEAR (10 cm/year)

0.4 INCHES PER YEAR (1.0 cm/yr)

0.4 INCHES PER YEAR (1.0 cm/yr)

1H

EPICENTER
3° 18' N
95° 47' E

MAGNITUDE 9
Multiple aftershocks of up to magnitude 7.3.

Sumatra
BANDA ACEH
20 SEC.
Focus

8 MIN.

24 MIN.

The wave reaches land

1 UNDERSEA EARTHQUAKE: Displacement of 50 feet (15 m) along the edge of the Indian Plate, 18 miles (30 km) below the seabed.

2 THE WAVE BEGINS: Large waves are detected northwest and southeast of the focus.

3 FIRST IMPACT: A 33-foot-high (10 m) wave destroys Banda Aceh, Indonesia, reaching 2.5 miles (4 km) inland.

The tsunami's advance.

A seismic station in Australia detected the seismic movement that later caused the great tsunami that struck the nearest coastlines with waves more than 33 feet (10 m) high. An hour and a half later, the tsunami reached Sri Lanka and Thailand. The tsunami had seven crests, which reached the coasts at 20-minute intervals. By the time the tsunami arrived at the coast of Africa hours later, the waves had been greatly diminished.

Risk Areas

A seismic area is found wherever there is an active fault, and these faults are very numerous throughout the world. These fractures are especially common near mountain ranges and mid-ocean ridges. Unfortunately, many population centers were built up in regions near these dangerous places, and, when an earthquake occurs, they become disaster areas. Where the tectonic plates collide, the risk is even greater.

Arctic Ocean

ASIA

Pacific Ocean

9.2
ALASKA, 1964
Lasted between three and five minutes and caused a tsunami responsible for 122 deaths.

Rocky Mountains

6.8
KOBE, 1995
The city of Kobe and nearby villages were destroyed in only 30 seconds.

8.1–8.7
ASSAM, 1897
More than 1,600 people died in northeast India.

Himalayas

Indo-Australian Plate

MOUNTAIN

TRENCH

Pacific Plate

Subduction zone

8.3
SAN FRANCISCO, 1906
Major fires contributed to the devastation of the city.

PACIFIC PLATE

8.1
MEXICO, 1985
Two days later there was a 7.6 aftershock. More than 11,000 people died.

PHILIPPINE PLATE

MARIANA TRENCH
The deepest marine trench on the planet, with a depth of 35,872 feet (10,934 m) below sea level. It is on the western side of the north Pacific and east of the Mariana Islands.

9.0
SUMATRA, 2004 TSUNAMI IN ASIA
An earthquake near the island of Sumatra created 33-foot (10-m) waves and a human tragedy.

Pacific Ocean

COCOS AND CARIBBEAN PLATES
Contact between these two plates is of the convergent type: the Cocos Plate moves under the Caribbean Plate, a phenomenon known as "subduction." This causes a great number of tremors and volcanoes.

Cocos Plate

Caribbean Plate

Indian Ocean

INDO-AUSTRALIAN PLATE

Indo-Australian Plate

NEW ZEALAND FAULT
A large fault in which the opposing plates slide past one another; it is a special type of fault called a "transform fault."

Pacific Plate

ANTARCTIC PLATE

Most vulnerable regions

They are unpredictable, and among the most destructive of natural phenomena. Earthquakes shake the earth. They open and move it, and, within a few seconds, they can turn a peaceful city into the worst disaster area, an area in which seismic activity and a high population density coincide. But in the open country, where earthquakes have much less effect, we can conclude that it is not earthquakes, but buildings, that kill people.

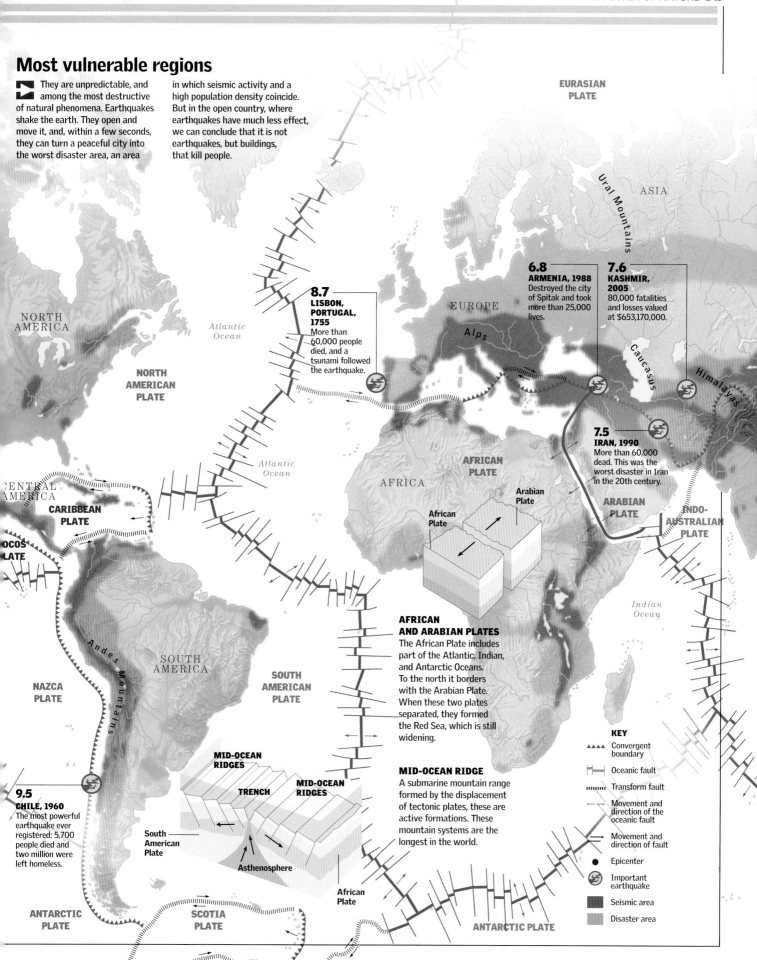

8.7
LISBON, PORTUGAL, 1755
More than 60,000 people died, and a tsunami followed the earthquake.

6.8
ARMENIA, 1988
Destroyed the city of Spitak and took more than 25,000 lives.

7.6
KASHMIR, 2005
80,000 fatalities and losses valued at $653,170,000.

7.5
IRAN, 1990
More than 60,000 dead. This was the worst disaster in Iran in the 20th century.

9.5
CHILE, 1960
The most powerful earthquake ever registered: 5,700 people died and two million were left homeless.

AFRICAN AND ARABIAN PLATES
The African Plate includes part of the Atlantic, Indian, and Antarctic Oceans. To the north it borders with the Arabian Plate. When these two plates separated, they formed the Red Sea, which is still widening.

MID-OCEAN RIDGE
A submarine mountain range formed by the displacement of tectonic plates, these are active formations. These mountain systems are the longest in the world.

MID-OCEAN RIDGES

TRENCH

MID-OCEAN RIDGES

South American Plate

Asthenosphere

African Plate

KEY

▲▲▲▲ Convergent boundary

Oceanic fault

Transform fault

→ Movement and direction of the oceanic fault

→ Movement and direction of fault

● Epicenter

⊚ Important earthquake

Seismic area

Disaster area

EURASIAN PLATE

ASIA

Ural Mountains

EUROPE

Alps

Caucasus

Himalayas

NORTH AMERICA

NORTH AMERICAN PLATE

Atlantic Ocean

Atlantic Ocean

CENTRAL AMERICA

CARIBBEAN PLATE

COCOS PLATE

AFRICAN PLATE

AFRICA

Arabian Plate

African Plate

ARABIAN PLATE

INDO-AUSTRALIAN PLATE

Indian Ocean

NAZCA PLATE

SOUTH AMERICA

Andes Mountains

SOUTH AMERICAN PLATE

ANTARCTIC PLATE

SCOTIA PLATE

ANTARCTIC PLATE

Historic Earthquakes

The Earth is alive. It moves, it shifts, it crashes, and quakes, and it has done so since its origin. Earthquakes vary from a soft vibration to violent and terrorizing movements. Many earthquakes have gone down in history as the worst natural catastrophes ever survived by humanity. Lisbon, Portugal, 1755; Valdivia, Chile, 1960; and Kashmir, Pakistan, 2005, are only three examples of the physical, material, and emotional devastation in which an earthquake can leave a population.

1995

KOBE, JAPAN

Magnitude	6.8 (Richter)
Fatalities	6,433
Material losses	$100 billion

The great earthquake of Hanshin that occurred on Jan. 17, 1995, in Kobe, a Japanese port, left behind more than 6,000 dead, 38,000 injured, and 319,000 people who had to be housed in more than 1,200 emergency shelters. The Nagata District was one of the hardest-hit areas. Almost 80 percent of the victims died because the old wooden homes crumbled in the generalized fires that followed the earthquake.

1755
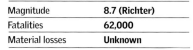

LISBON, PORTUGAL

Magnitude	8.7 (Richter)
Fatalities	62,000
Material losses	Unknown

It was the Day of the Dead, and, at 9:20 in the morning, almost the entire population of Lisbon was at church. While mass was celebrated, the earth quaked, and this earthquake would be one of the most destructive and lethal in history. The earthquake unleashed a tsunami that was felt from Norway to North America and that took the lives of those who had sought shelter in the river.

1906
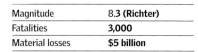

SAN FRANCISCO, U.S.

Magnitude	8.3 (Richter)
Fatalities	3,000
Material losses	$5 billion

The city was swept by the earthquake and by the fires that followed it. The quake was the result of the rupture of more than 40 miles (64 km) of the San Andreas fault. It is the greatest earthquake in the history of the United States: 300,000 people were left homeless, and property losses reached millions in 1906 dollars. Buildings collapsed, the fires spread for three days, and the water lines were destroyed.

1960

VALDIVIA, CHILE

Magnitude	9.5 (Richter)
Fatalities	5,700
Material losses	$500 million

Known as the Great Chilean Earthquake, this was the strongest earthquake of the 20th century. The surface waves produced were so strong that they were still being registered by seismometers 60 hours after the earthquake. The earthquake was felt in various parts of the planet, and a huge tsunami spread through the Pacific Ocean, killing more than 60 people in Hawaii. One of the most powerful earthquakes in memory, its aftershocks lasted for more than a week. More than 5,000 people died, and nearly two million people suffered damage and loss.

1985

MEXICO CITY, MEXICO

Magnitude	8.1 (Richter)
Fatalities	11,000
Material losses	$1 billion

The city shook on September 19. Two days later, there was an aftershock measuring 7.6 on the Richter scale. In addition to 11,000 deaths, there were 30,000 injured, and 95,000 people were left homeless. As the Cocos Plate slid under the North American Plate, the North American Plate fractured, or split, 12 miles (20 km) inside the crust. The vibrations of the ocean floor off the southwestern coast of Mexico provoked a tsunami and produced energy 1,000 times as great as that of an atomic bomb. Strong seismic waves reached as far east as Mexico City, a distance of 220 miles (350 km).

2004

SUMATRA, INDONESIA

Magnitude	9.0 (Richter)
Fatalities	230,507
Material losses	Incalculable

An earthquake whose epicenter crossed the island of Sumatra, Indonesia, took place on December 26. This earthquake generated a tsunami that affected the entire Indian Ocean, primarily the islands of Sumatra and Sri Lanka, and reached the coasts of India, Thailand, the Maldives, and even Kenya and Somalia. This was a true human tragedy, and the economic damages were incalculable.

2005

KASHMIR, PAKISTAN

Magnitude	7.6 (Richter)
Fatalities	80,000
Material losses	$595 million

Also known as the Indian Subcontinent Earthquake, the North Pakistan Earthquake, and the South Asian Earthquake. It occurred on Oct. 8, 2005, in the Kashmir region between India and Pakistan. Because schools were in session when the earthquake struck (9:20 a.m.), many of the victims were children, who died when their school buildings collapsed. It was the strongest earthquake experienced by the region for a century. Three million people lost their homes. The most heavily affected areas lost all their cattle. Entire fields disappeared under earth and rock. The epicenter was located near Islamabad, in the mountains of Kashmir, in an area governed by Pakistan.

AFTER THE HORROR. The world was shaken, looking at the horrendous images of how Kobe, the city by the sea, had been painfully broken to pieces.

4 A WORLD OF PLANTS

148

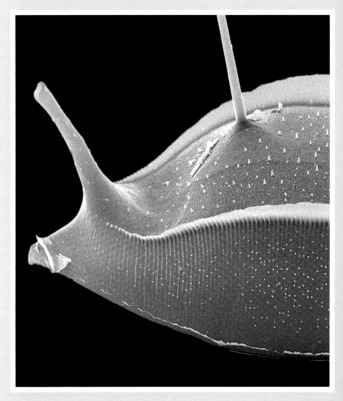

160

170

188

The Plant Kingdom

According to scientific evidence, the nearest relatives of plants are algae that lived on the shores of lagoons. Later, from these habitats, which were at times dry and at times damp, the first land plants emerged. Most had to adapt in order to prosper in a different environment. Such adaptation enabled them to achieve

PLANT LIFE

Leaves are the main organs for photosynthesis in land plants. After plants appeared on land more than 440 million years ago, the amount of photosynthesis taking place gradually increased.

amazing growth, as exemplified by the giant sequoia (*Sequoiadendron giganteum*), which can measure 260 feet (80 m) tall and 100 feet (30 m) in circumference at its base. Did you know that plants grow bigger as their cells multiply and expand? Many can grow 0.4 inch (1 cm) per day, and their growth can create enough pressure to open cracks in asphalt.

Kingdoms of the Quiet Life

Representing a vast array of life-forms, the plant kingdom includes approximately 300,000 species. Their most outstanding feature is the presence of chloroplasts with chlorophyll, a pigment that enables them to transform solar energy into chemical energy. They use this energy to produce their food. Plants need to attach themselves to a substrate (usually the ground), from which they can extract water and nutrients. This attachment, however, also keeps them from moving from place to place. Algae and fungi were once included in the plant kingdom, but they are now considered to be separate from plants and to belong to the kingdoms Protista and Fungi, respectively.

MOSS
Sphagnum sp.

RED MARINE ALGA
Rhodomela sp.

Algae

are commonly considered water plants, but this is not the case. Algae have neither roots nor stalks. Because they live in the water (freshwater or saltwater), they need no substrate. Some are microscopic, but large algae formations can be found in the ocean. Algae are classified into families depending on their color. Together green algae and plants make up the group of organisms called the "green line," whose members are characterized by having chloroplasts and by storing grains of starch in the cytoplasm as a reserve.

Bryophytes

include mosses and worts. Mosses have rhizoids rather than roots. They can also absorb water through their entire body surface. Bryophytes lack a means of surviving long periods of drought. When dry periods come, bryophytes enter a latent state. Because they have no system of veins for transporting nutrients, they can barely grow beyond 0.4 inch (1 cm) long. In order to reproduce they need to be near liquid water.

Plants

 The plant kingdom (Plantae) includes organisms whose characteristics include the presence of the pigment chlorophyll to convert solar energy into chemical energy for producing food from water and carbon dioxide. This ability is called "autotrophy." All plants, whether large or small, play an extremely important role in providing food for all other living beings. Plants cannot move from place to place, but their gametes, spores (cells that separate from a plant and can germinate), and seeds can move about, especially with the help of water and wind.

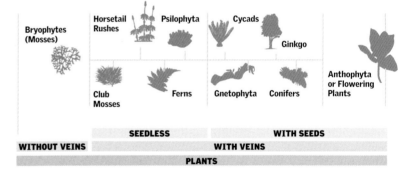

Green Algae

Bryophytes (Mosses)

Horsetail Rushes

Psilophyta

Cycads

Ginkgo

Club Mosses

Ferns

Gnetophyta

Conifers

Anthophyta or Flowering Plants

SEEDLESS — WITH SEEDS

WITHOUT VEINS — WITH VEINS

PLANTS

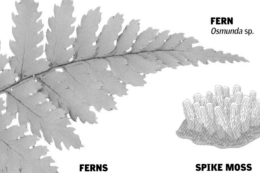

FERN
Osmunda sp.

Seedless

Ferns are the most common seedless plants today. Many are thought to have originated during the Devonian Period and reached their greatest splendor in the Carboniferous Period. Their tissues are simpler than those of plants with seeds, and their green stems have a large surface area, giving them a great capacity for photosynthesis. Ferns need water so that they can reproduce by means of spores. The spores are produced in spore cases called "sporangia," which grow on leaves called "sporophylls."

FERNS
are the most diverse group of seedless plants. Their origin dates back to the Devonian Period.

SPIKE MOSS
has scalelike leaves, some of which are clustered in the form of a spike.

PSILOPHYTA
are extremely simple plants; they lack roots and true leaves, but they have a stalk with veins.

HORSETAIL RUSHES
have roots, stems, and true leaves. The leaves are small and encircle the stems.

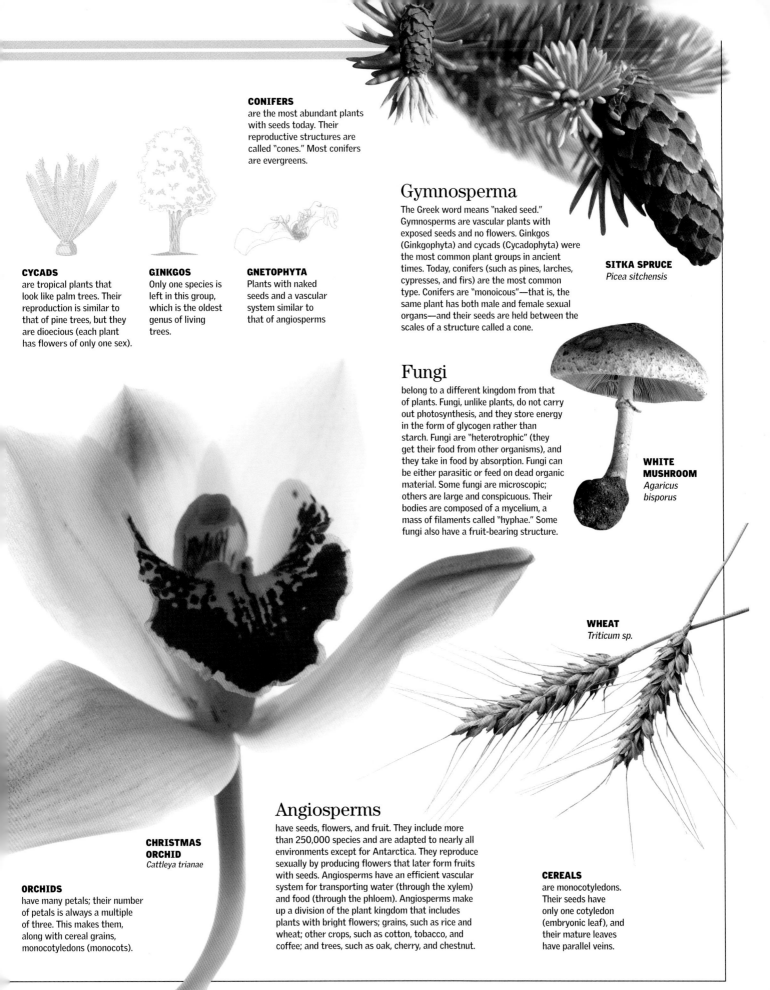

CONIFERS

are the most abundant plants with seeds today. Their reproductive structures are called "cones." Most conifers are evergreens.

Gymnosperma

The Greek word means "naked seed." Gymnosperms are vascular plants with exposed seeds and no flowers. Ginkgos (Ginkgophyta) and cycads (Cycadophyta) were the most common plant groups in ancient times. Today, conifers (such as pines, larches, cypresses, and firs) are the most common type. Conifers are "monoicous"—that is, the same plant has both male and female sexual organs—and their seeds are held between the scales of a structure called a cone.

SITKA SPRUCE
Picea sitchensis

CYCADS

are tropical plants that look like palm trees. Their reproduction is similar to that of pine trees, but they are dioecious (each plant has flowers of only one sex).

GINKGOS

Only one species is left in this group, which is the oldest genus of living trees.

GNETOPHYTA

Plants with naked seeds and a vascular system similar to that of angiosperms

Fungi

belong to a different kingdom from that of plants. Fungi, unlike plants, do not carry out photosynthesis, and they store energy in the form of glycogen rather than starch. Fungi are "heterotrophic" (they get their food from other organisms), and they take in food by absorption. Fungi can be either parasitic or feed on dead organic material. Some fungi are microscopic; others are large and conspicuous. Their bodies are composed of a mycelium, a mass of filaments called "hyphae." Some fungi also have a fruit-bearing structure.

WHITE MUSHROOM
Agaricus bisporus

WHEAT
Triticum sp.

Angiosperms

have seeds, flowers, and fruit. They include more than 250,000 species and are adapted to nearly all environments except for Antarctica. They reproduce sexually by producing flowers that later form fruits with seeds. Angiosperms have an efficient vascular system for transporting water (through the xylem) and food (through the phloem). Angiosperms make up a division of the plant kingdom that includes plants with bright flowers; grains, such as rice and wheat; other crops, such as cotton, tobacco, and coffee; and trees, such as oak, cherry, and chestnut.

CHRISTMAS ORCHID
Cattleya trianae

ORCHIDS

have many petals; their number of petals is always a multiple of three. This makes them, along with cereal grains, monocotyledons (monocots).

CEREALS

are monocotyledons. Their seeds have only one cotyledon (embryonic leaf), and their mature leaves have parallel veins.

Aquatic Plants

These plants are especially adapted for living in ponds, streams, lakes, and rivers—places where other land plants cannot grow. Although aquatic plants belong to many different families, they have similar adaptations and are therefore an example of adaptive convergence. They include submerged plants and floating plants; plants that may or may not be rooted at the bottom; amphibious plants, which have leaves both above and below the water's surface; and heliophilic plants, which have only their roots underwater.

A Vital Role

Aquatic plants play an important role in the ecosystem not only for crustaceans, insects, and worms but also for fish, birds, and mammals, because they are an important source of food and shelter for these categories of animals. Aquatic plants also play a major role in converting solar energy into the organic materials upon which many living things depend.

Rooted Plants with Floating Leaves

Such plants are often found in standing or slow-moving water. They have fixed rhizomes and petiolate leaves (leaves with a stalk that connects to a stem) that float on the surface of the water. Some of the plants have submerged leaves, some have floating leaves, and some have leaves outside the water, with each type having a different shape. In the case of floating leaves the properties of the upper surface are different from those of the lower surface, which is in contact with the water.

PARROT FEATHER
Myriophyllum aquaticum
This plant is native to temperate, subtropical, and tropical regions, and it is highly effective at oxygenating water.

TROPICAL WATER LILY
Victoria cruciana
It grows in deep, calm waters. Its leaves can measure up to 7 feet (2 m) across.

FLOATING LEAVES
The rhizomes are fixed, the leaves grow on long stalks, and the leaf surface floats on the water.

Upper Epidermis
Parenchyma
Aerenchyma
Lower Epidermis
Conduction Bundle
Air Chamber

YELLOW FLOATING HEART
Nymphoides peltata
It produces small creased yellow flowers all summer long.

Rooted Underwater Plants

The entire plant is submerged. The small root system serves only to anchor the plant since the stem can directly absorb water, carbon dioxide, and minerals. These plants are often found in flowing water. The submerged stems have no system of support—the water holds up the plant.

SAGO PONDWEED
Potamogeton densus
This water plant can be found in shallow depressions of clear-flowing streams.

HORNWORT
Ceratophyllum sp.
This plant has an abundance of fine leaves that form a conelike structure on each stem.

They produce and release oxygen as a result of photosynthesis.

Aquatic but Modern

The evolutionary history of plants began in water environments. They later conquered land by means of structures such as roots. Modern aquatic plants are not a primitive group, however. On the contrary, they have returned to the water environment by acquiring highly specialized organs and tissues. For example, some tissues have air pockets that enable the plant to float.

Aerenchyma

is always found in floating organisms. This tissue has an extensive system of intercellular spaces through which gases are diffused.

Aerenchyma
Epidermis
Air Chamber

Submerged stems have no support system because the water holds up the plant. Their limiting factor is oxygen availability, so the aerenchyma helps make this substance available to the plant.

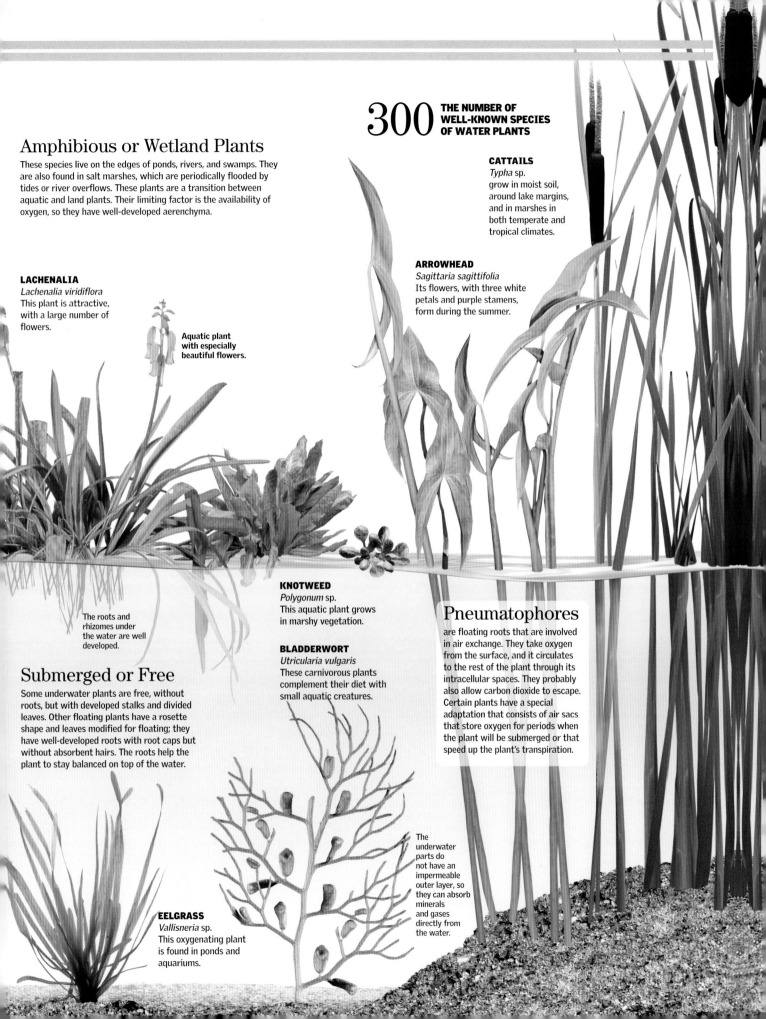

Amphibious or Wetland Plants

These species live on the edges of ponds, rivers, and swamps. They are also found in salt marshes, which are periodically flooded by tides or river overflows. These plants are a transition between aquatic and land plants. Their limiting factor is the availability of oxygen, so they have well-developed aerenchyma.

300 **THE NUMBER OF WELL-KNOWN SPECIES OF WATER PLANTS**

CATTAILS
Typha sp.
grow in moist soil, around lake margins, and in marshes in both temperate and tropical climates.

ARROWHEAD
Sagittaria sagittifolia
Its flowers, with three white petals and purple stamens, form during the summer.

LACHENALIA
Lachenalia viridiflora
This plant is attractive, with a large number of flowers.

Aquatic plant with especially beautiful flowers.

The roots and rhizomes under the water are well developed.

Submerged or Free

Some underwater plants are free, without roots, but with developed stalks and divided leaves. Other floating plants have a rosette shape and leaves modified for floating; they have well-developed roots with root caps but without absorbent hairs. The roots help the plant to stay balanced on top of the water.

KNOTWEED
Polygonum sp.
This aquatic plant grows in marshy vegetation.

BLADDERWORT
Utricularia vulgaris
These carnivorous plants complement their diet with small aquatic creatures.

Pneumatophores

are floating roots that are involved in air exchange. They take oxygen from the surface, and it circulates to the rest of the plant through its intracellular spaces. They probably also allow carbon dioxide to escape. Certain plants have a special adaptation that consists of air sacs that store oxygen for periods when the plant will be submerged or that speed up the plant's transpiration.

The underwater parts do not have an impermeable outer layer, so they can absorb minerals and gases directly from the water.

EELGRASS
Vallisneria sp.
This oxygenating plant is found in ponds and aquariums.

Conquest of Land

The movement of plants from shallow water onto land is associated with a series of evolutionary events. Certain changes in the genetic makeup of plants enabled them to face the new and extreme conditions found on the Earth's surface. Although land habitats offered plants direct exposure to sunlight, they also presented the problem of transpiration and the loss of water that it produces. This difficulty had to be overcome before plants could spread over land.

Vital Changes

Roots are among the most important adaptations for plants' success in land habitats. Root systems anchor the plant in the substrate and serve as a pathway for water and mineral nutrients to enter it. Besides roots, the development of a cuticle (skin membrane) to cover the entire plant's surface was crucial. Cells in the epidermis produce this waterproof membrane, which helps the plant tolerate the heat generated by sunlight and the wear and loss of water caused by the wind. This protection is interrupted by pores, which allow for gas exchange.

Green Revolution

Leaves are the main organs for photosynthesis in land plants. After plants appeared on land more than 440 million years ago, the amount of photosynthesis taking place gradually increased. This increase is believed to be one of the reasons the concentration of carbon dioxide in the atmosphere decreased. As a result, the Earth's average temperature also decreased.

50,000
SPECIES OF FUNGUS LIVE ALONGSIDE LAND-DWELLING PLANTS.

MALE FERN
Dryopteris filix-mas
These vascular plants need liquid water to reproduce.

MOSS
Sphagnum sp.
Bryophytes are the simplest of all land plants.

Epiphytes

grow on plants or on some other supporting surface. Their anatomy includes secondary adaptations that enable them to live without being in contact with the soil.

Grasses

take advantage of long hours of summer daylight to grow and reproduce. Their stalks do not have reinforcing tissues that would enable them to remain erect.

SWEET VIOLET
Viola odorata
This plant's spring flowers have a pleasant scent.

STEMLESS SOW THISTLE
Sonchus acaulis
These plants lack a stem.

Giants

Trees are distinguished by their woody trunks. As a tree grows from a tender shoot, it develops a tissue that gives it strength, enabling it to grow over 330 feet (100 m) tall. Trees are found in the principal terrestrial ecosystems.

360 Feet (110 M)
THE HEIGHT REACHED BY SOME SEQUOIA SEMPERVIREN TREES

CHESTNUTS
Castanea sp.

WALNUTS
Juglans sp.

BEECHES
Fagus sp.

MAPLES
Acer sp.

OAKS
Quercus sp.

LINDENS
Tilia sp.

Anatomy of a Tree

The oak tree is the undisputed king of the Western world. It is known for its lobed leaves and the large cap of its acorn, a nut found on all trees of the genus *Quercus*. The tree's main trunk grows upward and branches out toward the top. Oaks are a large group, containing many types of deciduous trees. Under optimal conditions oaks can grow to a height of more than 130 feet (40 m) and live an average of 600 years.

The leaves absorb CO₂ and produce sugars by means of photosynthesis.

Transpiration (the loss of water vapor) in the leaves pulls the xylem sap upward.

CLIMATE
Trees grow in any place where there is sufficient water in the soil.

Flowers

The tree produces hanging male flowers, whereas female flowers are hidden among the leaves.

Buds

are formed by protective scales that fall off in the spring. They grow into new leaves and branches.

SUMMER
The oak blossoms. It increases in height, and its trunk grows thicker.

SPRING
The cycle begins as the first leaves appear.

WINTER
The leaves fall away; the tree is dormant until spring.

FALL
Low temperatures weaken the branches.

Oak-tree Products

The bark is rich in tannin, which is used in curing leather and as an astringent. The wood is strong and resists rotting.

ENERGY SOURCE
The chlorophyll traps energy from sunlight and uses it to convert water and carbon dioxide into food.

SURFACE
Mosses use the bark of oak trees as a source of moisture.

Roots

grow sideways to form a deep, broad root system.

Absorption of Water and Minerals

The xylem transports water and minerals from the roots to the rest of the tree.

The phloem transports sugars from the leaves to the rest of the tree.

Woodpeckers drill holes in the tree with their beaks as they look for insects.

Growth Rings

Trunk

The trunk is strong and grows straight upward. The top of the tree widens with branches, which may be twisted, knotted, or bent.

Leaves

are arranged one leaf to a stem on alternating sides of the twig. They have rounded lobes on either side of the main vein.

SUMMER
The leaves undertake photosynthesis, and the rest of the tree uses the sugars it produces.

FALL
The cells at the end of each leaf stem weaken.

WINTER
The leaf falls away, and the tree remains dormant.

SPRING
New leaves begin to replace the old ones.

Beginnings

In its first year of life an oak tree's roots can grow nearly 5 feet (1.5 m).

600 years

THE AVERAGE LIFE SPAN OF AN OAK

— Achene: A hard seed that does not split open at maturity

— Remains of the Carpel (female reproductive part)

Seeds

Some species have sweet-tasting seeds; others are bitter.

Acorns

have dark stripes along their length. Their caps have flat scales.

Feeding on Light

An important characteristic of plants is their ability to use sunlight and the carbon dioxide in the air to manufacture their own complex nutrients. This process, called "photosynthesis," takes place in chloroplasts, cellular components that contain the necessary enzyme machinery to transform solar energy into chemical energy. Each plant cell can have between 20 and 100 oval-shaped chloroplasts. Chloroplasts can reproduce themselves, suggesting that they were once autonomous organisms that established a symbiosis, which produced the first plant cell.

Why Green?

Leaves absorb energy from visible light, which consists of different colors. The leaves reflect only the green light.

Leaves

are made of several types of plant tissues. Some serve as a support, and some serve as filler material.

Algae

perform photosynthesis underwater. Together with water plants, they provide most of the atmosphere's oxygen.

O_2 **IS RELEASED BY PLANTS INTO THE EARTH'S ATMOSPHERE**

Plant Cells

have three traits that differentiate them from animal cells: cell walls (which are made up of 40 percent cellulose), a large vacuole containing water and trace mineral elements, and chloroplasts containing chlorophyll. Like an animal cell, a plant cell has a nucleus.

CHLOROPHYLL is the most abundant pigment in leaves.

WATER Photosynthesis requires a constant supply of water, which reaches the leaves through the plant's roots and stem.

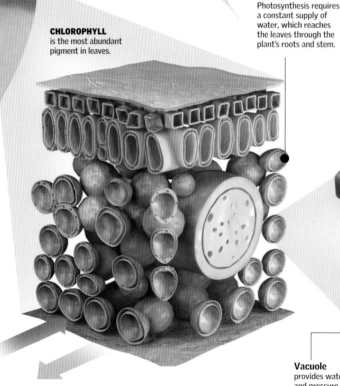

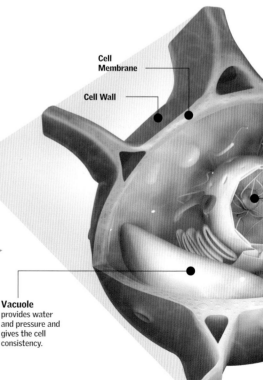

Cell Membrane

Cell Wall

Plant Tissues

The relative stiffness of plant cells is provided by cellulose, the polysaccharide formed by the plant's cell walls. This substance is made of thousands of glucose units, and it is very difficult to hydrolyze (break down in water).

CARBON DIOXIDE is absorbed by plant cells to form sugars by means of photosynthesis.

OXYGEN is a by-product of photosynthesis. It exits the surface of the leaves through their stoma (two-celled pores).

Vacuole provides water and pressure and gives the cell consistency.

Stages of the Process

Photosynthesis takes place in two stages. The first, called photosystem II, depends directly on the amount of light received, which causes the chlorophyll to release electrons. The resulting gaps are filled by electrons of water, which breaks down and releases oxygen and ionized hydrogen ($2H^+$).

1 ATP formation is powered by the movement of electrons into receptor molecules in a chain of oxidation and reduction reactions.

2 In photosystem I light energy is absorbed, sending electrons into other receptors and making NADPH out of NADP+.

3 The ATP and NADPH obtained are the net gain of the system, in addition to oxygen. Two water molecules are split apart in the process, but one is regenerated when the ATP is formed.

ATP: Adenosine Triphosphate.
ADP: Adenosine Diphosphate.
NADP: Nicotinamide Adenine Dinucleotide Phosphate.
NADPH: Nicotinamide Adenine Dinucleotide Phosphate Hydrogen.

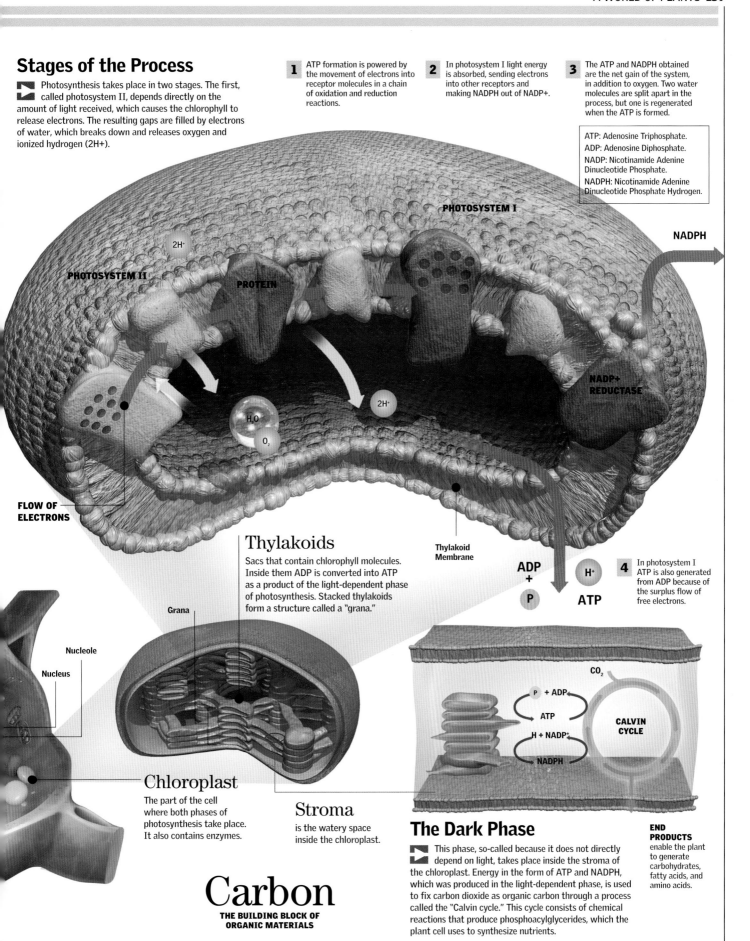

PHOTOSYSTEM I

NADPH

$2H^+$

PHOTOSYSTEM II

PROTEIN

H_2O
O_2

$2H^+$

NADP+ REDUCTASE

FLOW OF ELECTRONS

Thylakoids

Sacs that contain chlorophyll molecules. Inside them ADP is converted into ATP as a product of the light-dependent phase of photosynthesis. Stacked thylakoids form a structure called a "grana."

Thylakoid Membrane

ADP + P

H+

ATP

4 In photosystem I ATP is also generated from ADP because of the surplus flow of free electrons.

Grana

Nucleole

Nucleus

Chloroplast

The part of the cell where both phases of photosynthesis take place. It also contains enzymes.

Stroma

is the watery space inside the chloroplast.

CO_2

P + ADP

ATP

H + NADP+

NADPH

CALVIN CYCLE

The Dark Phase

This phase, so-called because it does not directly depend on light, takes place inside the stroma of the chloroplast. Energy in the form of ATP and NADPH, which was produced in the light-dependent phase, is used to fix carbon dioxide as organic carbon through a process called the "Calvin cycle." This cycle consists of chemical reactions that produce phosphoacylglycerides, which the plant cell uses to synthesize nutrients.

END PRODUCTS enable the plant to generate carbohydrates, fatty acids, and amino acids.

Carbon
THE BUILDING BLOCK OF ORGANIC MATERIALS

From Algae to Ferns

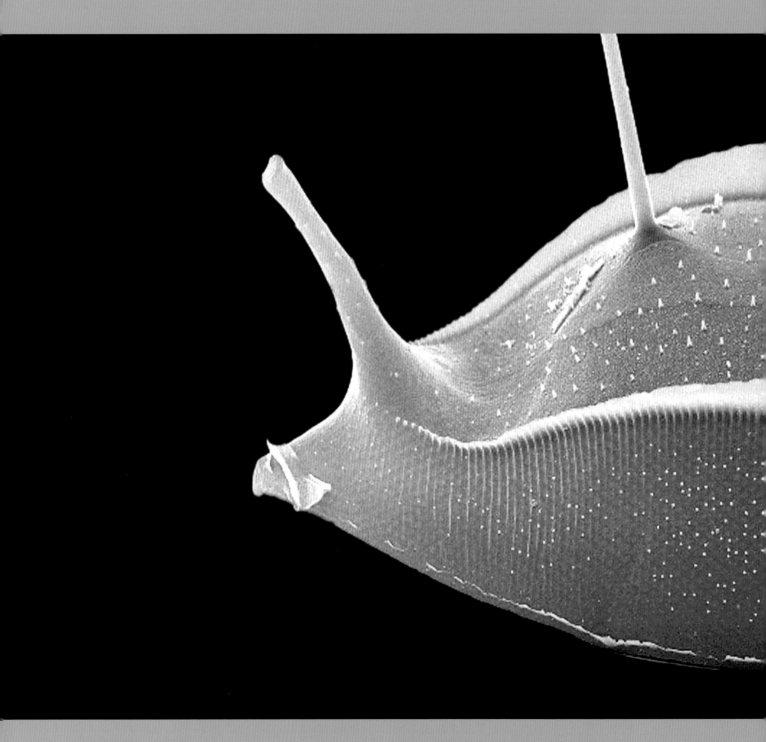

Algae (including seaweed) do not belong to the plant kingdom, because they do not have all the characteristics and functions of plants. Algae have neither roots nor stems. Because they live in water, they do not need these structures for absorbing water. Algae grow on the sea-floor or on the surface of

DIATOMACEOUS ALGAE
The scientific name of this type of
single-celled algae is *Biddulphia laevis*.
It is usually found close to the surface
of very shallow bodies of water.

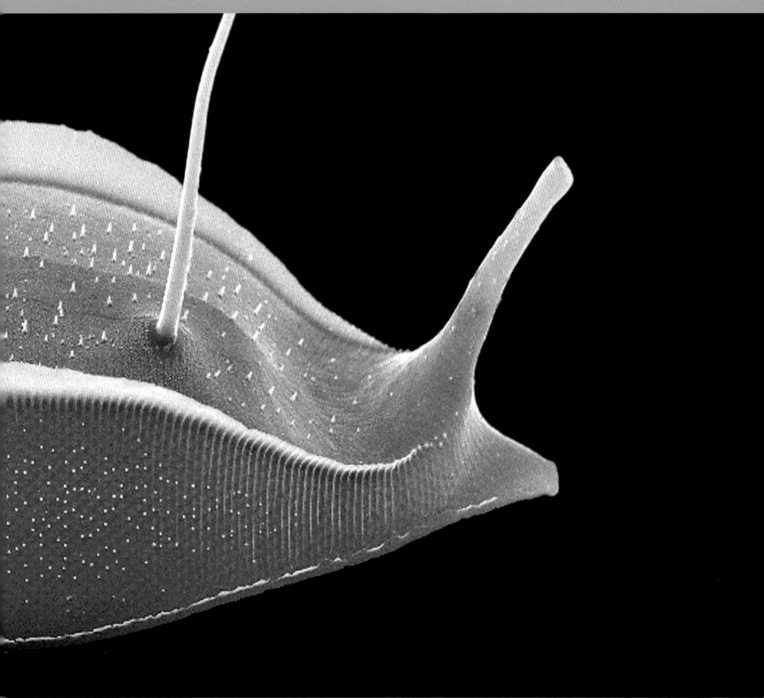

rocks in the ocean, in rivers, and in lakes.
Their shape and color are extremely varied.
The annual world harvest of algae is estimated
at more than 1 million tons in dry weight.

Asian countries (Japan and China) produce
80 percent of the world's harvest. Algae
are used in agriculture, the food industry,
pharmaceuticals, preservatives, and medicine.

Colors of Life

A lgae are living things that manufacture their own food using photosynthesis. Their color is related to this process, and it has been used as a way of classifying them. They are also grouped according to the number of cells they have. There are many kinds of one-celled algae. Some algae form colonies, and others have multicellular bodies. Some types of brown seaweed can reach a length of more than 150 feet (45 m).

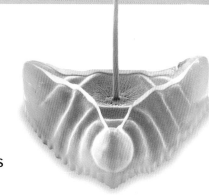

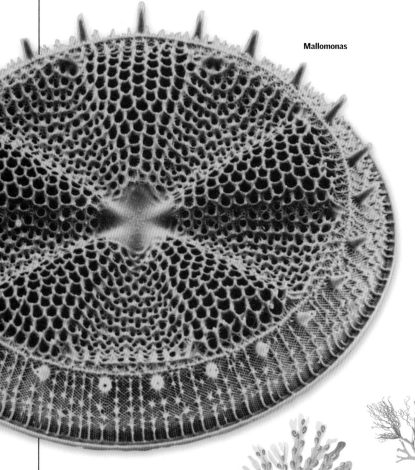

Mallomonas

Single-celled Organisms

often have flagella that enable them to move through the water. Most have the ability to ingest solid material through phagocytosis. Single-celled algae include some distinctive groups. Diatoms are covered with a protective shell made of silicon. Some single-celled algae, namely red algae, can thrive at relatively high temperatures. Red algae is unique among eukaryote organisms in its ability to live inside thermal water vents.

GREAT OPPORTUNISTS
Single-celled algae live near the surface of bodies of water. When they find an area with light and the nutrients necessary for development, they use asexual reproduction to multiply and colonize the area.

Fucus vesiculosus

Dictyota dichotoma f. *implexa*

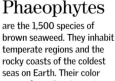

① Phaeophytes

are the 1,500 species of brown seaweed. They inhabit temperate regions and the rocky coasts of the coldest seas on Earth. Their color comes from the pigment fucoxanthin, a xanthophyll that masks the green color of their chlorophyll.

Dictyota dichotoma (Hudson) J.V. Lamouroux

Cystoseira amantacea var. stricta

Ectocarpus siliculosus

Multicelled Organisms

This group of algae includes multicelled structures. They form colonies with mobile, single-celled algae that group together more or less regularly in a shared mucilaginous capsule. They can also appear in threadlike shapes, which branch off, or in bulky shapes, which are made up of layers of cells with a particular degree of cellular differentiation, that together are called a "thallus."

2 Chlorophytes

constitute the group of green algae. The majority of species are microscopic, single-celled organisms with flagella. Others form into filaments, and yet others form large multicellular bodies. The group Ulvophyceae includes sea lettuce, which resembles a leaf of lettuce and is edible. The group Charophyceae includes stoneworts, which contain calcium carbonate deposits. The chlorophytes are linked evolutionally with plants because they contain the same forms of chlorophyll, and their cell walls contain cellulose.

Micrasterias rotata

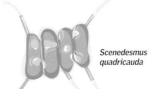

Scenedesmus quadricauda

Micrasteria staurastrum

Acetabularia crenulata

Pinnularia borealis

Chlamydomonas

6,000

DIFFERENT SPECIES
have been classified within this group of green algae, or chlorophytes.

3 Rhodophytes

are characterized by their phycoerythrin pigments, which give the algae a reddish color by masking their chlorophyll's green color. Most rhodophytes grow below the intertidal zone near tropical and subtropical coasts. They are distributed throughout the principal oceans of the world and grow mainly in shaded areas in warm, calm water.

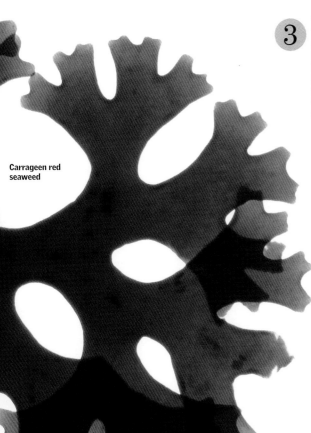

Carrageen red seaweed

Hypoglossum hypoglossoides

Bangia atropurpurea

Nitophyllum punctatum

Halymenia floresia

Apoglossum ruscifolium

How Algae Reproduce

The reproduction of algae can be sexual or asexual in alternating phases, depending on the species and on environmental conditions. Vegetative multiplication occurs through fragmentation or through the production of spores. In sexual reproduction the fertilization of the gametes (sexual cells) produces a zygote that will give rise to a new alga. During asexual reproduction there is no genetic exchange, and the algae produced are clones of the original. Sexual reproduction, in contrast, produces algae with new characteristics that may help them to better adapt to their environment.

Asexual

Asexual reproduction does not involve fertilization. It can take place in either of two ways. In fragmentation, segments of an alga become detached from its body, and, since the alga does not have any specialized organs, the segments continue to grow as long as environmental conditions remain favorable. The other form of asexual reproduction is by means of spores, special cells that form from a normal cell. Some algae spores have one or more filaments, or flagella, that allow the alga to swim freely. When the appropriate environmental conditions are found, the spores germinate into new algae.

ZOOSPORE
A structure that can produce a new individual asexually

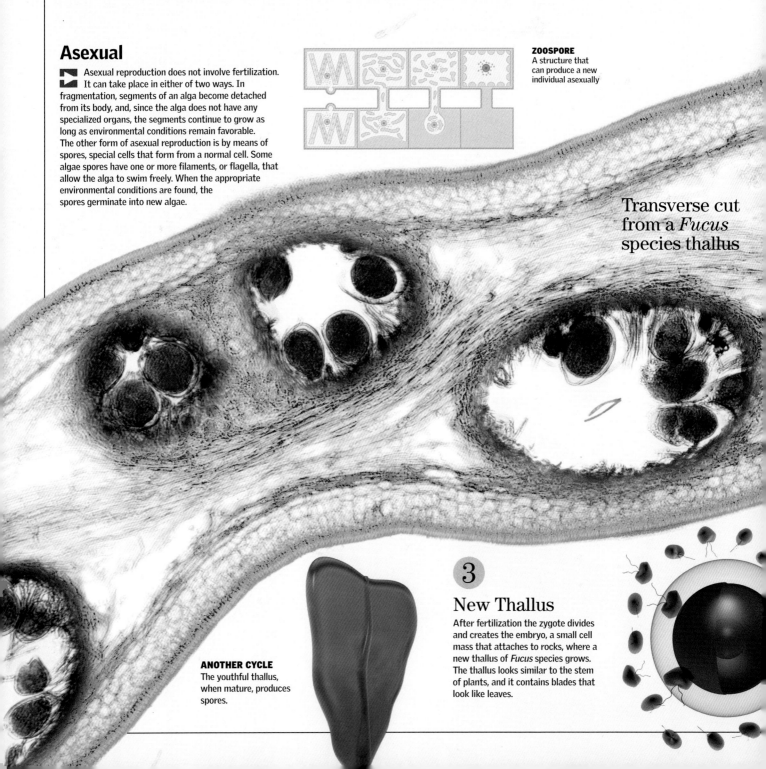

Transverse cut from a *Fucus* species thallus

ANOTHER CYCLE
The youthful thallus, when mature, produces spores.

3 New Thallus

After fertilization the zygote divides and creates the embryo, a small cell mass that attaches to rocks, where a new thallus of *Fucus* species grows. The thallus looks similar to the stem of plants, and it contains blades that look like leaves.

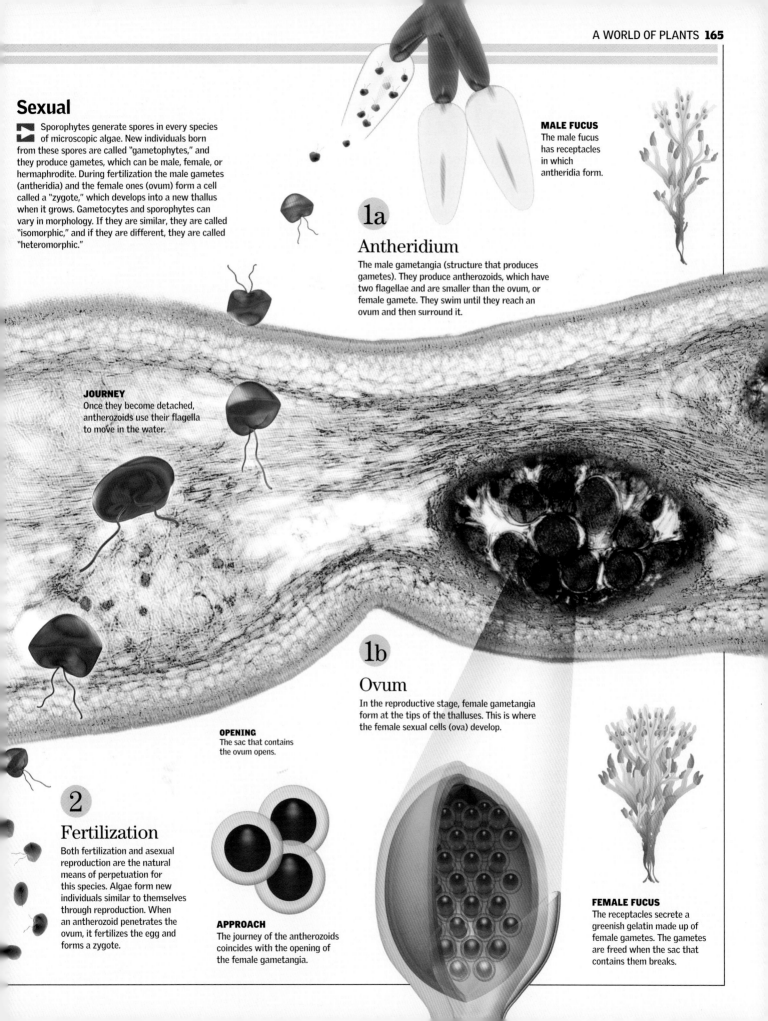

Sexual

Sporophytes generate spores in every species of microscopic algae. New individuals born from these spores are called "gametophytes," and they produce gametes, which can be male, female, or hermaphrodite. During fertilization the male gametes (antheridia) and the female ones (ovum) form a cell called a "zygote," which develops into a new thallus when it grows. Gametocytes and sporophytes can vary in morphology. If they are similar, they are called "isomorphic," and if they are different, they are called "heteromorphic."

MALE FUCUS
The male fucus has receptacles in which antheridia form.

1a
Antheridium

The male gametangia (structure that produces gametes). They produce antherozoids, which have two flagellae and are smaller than the ovum, or female gamete. They swim until they reach an ovum and then surround it.

JOURNEY
Once they become detached, antherozoids use their flagella to move in the water.

1b
Ovum

In the reproductive stage, female gametangia form at the tips of the thalluses. This is where the female sexual cells (ova) develop.

OPENING
The sac that contains the ovum opens.

2
Fertilization

Both fertilization and asexual reproduction are the natural means of perpetuation for this species. Algae form new individuals similar to themselves through reproduction. When an antherozoid penetrates the ovum, it fertilizes the egg and forms a zygote.

APPROACH
The journey of the antherozoids coincides with the opening of the female gametangia.

FEMALE FUCUS
The receptacles secrete a greenish gelatin made up of female gametes. The gametes are freed when the sac that contains them breaks.

Terrestrial and Marine Algae

As long as there is water, the survival of an alga is assured. Algae are found both in the oceans and in freshwater, but not all can survive in both environments. Depth, temperature, and salt concentrations of water are characteristics that determine whether algae can live in a given area. Algae can be green, brown, or red. Of the three, red algae are found in the deepest waters. Some species of algae can live outside water, but they are nevertheless found in humid places, such as in mud or on stone walls or rocks.

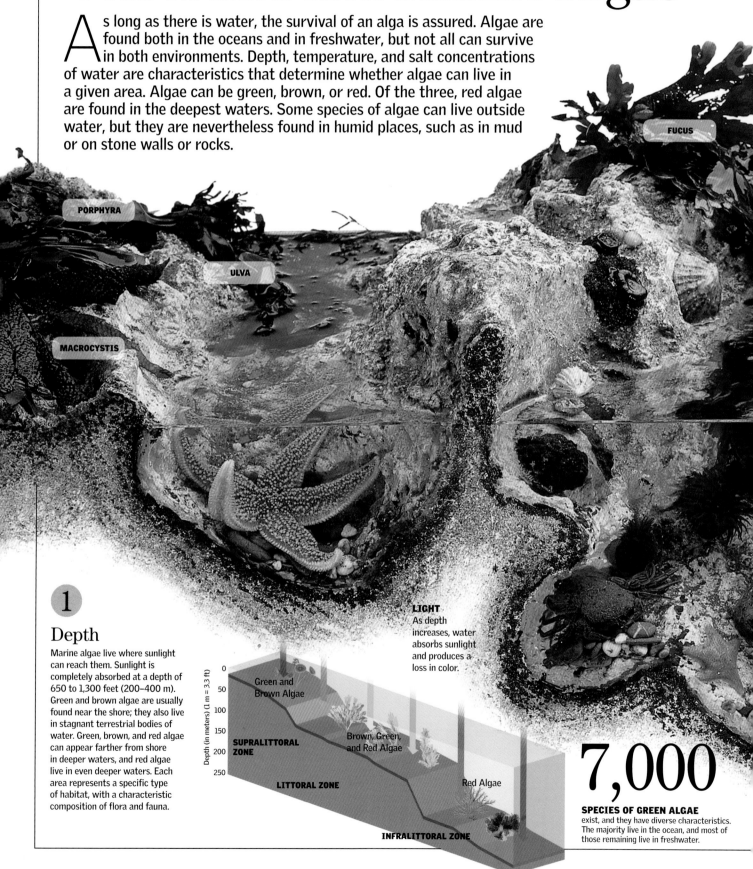

FUCUS

PORPHYRA

ULVA

MACROCYSTIS

LIGHT
As depth increases, water absorbs sunlight and produces a loss in color.

1

Depth

Marine algae live where sunlight can reach them. Sunlight is completely absorbed at a depth of 650 to 1,300 feet (200–400 m). Green and brown algae are usually found near the shore; they also live in stagnant terrestrial bodies of water. Green, brown, and red algae can appear farther from shore in deeper waters, and red algae live in even deeper waters. Each area represents a specific type of habitat, with a characteristic composition of flora and fauna.

Depth (in meters) (1 m = 3.3 ft)

0
50
100
150
200
250

Green and Brown Algae

SUPRALITTORAL ZONE

Brown, Green, and Red Algae

LITTORAL ZONE

Red Algae

INFRALITTORAL ZONE

7,000

SPECIES OF GREEN ALGAE
exist, and they have diverse characteristics. The majority live in the ocean, and most of those remaining live in freshwater.

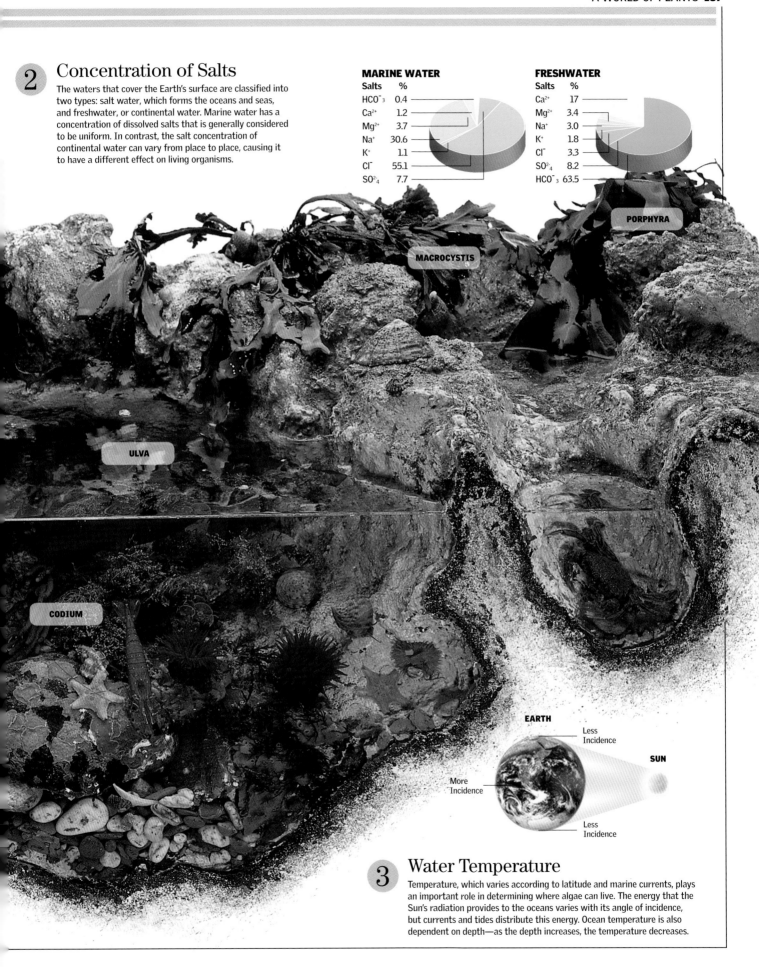

② Concentration of Salts

The waters that cover the Earth's surface are classified into two types: salt water, which forms the oceans and seas, and freshwater, or continental water. Marine water has a concentration of dissolved salts that is generally considered to be uniform. In contrast, the salt concentration of continental water can vary from place to place, causing it to have a different effect on living organisms.

MARINE WATER

Salts	%
HCO^-_3	0.4
Ca^{2+}	1.2
Mg^{2+}	3.7
Na^+	30.6
K^+	1.1
Cl^-	55.1
SO^2_4	7.7

FRESHWATER

Salts	%
Ca^{2+}	17
Mg^{2+}	3.4
Na^+	3.0
K^+	1.8
Cl^-	3.3
SO^2_4	8.2
HCO^-_3	63.5

PORPHYRA

MACROCYSTIS

ULVA

CODIUM

EARTH

Less Incidence

More Incidence

SUN

Less Incidence

③ Water Temperature

Temperature, which varies according to latitude and marine currents, plays an important role in determining where algae can live. The energy that the Sun's radiation provides to the oceans varies with its angle of incidence, but currents and tides distribute this energy. Ocean temperature is also dependent on depth—as the depth increases, the temperature decreases.

Dispersion of Spores

The fern is one of the oldest plants. Ferns have inhabited the surface of the Earth for 400 million years. Their leaves have structures called "sori" that contain the sporangium, which houses the spores. When the sori dry up, they release the spores into the air. Once on the ground, the spores germinate as gametophytes. In times of rain and abundant moisture the male cells of the gametophyte are able to swim to reach female gametes, which they fertilize to form a zygote that will grow as a sporophyte.

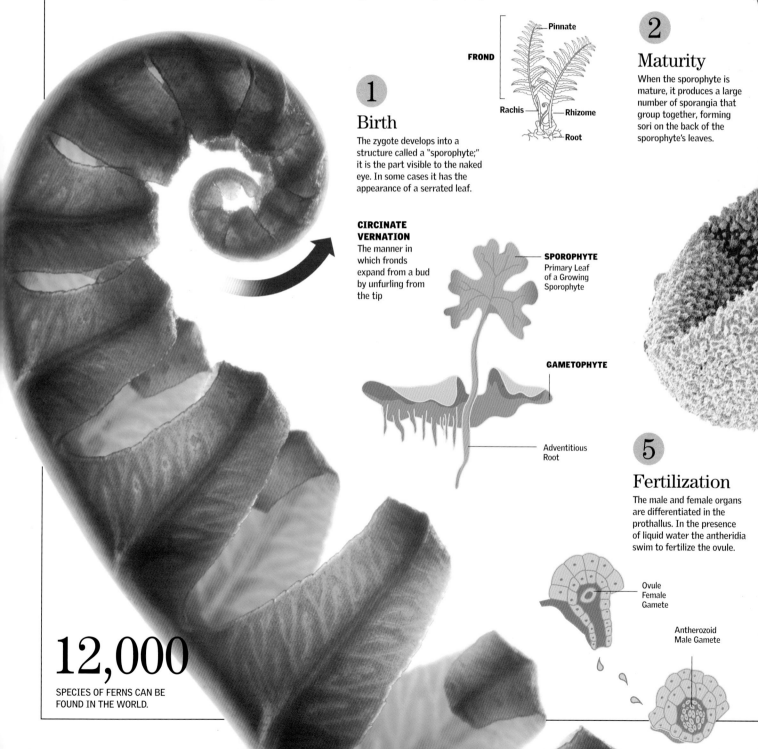

FROND
- Pinnate
- Rachis
- Rhizome
- Root

1

Birth

The zygote develops into a structure called a "sporophyte;" it is the part visible to the naked eye. In some cases it has the appearance of a serrated leaf.

CIRCINATE VERNATION
The manner in which fronds expand from a bud by unfurling from the tip

SPOROPHYTE
Primary Leaf of a Growing Sporophyte

GAMETOPHYTE

Adventitious Root

2

Maturity

When the sporophyte is mature, it produces a large number of sporangia that group together, forming sori on the back of the sporophyte's leaves.

5

Fertilization

The male and female organs are differentiated in the prothallus. In the presence of liquid water the antheridia swim to fertilize the ovule.

Ovule
Female
Gamete

Antherozoid
Male Gamete

12,000

SPECIES OF FERNS CAN BE FOUND IN THE WORLD.

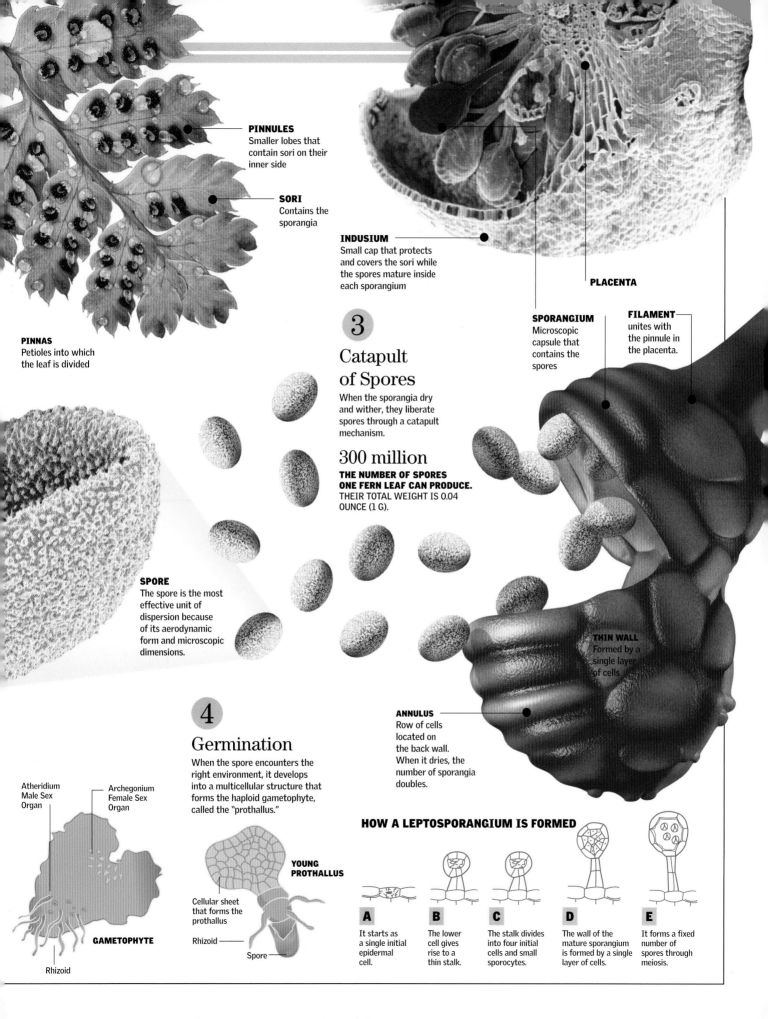

PINNULES
Smaller lobes that contain sori on their inner side

SORI
Contains the sporangia

INDUSIUM
Small cap that protects and covers the sori while the spores mature inside each sporangium

PLACENTA

PINNAS
Petioles into which the leaf is divided

SPORANGIUM
Microscopic capsule that contains the spores

FILAMENT
unites with the pinnule in the placenta.

3

Catapult of Spores

When the sporangia dry and wither, they liberate spores through a catapult mechanism.

300 million

THE NUMBER OF SPORES ONE FERN LEAF CAN PRODUCE. THEIR TOTAL WEIGHT IS 0.04 OUNCE (1 G).

SPORE
The spore is the most effective unit of dispersion because of its aerodynamic form and microscopic dimensions.

THIN WALL
Formed by a single layer of cells

4

Germination

When the spore encounters the right environment, it develops into a multicellular structure that forms the haploid gametophyte, called the "prothallus."

ANNULUS
Row of cells located on the back wall. When it dries, the number of sporangia doubles.

Atheridium Male Sex Organ

Archegonium Female Sex Organ

YOUNG PROTHALLUS

Cellular sheet that forms the prothallus

Rhizoid

Spore

GAMETOPHYTE

Rhizoid

HOW A LEPTOSPORANGIUM IS FORMED

A
It starts as a single initial epidermal cell.

B
The lower cell gives rise to a thin stalk.

C
The stalk divides into four initial cells and small sporocytes.

D
The wall of the mature sporangium is formed by a single layer of cells.

E
It forms a fixed number of spores through meiosis.

Seed Plants

Unlike animals, plants are limited in their ability to seek favorable conditions for life and growth. Consequently, they have evolved in different ways to reproduce and increase their population through seeds. A seed must arrive at an appropriate location at the best time for germination. Each species achieves its

THE POLLEN REACHES THE STIGMA
This is the first step toward forming a seed. In this magnified image the grains of pollen can be seen on the stigma of wolfsbane (*Arnica montana*).

objective in a different way. Some produce a great number of seeds; others wrap their seeds in a layer of hard material that softens with rain and winter's cold to germinate in spring.

In this chapter you will find how this process takes place, step by step, from pollination to the formation of a new plant.

Seeds, To and Fro

Reproduction from seeds is the most prominent evolutionary advantage in plants' conquest of the terrestrial environment. The seed shelters the embryo of the future plant with protective walls. The embryo is accompanied by tissues that provide enough nutrients for it to begin to develop. Optimal temperature and an appropriate quantity of water and air are the factors that stimulate the seed to awaken to a marvelous cycle of development and growth that will culminate in the generation of new seeds.

 AWAKENING OF THE SEED
Seeds, such as those of the field, or corn, poppy (*Papaver rhoeas*), leave their latent stage when they hydrate and receive enough light and air. Their protective coverings open and the embryo grows thanks to the energy provided by its cotyledons, or seed leaves.

 TROPISM
Because of gravity, amyloplasts are always located in the lower part of cells. They produce a stimulus that encourages the root to grow toward the earth, a process called "geotropism."

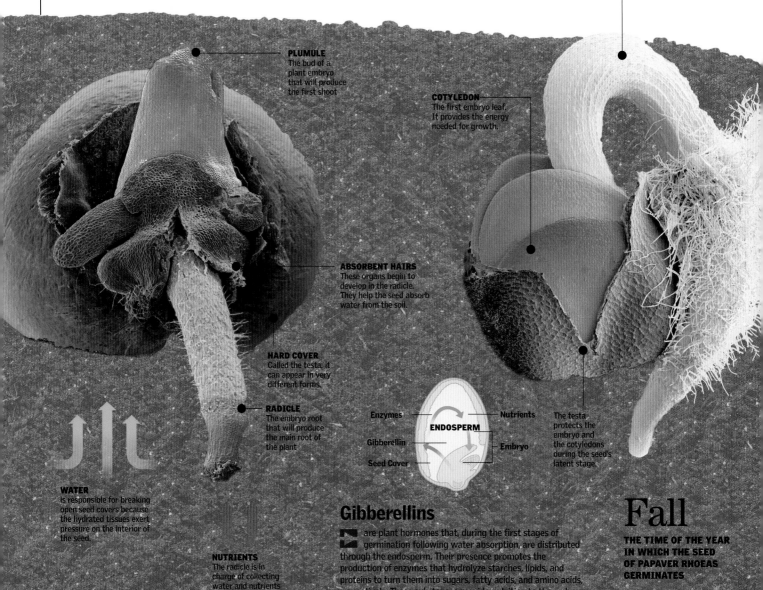

Cell multiplication allows the stem to grow.

PLUMULE
The bud of a plant embryo that will produce the first shoot

COTYLEDON
The first embryo leaf. It provides the energy needed for growth.

ABSORBENT HAIRS
These organs begin to develop in the radicle. They help the seed absorb water from the soil.

HARD COVER
Called the testa, it can appear in very different forms.

RADICLE
The embryo root that will produce the main root of the plant

Enzymes | Nutrients
ENDOSPERM
Gibberellin | Embryo
Seed Cover

The testa protects the embryo and the cotyledons during the seed's latent stage.

WATER
is responsible for breaking open seed covers because the hydrated tissues exert pressure on the interior of the seed.

NUTRIENTS
The radicle is in charge of collecting water and nutrients present in the soil.

Gibberellins

are plant hormones that, during the first stages of germination following water absorption, are distributed through the endosperm. Their presence promotes the production of enzymes that hydrolyze starches, lipids, and proteins to turn them into sugars, fatty acids, and amino acids, respectively. These substances provide nutrition to the embryo and later to the seedling.

Fall

THE TIME OF THE YEAR IN WHICH THE SEED OF PAPAVER RHOEAS GERMINATES

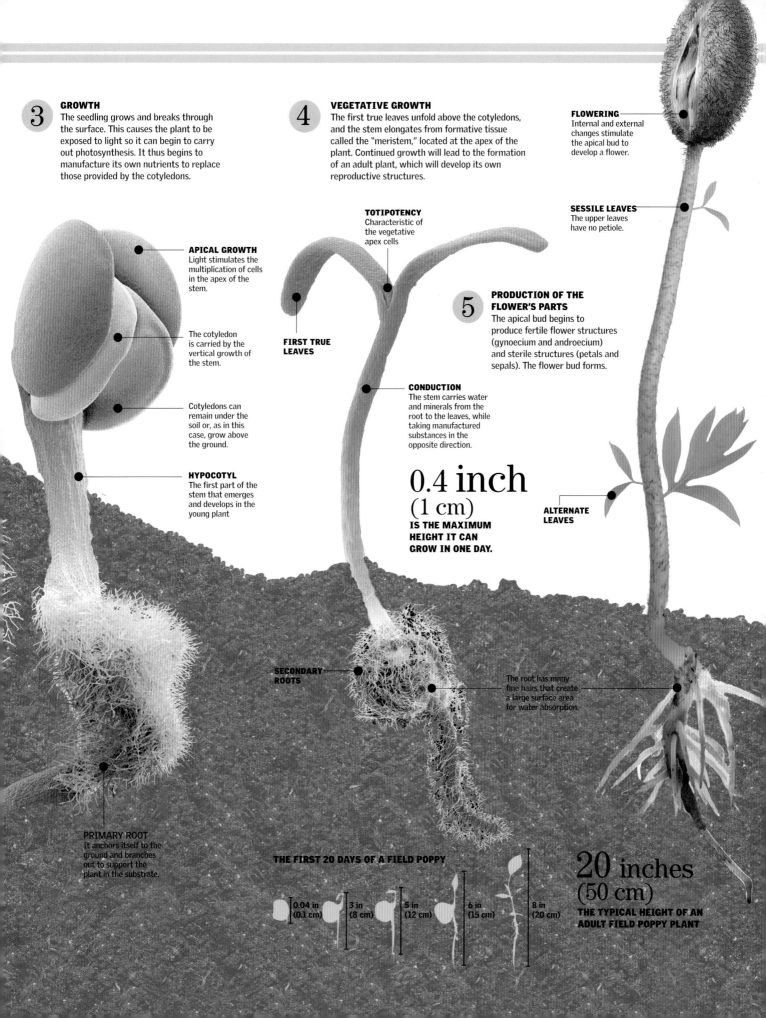

3 **GROWTH**
The seedling grows and breaks through the surface. This causes the plant to be exposed to light so it can begin to carry out photosynthesis. It thus begins to manufacture its own nutrients to replace those provided by the cotyledons.

APICAL GROWTH
Light stimulates the multiplication of cells in the apex of the stem.

The cotyledon is carried by the vertical growth of the stem.

Cotyledons can remain under the soil or, as in this case, grow above the ground.

HYPOCOTYL
The first part of the stem that emerges and develops in the young plant

PRIMARY ROOT
It anchors itself to the ground and branches out to support the plant in the substrate.

4 **VEGETATIVE GROWTH**
The first true leaves unfold above the cotyledons, and the stem elongates from formative tissue called the "meristem," located at the apex of the plant. Continued growth will lead to the formation of an adult plant, which will develop its own reproductive structures.

TOTIPOTENCY
Characteristic of the vegetative apex cells

FIRST TRUE LEAVES

CONDUCTION
The stem carries water and minerals from the root to the leaves, while taking manufactured substances in the opposite direction.

5 **PRODUCTION OF THE FLOWER'S PARTS**
The apical bud begins to produce fertile flower structures (gynoecium and androecium) and sterile structures (petals and sepals). The flower bud forms.

0.4 inch
(1 cm)
IS THE MAXIMUM HEIGHT IT CAN GROW IN ONE DAY.

SECONDARY ROOTS

The root has many fine hairs that create a large surface area for water absorption.

FLOWERING
Internal and external changes stimulate the apical bud to develop a flower.

SESSILE LEAVES
The upper leaves have no petiole.

ALTERNATE LEAVES

THE FIRST 20 DAYS OF A FIELD POPPY

0.04 in (0.1 cm) | 3 in (8 cm) | 5 in (12 cm) | 6 in (15 cm) | 8 in (20 cm)

20 inches
(50 cm)
THE TYPICAL HEIGHT OF AN ADULT FIELD POPPY PLANT

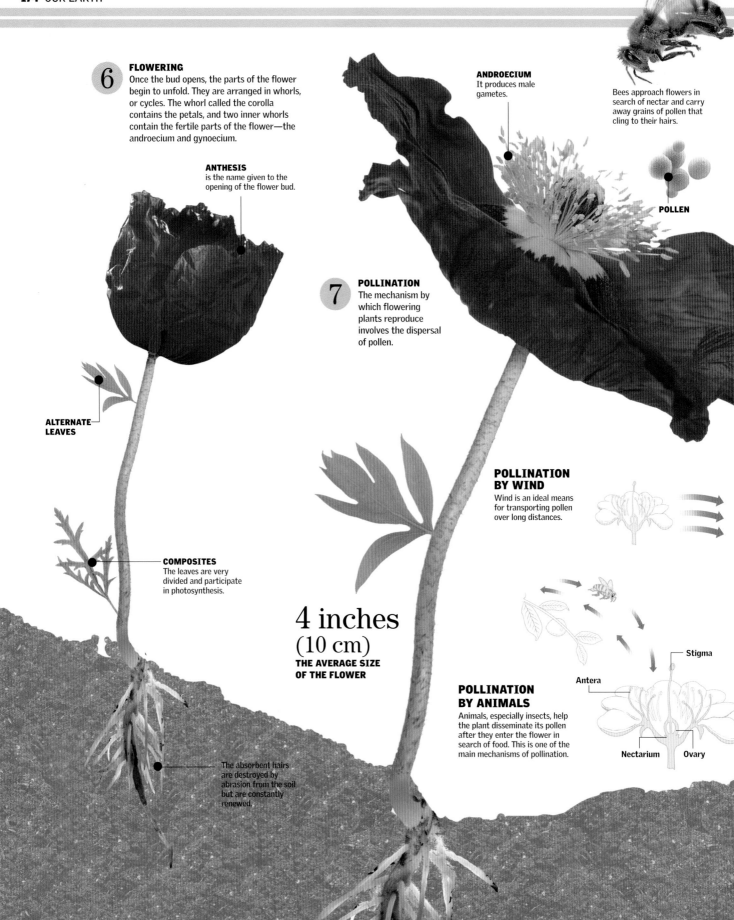

6 FLOWERING
Once the bud opens, the parts of the flower begin to unfold. They are arranged in whorls, or cycles. The whorl called the corolla contains the petals, and two inner whorls contain the fertile parts of the flower—the androecium and gynoecium.

ANTHESIS
is the name given to the opening of the flower bud.

ALTERNATE LEAVES

COMPOSITES
The leaves are very divided and participate in photosynthesis.

The absorbent hairs are destroyed by abrasion from the soil but are constantly renewed.

ANDROECIUM
It produces male gametes.

Bees approach flowers in search of nectar and carry away grains of pollen that cling to their hairs.

POLLEN

7 POLLINATION
The mechanism by which flowering plants reproduce involves the dispersal of pollen.

POLLINATION BY WIND
Wind is an ideal means for transporting pollen over long distances.

4 inches
(10 cm)
THE AVERAGE SIZE OF THE FLOWER

POLLINATION BY ANIMALS
Animals, especially insects, help the plant disseminate its pollen after they enter the flower in search of food. This is one of the main mechanisms of pollination.

Stigma

Antera

Nectarium   **Ovary**

FRUIT
After fertilization, the ovary and adjacent tissues become the fruit.

STAMENS

8 FRUIT
The seeds develop inside the fruit. Each seed can develop a new seedling.

FRUIT

SEEDS

9 RIPE FRUIT
The fruits scatter the seeds. Field poppies have dry fruits that open when they mature. This facilitates the dispersion of the seed by air.

POPPY SEEDS

10 DISPERSION
The fruit of a field poppy is a capsule with small openings at the top that help scatter the seeds.

11 SEED
Each seed distributed by air, water, or an animal can, under the right environmental conditions, germinate and develop into a new seedling.

3,000
SEEDS CAN BE CONTAINED IN ONE RIPE FIELD POPPY FRUIT.

Something in Common

When a seed encounters the right conditions, it can begin its life cycle. Even though every species of plant with flowers has its own particular life cycle, the various stages of the cycle represented here are typical of angiosperms in general.

Stems: More Than a Support

Stems, which occur in a variety of shapes and colors, support a plant's leaves and flowers. They keep it from breaking apart in the wind, and they determine its height. In addition, stems are also responsible for distributing the water and minerals absorbed by a plant's roots. Stems contain conducting vessels through which water and nutrients circulate. In trees and bushes, stems are woody for better support.

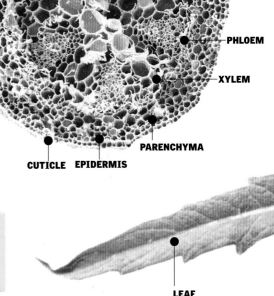

CROSS SECTION OF A NEW STEM

PHLOEM

XYLEM

PARENCHYMA

CUTICLE   EPIDERMIS

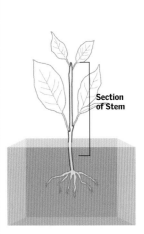

Section of Stem

IN THE AIR
Stems are usually branched, as seen in trees and bushes.

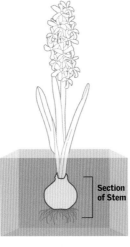

Section of Stem

IN THE GROUND
Certain types of stems have unusual characteristics.

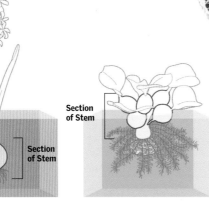

Section of Stem

IN THE WATER
The stem of an aquatic plant can lie underwater.

LEAF

Development of Stems in Different Mediums

Stems have widely varying sizes and shapes that reflect different adaptations to the environment. Palm trees and wheat are two good examples that show how different mediums can modify the stem through evolution. Palm trees are the tallest nonwoody plants. They grow tall because they must compete with many other plants for sunlight. In contrast, wheat is typical of areas with a cold climate and a short growing season. It develops a relatively short stem. This enables it to survive the physical assault of the dry wind and the loss of leaves.

SPROUTS
grow from the eyes.

TUBER
An underground stem composed mainly of parenchymatic cells filled with starch. The potato's small depressions are actually axillary eyes. In an onion, another example of a plant with an underground stem, starch accumulates not in tubers but in thick leaves that grow around the stem.

COMMON POTATO
Solanum tuberosum

AXILLARY EYES
are grouped in a spiral pattern along the potato.

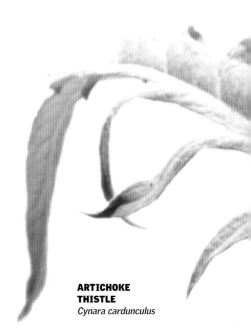

ARTICHOKE THISTLE
Cynara cardunculus

Circulation

Because the stem is the link between the roots, which absorb water and minerals, and the leaves, which produce food, the stem's veined tissues are connected to the roots and leaves. It functions as a transport system for interchanging substances. The stem and its branches hold the leaves up to receive light and support the plant's flowers and fruit. Some stems have cells with chlorophyll that carry out photosynthesis; others have specialized cells for storing starch and other nutrients.

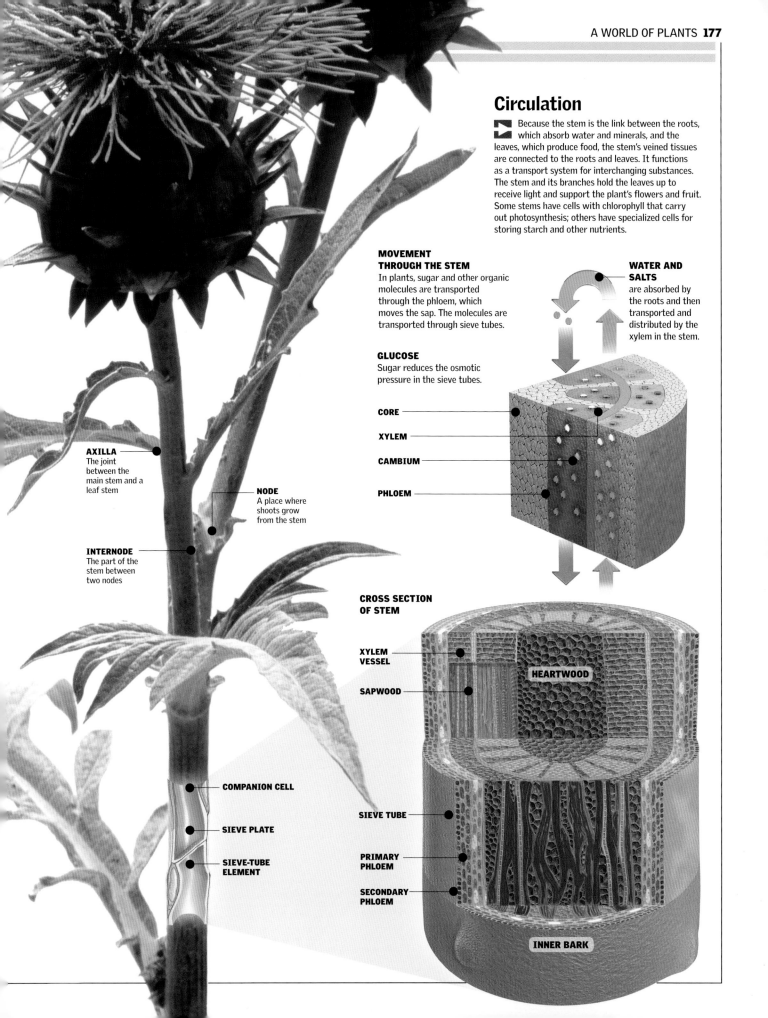

MOVEMENT THROUGH THE STEM
In plants, sugar and other organic molecules are transported through the phloem, which moves the sap. The molecules are transported through sieve tubes.

WATER AND SALTS
are absorbed by the roots and then transported and distributed by the xylem in the stem.

GLUCOSE
Sugar reduces the osmotic pressure in the sieve tubes.

CORE

XYLEM

CAMBIUM

PHLOEM

AXILLA
The joint between the main stem and a leaf stem

NODE
A place where shoots grow from the stem

INTERNODE
The part of the stem between two nodes

CROSS SECTION OF STEM

XYLEM VESSEL

SAPWOOD

HEARTWOOD

COMPANION CELL

SIEVE PLATE

SIEVE-TUBE ELEMENT

SIEVE TUBE

PRIMARY PHLOEM

SECONDARY PHLOEM

INNER BARK

Energy Manufacturers

The main function of leaves is to carry out photosynthesis. Their shape is specialized to capture light energy and transform it into chemical energy. Their thinness minimizes their volume and maximizes their surface area that is exposed to the Sun. However, there are a great many variations on this basic theme, which have evolved in association with different types of weather conditions.

EDGES (MARGINS)
Species are distinguished by a wide variety of edges: smooth, jagged, and wavy.

VEINS
Flowering plants (division Angiosperma) are often distinguished by the type of veins they have: parallel veins in monocots and branching veins in dicots.

PRIMARY VEINS
The products of photosynthesis circulate through the veins from the leaves to the rest of the body.

LEAF SURFACE
Colorful, usually green, with darker shades on the upper, or adaxial, side. The veins can be readily seen.

RACHIS

LEAF STEM (PETIOLE)

ACER SP.
This genus includes trees and bushes easily distinguishable by their opposite and lobed leaves.

Simple Leaves
In most monocotyledon plants the leaf is undivided. In some cases it may have lobes or notches in its side, but these divisions do not reach all the way to the primary vein of the leaf.

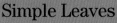

Compound Leaves
When the leaf is divided from the primary vein, it forms separate leaflets. A compound leaf is called "palmate "when the leaflets are arranged like the fingers on a hand and "pinnate" when they grow from the sides of the leaf stem like the barbs of a feather.

CROSS-SECTION
In general, upon sectioning a leaf, one can observe that it possesses the same tissues as the rest of the body of the plant. The distribution of tissues varies with each species.

CONDUCTING TISSUE
is made of live cells (phloem) and dead cells (xylem).

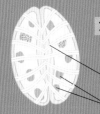

1 The stomatic apparatus is closed. No air can enter or leave the leaf. This prevents excessive transpiration, which could damage the plant.

Thickened cell walls in the area of the pore

Cellulose microfibers

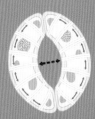

2 The stomatic apparatus is open. The stomatic cells are swollen. As tension increases, the cellular form is modified and is able to exchange gases.

PLANTS AND THE ENVIRONMENT
The flow of carbon dioxide and water vapor between the plant and the environment is essential for the photosynthetic process. This exchange can be affected by internal or external factors, such as changes in light, temperature, or humidity. In response to these stimuli, the stomas can open or close.

BASIC TISSUE
is formed by live cells that give structure to the leaf and usually contain some chloroplasts.

EPIDERMAL TISSUE
is composed of live cells. It surrounds all the parts of the leaf and the plant. It produces a substance that forms the cuticle.

Change and Its Advantages

Conifers possess an interesting modification in their leaves. In these gymnosperms, evolution directed the abrupt reduction of surface foliage area. This gave them an adaptive advantage over plants whose leaves have a large surface area: less resistance to wind and less transpiration in arid climates. In addition, they are able to avoid the excessive weight that would result from the accumulation of snow on large leaves.

TENDRILS
The leaves of climbing plants, such as the grapevine, have these adaptive modifications.

VASCULAR BUNDLE
Formed by phloem and xylem

RESIN
functions to prevent freezing. It circulates through the resin ducts.

EPIDERMIS
Cells with thick walls and a thick cuticle

CONIFERS
Needle-shaped leaves are characteristic of conifers. They are usually oval or triangular. A hypodermis, which is enclosed by the epidermis, is broken only in the stomas.

Functional Beauty

Flowers are not simply beautiful objects; they are also the place where the reproductive organs of angiosperms are located. Many are hermaphroditic, meaning that they contain both the male reproductive apparatus (the androecium) and the female (the gynoecium). The process of pollination is carried out through external agents, such as insects, birds, wind, and water. Following fertilization, flowers produce seeds in their ovaries. The floral parts are arranged in circular or spiral patterns.

GYNOECIUM
The female reproductive system. It is formed by carpels and includes the ovary, ovules, style, and stigma.

STIGMA
It can be simple or divided. It secretes a sticky liquid that captures the pollen. Some are also covered with hair.

Classification

Plants with flowers are classified as dicotyledons or monocotyledons. The first group has seeds with two cotyledons, and the second has seeds with only one. Each represents a different evolutionary line. They are differentiated by the structure of their organs. The cotyledon contains nutrients that the embryo utilizes during its growth until its true leaves appear. When a seed germinates, the first thing that appears is the root. In monocotyledons the stem and the radicle are protected by a membrane; the dicotyledons lack this protection, and the stem pushes itself through the soil.

Dicotyledons

In this class of plants each whorl of the flower is arranged in groups of four or five parts. In dicotyledons, the sepal is small and green, the petals are large and colorful, and the leaves are wide. The vascular ducts are cylindrical.

FLORAL DIAGRAM

Monocotyledons

Each whorl of these flowers contains three parts, and their sepals and petals are generally not differentiated from one another. The majority are herbaceous plants with scattered vascular conduits. They are the most evolved species of angiosperms.

FLORAL DIAGRAM

OVARY
The ovary is found in the receptacle at the base of the gynoecium, inside the carpels. The pollen tube extends into the ovary and penetrates the ovule.

CARPEL
The carpel consists of modified leaves that together form the gynoecium. It contains a stigma, a style, and an ovary. Ovules are produced in the ovary.

LEAVES
In dicotyledons, leaves have various forms, and they contain a network of veins that connect with a primary vein.

LEAVES
Plants with only one cotyledon have large and narrow leaves, with parallel veins and no petiole.

ROOT
In dicotyledons, the main root penetrates the ground vertically as a prolongation of the stem, and secondary roots extend from it horizontally. It can be very deep and long-lived.

ANDROECIUM
The male reproductive system. It is formed by a group of stamens, each of which consists of an anther supported by a filament. The base may contain glands that produce nectar.

ANTHER
A sac where grains of pollen (the male gametes) are produced

FILAMENT
Its function is to sustain the anther.

Whorls
Most flowers have four whorls. In a typical flower the outermost whorl is the calyx, followed by the corolla, the androecium (which can have two parts), and the gynoecium. When a flower has all four whorls, it is considered complete; it is incomplete when it lacks at least one of them. Plants that have an androecium and a gynoecium, but in separate flowers, are called "monoecious." If the flower lacks a sepal and petals, it is said to be naked.

250,000
THE NUMBER OF KNOWN SPECIES OF ANGIOSPERM PLANTS, THOUGH ONLY 1,000 SPECIES HAVE ECONOMIC IMPORTANCE. ABOUT TWO THIRDS OF THESE SPECIES ARE NATIVE TO THE TROPICS.

STYLE
Some styles are solid, others hollow. Their number depends on the number of carpels. The pollen tube grows through the style. In corn the tube can reach a length of 15 inches (40 cm).

COROLLA
A grouping of petals. If its parts are separated, they are simply called petals; if they are united, the plant is described as "gamopetalous."

PETAL
It typically has a showy color to attract pollinating insects or other animals.

CALYX
The grouping of sepals that protects the other parts of the flower. Together with the corolla it forms the perianth. The sepals may be separate or united; in the latter case the plant is called "gamosepalous."

SEPAL
Each of the modified leaves that protect the flower in its first stage of development. They also prevent insects from gaining access to the nectar without completing their pollinating function. Sepals are usually green.

OVARY
The ovary is found in the receptacle in the base of the gynoecium, inside the carpels. The pollen tube, which conducts the pollen to the ovule, extends to the ovary.

TEPAL
In monocotyledonous plants, the petals and sepals are usually the same. In this case they are called "tepals," and the group of tepals is called a "perianth."

ROOT
In monocotyledons, all the roots branch from the same point, forming a kind of dense hair. They are generally superficial and short-lived.

Pollination

The orchid, whose scientific name *Ophrys apifera* means "bee orchid," is so-called because of the similarity between the texture of its flowers and the body of a bee. Orchids' flowers are large and very colorful, and they secrete a sugary nectar that is eaten by many insects. The orchid is an example of a "zoomophilous" species; this means that its survival is based on attracting birds or insects that will transport its pollen to distant flowers and fertilize them.

CAUDICLE
At times it closes, covering the pollinia.

ODOR
The odor is similar to bee pheromones.

POLLINIUM
A small clump of closely packed pollen grains

1
Attraction
When a flower opens, a liquid drips on its lower petal and forms a small pool. The liquid gives off an intense aroma that attracts bees.

POLLINATING INSECT
Male Bee
Gorytes sp.

3
The Load
While passing through the narrow tunnel, the bee brushes the pollinarium, and pollen sticks to the bee.

2
The Fall
Excited by the perfume and the texture, the bee enters the flower, and in this pseudo-copulation it usually falls into the pool and becomes trapped. It cannot fly and can only escape by climbing the flower's stamens.

Bee Orchid
Ophyrys apifera

NECTAR
A sugary liquid that is somewhat sticky

LABELLUM
Its form imitates the abdomen of the bee.

POLLINIA
Small clumps of
pollen grains housed
in a compartment of
the anther

**0.008 TO
0.08 INCH
(0.2-2 MM)**

POLLINARIUM
Grouping of two, four,
six, or eight pollinia

**GRAIN OF
POLLEN**

Pollen

Each grain contains a male gamete.

12,000
THE NUMBER OF SEEDS
THAT A SINGLE FERTILIZED
ORCHID PRODUCES

CORBICULUM
Organ for the
transport of pollen

COLORATION
is one of the
factors of
attraction.

④ Transfer

The bee takes off toward
other flowers, with
pollen from the orchid
stuck to its back.

LOBULES
They have
fine, silky hairs
that attract the
bees.

⑤ Toward a Destination

When it arrives at another
flower of the same species,
the bee repeats the incursion
and bumps the flower's
stigmas (female organs),
depositing pollen that is
capable of fertilizing it.

CAMOUFLAGE
Some plants that rely on insects for
pollination acquire the appearance
of the animal species on which they
depend for survival. Each orchid has
its own pollinating insect.

Bearing Fruit

Once the flower is fertilized, its ovary matures and develops, first to protect the seed forming within it and then to disperse the seed. The stigmas and anthers wither, and the ovary transforms into fruit. Its wall forms the cover, or "pericarp." Fruits and seeds are of great economic importance because of their key role in human nutrition. The endosperms of some seeds are rich in starch, proteins, fats, and oils.

Simple Fruits

come from a single flower. They may contain one or more seeds and be dry or fleshy. Among them are drupes, berries, and pomes.

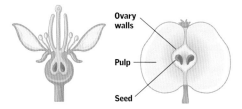

Ovary walls
Pulp
Seed

A POMES
are fleshy fruits that come from epigynous flowers, or flowers whose enclosed ovaries lie below the place where the other parts of the flower are attached. The floral receptacle thickens and forms an edible mesocarp. Apples are one example.

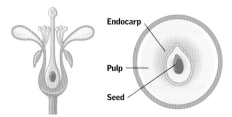

Endocarp
Pulp
Seed

B DRUPES
are fleshy fruits, leathery or fibrous, which are surrounded by a woody endocarp with a seed in its interior. They are generally derived from hypogynous flowers—flowers whose ovaries lie above the point where the other flower parts are attached. An example is the peach.

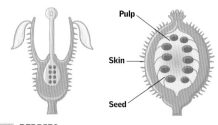

Pulp
Skin
Seed

C BERRIES
When they mature, berries generally have a bright color and a fleshy or juicy mesocarp. They come from either epigynous or hypogynous flowers. The grape is an example.

Oranges

Like other citrus fruits, oranges are similar to berries. Their seeds may propagate when the fruit rots and exposes them or when an animal eats the fruit and then defecates the seeds.

14%
THE PROPORTION OF AN IMMATURE CITRUS FRUIT THAT IS MADE UP OF THE FLAVONOID GLYCOSIDE (HESPERIDIN)

SEEDS

CENTRAL AXIS

LOCULES

SEPTA

VESICLES

ENDOCARP
The part of the pericarp that contains the seeds. It is formed in parts, or sections.

MESOCARP
A fleshy structure that is relatively solid.

Section

A sac that fills with juices (reserves of water and sugar) produced by the ovary walls

Peel

It consists of the mesocarp and exocarp of the fruit. It is soft and secretes oils and acids. However, in the case of a nut, its hard "peel" is its endocarp.

Multiple Fruits

are those that develop from the carpels of more than one flower, in a condensed inflorescence. When they mature, they are fleshy. An example is the fig.

FIG
Condensed fruit

BLACKBERRY
In this aggregate fruit, each berry is a fruit.

1 **AGGREGATE FRUIT**
The fruit is made of numerous drupelets that grow together.

2 **SYCONIUM**
The fruit axis dilates and forms a concave receptacle with the shape of a cup or bottle.

Dry Fruits

are simple fruits whose pericarps dry as they mature. They include follicles (magnolias), legumes (peanuts, fava beans, peas), pods (radishes), and the fruits of many other species, including the majority of cereals and the fruits of trees such as maple and ash. Most dehiscent fruits (fruits that break open to expose their seeds) are dry fruits.

Exocarp

Mesocarp

Endocarp

— ABORTED SEEDS

EXOCARP

The skin, or external part, of the fruit.

Conifers

Are effectively the most representative of the gymnosperms, a group of plants with seeds but not flowers. Through the fossil record it is known that conifers have existed for more than 390 million years. Their leaves are usually needle-shaped and perennial. They are woody plants that reproduce by means of seeds that contain tissues and an embryo that grows until it becomes an adult plant.

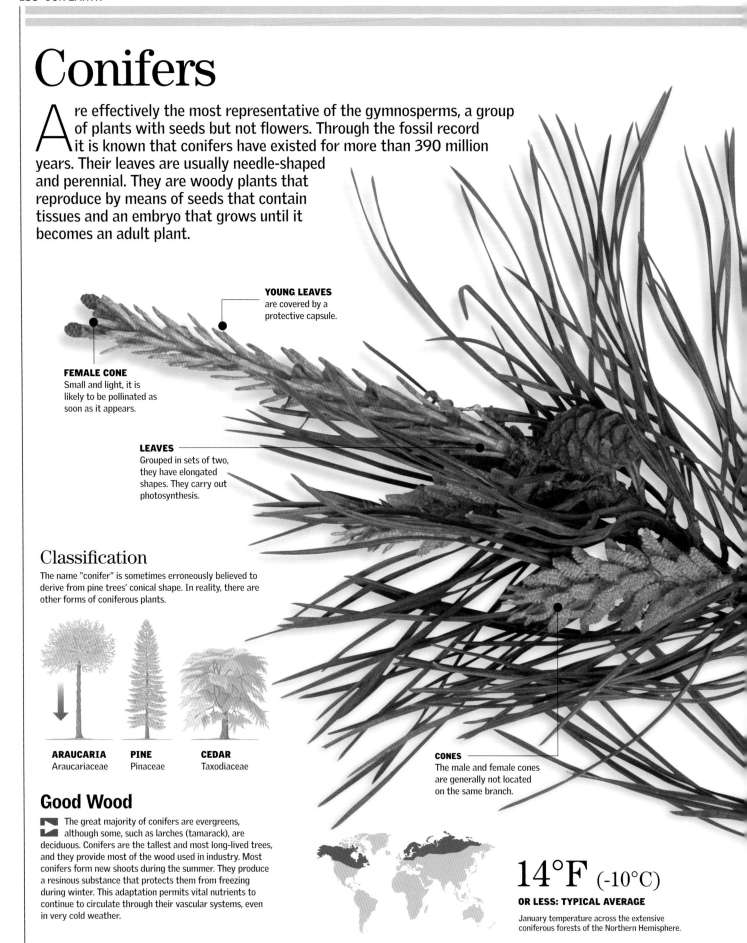

YOUNG LEAVES
are covered by a protective capsule.

FEMALE CONE
Small and light, it is likely to be pollinated as soon as it appears.

LEAVES
Grouped in sets of two, they have elongated shapes. They carry out photosynthesis.

CONES
The male and female cones are generally not located on the same branch.

Classification

The name "conifer" is sometimes erroneously believed to derive from pine trees' conical shape. In reality, there are other forms of coniferous plants.

ARAUCARIA
Araucariaceae

PINE
Pinaceae

CEDAR
Taxodiaceae

Good Wood

The great majority of conifers are evergreens, although some, such as larches (tamarack), are deciduous. Conifers are the tallest and most long-lived trees, and they provide most of the wood used in industry. Most conifers form new shoots during the summer. They produce a resinous substance that protects them from freezing during winter. This adaptation permits vital nutrients to continue to circulate through their vascular systems, even in very cold weather.

14°F (-10°C)

OR LESS: TYPICAL AVERAGE

January temperature across the extensive coniferous forests of the Northern Hemisphere.

LEAFLET

SCALE

Bract Scale

Cuticle

Gametophyte

Pine Cones

The female cone contains ovules that are situated among its ovuliferous scales. The cones are woody and are usually found in the upper branches of the tree. The male cones are not woody and are usually found in the lower branches. When the ovules of a female cone are pollinated, the resulting seeds need about three years to mature inside the cone. Mature ovules are popularly called pine nuts.

DISPERSION
The ovuliferous scales generate a greenish gelatin containing the female gametes. The gametes are freed when the sac that contains them opens. A forest fire can promote reproduction by causing the sac to open.

Bract
Scales

Ovuliferous
Scales

MATURE CONE
Three years after the cone appears, its seeds are ready to disseminate.

CLOSED

OPEN

Pine Nuts

Pine nuts have long been used with honey and sugar to make pastries. When summer arrives, harvested pine cones are placed in the sun, which causes them to open. The pine nuts are then shaken loose from their cones and gathered. In traditional processing the pine nuts are soaked in water to remove their outer covering, which floats to the surface. The pine nuts are then run between two closely spaced mechanical rollers to crack their inner shells. Finally, the pine-nut meat is separated from the shell by hand.

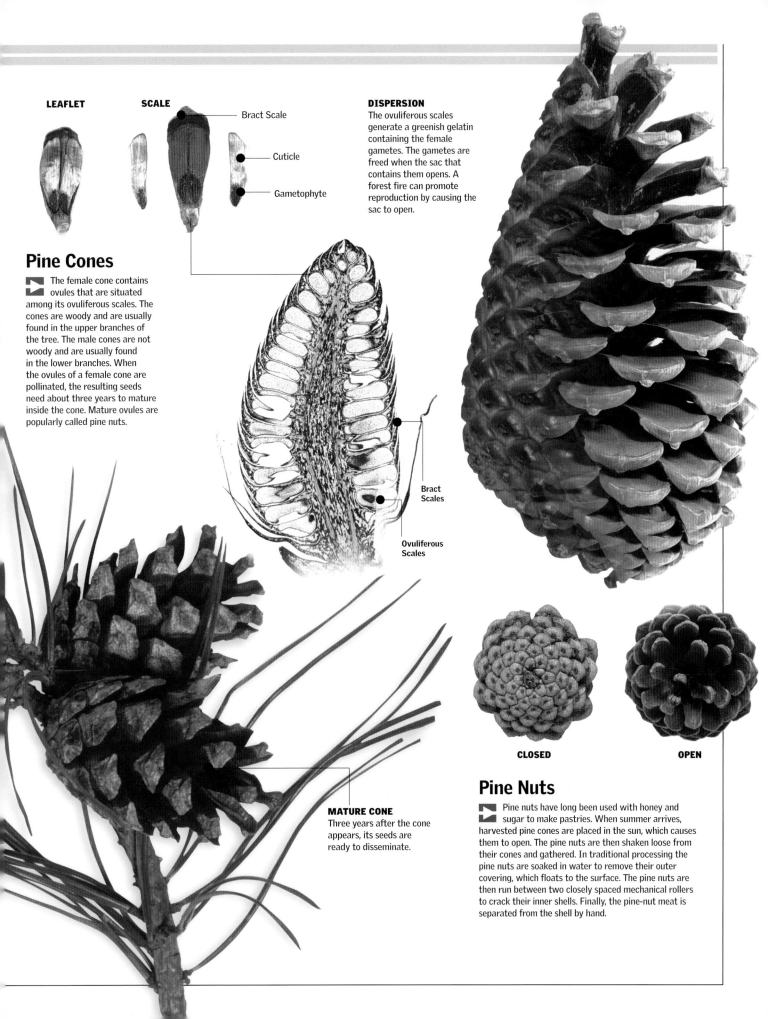

Fungi

For nearly a billion years the ability of fungi to break down substances has been important to life on Earth. These life-forms break down carbon compounds and return carbon and other elements to the environment to be used by other organisms. They interact with roots, enabling them to better absorb water and

AMANITA MUSCARIA
The quintessential toadstool has unpleasant psychoactive effects. Depending on the dose, they range from dizziness, muscle cramps, and vomiting to amnesia.

mineral nutrients. For many years fungi were classified within the plant kingdom. However, unlike plants, they cannot produce their own food. Fungi can develop in all sorts of environments, especially damp and poorly lit places. Many are parasites, and some fungi are pathogens—they can cause sickness in humans, animals, or plants.

Another World

For many years fungi were classified within the plant kingdom. However, unlike plants, they are "heterotrophic"—unable to produce their own food. Some fungi live independently, whereas others are parasitic. Like animals, they use glycogen for storing reserves of energy, and their cell walls are made of chitin, the substance from which insects' outer shells are made.

Fungi: A Peculiar Kingdom

Fungi can develop in all sorts of environments, especially damp and poorly lit places, up to elevations of 13,000 feet (4,000 m). They are divided into four large phyla, in addition to a group of fungi called "imperfect" because they generally do not reproduce sexually. At present, 15,000 species of fungi fall into this category. DNA analysis has recently reclassified them as Deuteromycetes.

Chytridiomycota

are the only fungi that, at some point in their lives, have mobile cells—male and female gametes, which they release into water in order to reproduce. They live in water or on land, feeding on dead material or living as parasites on other living organisms. Their cell walls are made of chitin.

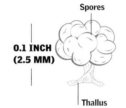

0.1 INCH (2.5 MM)

Spores

Thallus

VARIETY
There are great anatomical differences among the Chytridiomycetes. In the same reproductive phase they can produce haploid and diploid spores.

39° to 140°F
(4°– 60°C)
THE TEMPERATURE RANGE IN WHICH MOST FUNGI CAN LIVE IN HUMID CLIMATES

Deuteromycota

are also called "imperfect fungi" because they are not known to have a form of sexual reproduction. Many live as parasites on plants, animals, or humans, causing ringworm or mycosis on the skin. Others–such as Penicillium, which produces penicillin, and Cyclospora–have great medicinal and commercial value.

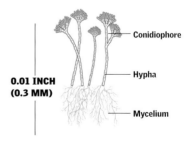

Conidiophore

Hypha

Mycelium

0.01 INCH (0.3 MM)

OF UNKNOWN SEX
In Deuteromycetes, conidia are tiny spores that function asexually. They are contained in structures called conidiophores.

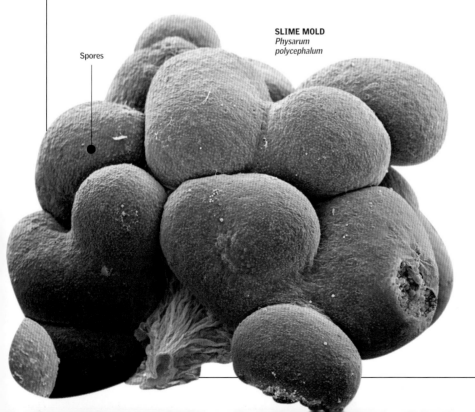

Spores

SLIME MOLD
Physarum polycephalum

Basidiomycota

This phylum, which includes mushrooms, is the most familiar of the fungi. The mushroom's reproductive organ is its cap. Its branches grow underground or into some other organic substrate.

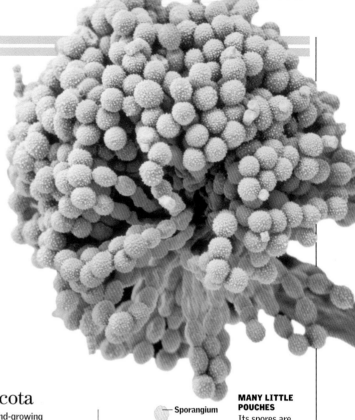

BLACK BREAD MOLD
Rhizopus stolonifer

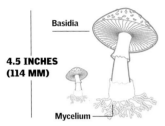

4.5 INCHES (114 MM)

Basidia

Mycelium

CAPPED MUSHROOMS
With its recognizable shape, the mushroom's cap protects the basidia, which produce spores.

CHANTERELLE MUSHROOM
Cantharellus cibarius

80,857
different species
HAVE BEEN IDENTIFIED IN THE FUNGI KINGDOM. THERE ARE BELIEVED TO BE APPROXIMATELY 1,500,000 SPECIES.

Zygomycota

is a phylum of land-growing fungi that reproduce sexually with zygosporangia, diploid cells that do not break their cell walls until conditions are right for germinating. They also reproduce asexually. Most zygomycetes live in the soil and feed on plants or dead animal matter. Some live as parasites on plants, insects, or small land animals.

0.01 INCH (0.3 MM)

Sporangium

Sporangiophore

Mycelium

MANY LITTLE POUCHES
Its spores are formed when two gametes of opposite sexes fuse. It can also reproduce asexually, when the sporangium breaks and releases spores.

Ascus with Ascospores

Ascomycota

is the phylum with the most species in the Fungi kingdom. It includes yeasts and powdery mildews, many common black and yellow-green molds, morels, and truffles. Its hyphae are partitioned into sections. Their asexual spores (conidia) are very small and are formed at the ends of special hyphae.

EXPLOSIVE
At maturity the asci burst. The explosion releases their sexual spores (ascospores) into the air.

Ascus

Hypha

0.6 INCH (15 MM)

Ascocarp

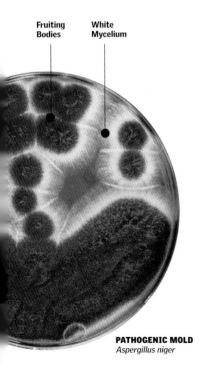

Fruiting Bodies

White Mycelium

ERGOT
Claviceps purpurea

PATHOGENIC MOLD
Aspergillus niger

The Diet of Fungi

Fungi do not ingest their food like animals. On the contrary, they absorb it after breaking it down into small molecules. Most of them feed on dead organic material. Other fungi are parasites, which feed on living hosts, or predators, which live off the prey they trap. Many others establish relationships of mutual benefit with algae, bacteria, or plants and receive organic compounds from them.

Chemical Transformation

The organic or inorganic substances that fungi feed on are absorbed directly from the environment. Fungi first secrete digestive enzymes onto the food source. This causes a chemical transformation that results in simpler, more easily assimilated compounds. Basidiomycetes are classified according to their diet. For example, they colonize different parts of a tree depending on the nutrients they require.

CAP
Besides being easy to spot, the cap is the fertile part of basidiomycetes; it contains spores.

PARASITES
Fungi such as *Ceratocystis ulmi* and *Agrocybe aegerita* (shaded areas on the leaf) live at the expense of other plants, which they can even kill. Others live parasitically off animals.

SAPROBES
There is no organic material that cannot be broken down by this type of fungus. They actually live on the dead parts of other plants, so they cause no harm to the host.

SYMBIOTIC
While feeding off the plant, they help it to obtain water and mineral salts more easily from the soil. Each species has its own characteristics.

Fungi of the genus *Amanita*, including the poisonous *A. muscaria* shown here, have the well-known mushroom shape with a mushroom cap.

MYCELIUM
When a mushroom spore finds the right medium, it begins to generate a network of hyphae, branching filaments that extend into the surrounding medium. This mass of hyphae is called a "mycelium." A mushroom forms when threads of the mycelium are compacted and grow upward to create a fruiting body.

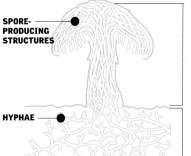

SPORE-PRODUCING STRUCTURES

HYPHAE

FRUITING BODY
The basidiocarp, or mushroom cap, generates new spores.

VEGETATIVE MYCELIUM
It is made of branches of threadlike hyphae that grow underground.

Cuticle

The skin, or membrane, that covers the cap, or pileus, is called the cuticle. It can have a variety of colors and textures, such as velvety, hairy, scaly, threadlike, fibrous, fuzzy, smooth, dry, or slimy.

GILLS
are the structures that produce spores. Their shape varies according to the species.

BASIDIA
are fine structures that contain groups of four cells, which are able to reproduce.

Basidium

Basidiospore

HYMENIUM
It is located on the underside of the cap. It contains very fine tissues that produce spores. Its structure can consist of tubes, wrinkles, hairlike projections, or even needles.

DETAIL OF A GILL

Life Cycle of a Fungus

Fungi produce spores during sexual or asexual reproduction. Spores serve to transport the fungus to new places, and some help the fungus to survive adverse conditions.

Development of the fruit-bearing body

Hyphae formation

Spore formation by fertilization

Release of spores

RING
Also known as the veil, it protects part of the hymenium in young fungi.

Growth

At birth the fruiting body of the species *Amanita muscaria* looks like a white egg. It grows and opens slowly as the mushroom's body unfolds. As it grows the cap first appears completely closed. During the next several days it opens like an umbrella and acquires its color.

HALLUCINOGENIC MUSHROOM
Psilocybin sp.

STEM
Cylindrical in shape, it holds up the cap and reveals important information for identifying the species.

Did You Know?

Fungi can break down an impressive variety of substances. For example, a number of species can digest petroleum, and others can digest plastic. Fungi also provided the first known antibiotic, penicillin. They are now a basic source of many useful medical compounds. Scientists are studying the possibility of using petroleum-digesting fungi to clean up oil spills and other chemical disasters.

VOLVA
The volva is made of the remains of the early rings that have fallen off. It differs from species to species.

Strobilurus esculentus
lives on the cones of various pine trees.

Pathogens

Fungi that are able to cause illnesses in people, animals, or plants are called "pathogens." The nocive, or toxic, substances that these organisms produce have negative effects on people and cause significant damage to agriculture. One reason these pathogens are so dangerous is their high tolerance to great variations in temperature, humidity, and pH. *Aspergillus* is a genus of fungi whose members create substances that can be highly toxic.

CONIDIA CHAIN
Conidia are asexual spores that form at the ends of the hyphae. In this case they group together in chains.

CONIDIA
are so small that they spread through the air without any difficulty.

PHIALIDES
are cells from which conidia are formed.

900
THE NUMBER OF ASPERGILLUS SPECIES. THEY HAVE BEEN CLASSIFIED INTO 18 GROUPS. MOST OF THESE SPECIES ARE ASSOCIATED WITH HUMAN ILLNESSES, SUCH AS ASPERGILLOSIS.

CONIDIOPHORE
The part of the mycelium of the fruiting, or reproductive, body in which asexual spores, or conidia, are formed

ALLERGENICS
Aspergillus flavus

This species is associated with allergic reactions in people with a genetic predisposition to this allergy. They also cause the contamination of seeds, such as peanuts. They produce secondary metabolites, called "micotoxins," that are very toxic.

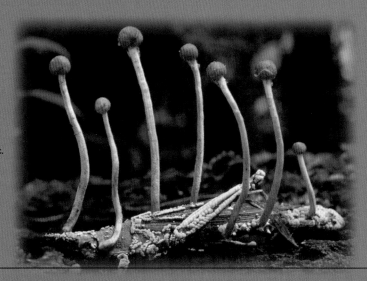

SAPROBIA
Aspergillus sp.

In addition to the pathogen species, there are some species of *Aspergillus* that decompose the organic matter of dead insects, thus incorporating nutrients into the soil.

Aspergillum

Aspergillus are "imperfect" fungi, or deuteromycetes, that are characterized by having reproductive structures called "conidial heads." The head is composed of a vesicle that is surrounded by a crown of phialides shaped like a bottle, at the end of which spore chains form.

CONIDIAL HEAD
Has a greenish mycelium and short and abundant conidiophores.

BREAD MOLD
Aspergillus niger

The fruiting body is yellowish white, but it will turn black when the conidia mature. Its conidiophores are large and have phialides that cover all its conidial head vesicle. They can be found in mold-covered food.

12

SPECIES ARE ASSOCIATED WITH HUMAN ILLNESSES. ASPERGILLUS FUMIGATUS, A. FLAVUS, A. NIGER, AND A. TERREUS ARE EXAMPLES.

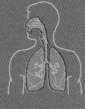

OPPORTUNISTIC
Aspergillus fumigatus

This pathogen can affect people whose immune systems are weakened. It can cause serious invasive diseases.

5 WEATHER AND CLIMATE

198

208

220

238

Climatology

The constantly moving atmosphere, the oceans, the continents, and the great masses of ice are the principal components of the environment. All these constitute what is called the "climatic system;" they permanently interact with one another and transport water (as liquid or vapor), electromagnetic radiation, and

SATELLITE IMAGE
In this image of the Earth, one clearly sees the movement of water and air, which causes, among other things, temperature variations.

heat. Within this complex system, one of the fundamental variables is temperature, which experiences the most change and is the most noticeable. The wind is important because it carries heat and moisture into the atmosphere. Water, with all its processes (evaporation, condensation, convection), also plays a fundamental role in Earth's climatic system.

Global Equilibrium

The Sun's radiation delivers a large amount of energy, which propels the Earth's extraordinary mechanism called the "climatic system." The components of this complex system are the atmosphere, hydrosphere, lithosphere, cryosphere, and biosphere. All these components are constantly interacting with one another via an interchange of materials and energy. Weather and climatic phenomena of the past—as well as of the present and the future—are the combined expression of Earth's climatic system.

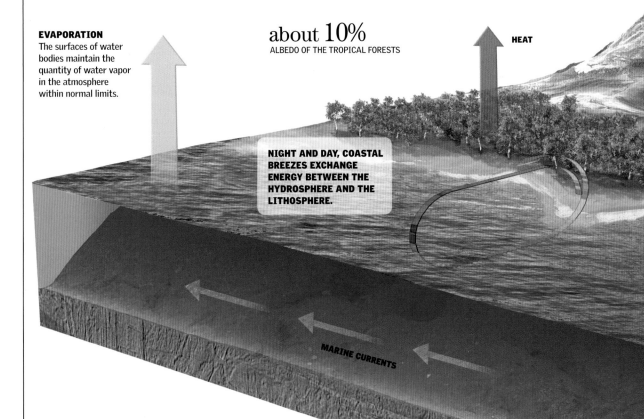

Atmosphere

Part of the energy received from the Sun is captured by the atmosphere. The other part is absorbed by the Earth or reflected in the form of heat. Greenhouse gases heat up the atmosphere by slowing the release of heat to space.

Biosphere

Living beings (such as plants) influence weather and climate. They form the foundations of ecosystems, which use minerals, water, and other chemical compounds. They contribute materials to other subsystems.

WINDS
The atmosphere is always in motion. Heat displaces masses of air, and this leads to the general circulation of the atmosphere.

PRECIPITATION
Water condensing in the atmosphere forms droplets, and gravitational action causes them to fall on different parts of the Earth's surface.

EVAPORATION
The surfaces of water bodies maintain the quantity of water vapor in the atmosphere within normal limits.

about 10%
ALBEDO OF THE TROPICAL FORESTS

HEAT

NIGHT AND DAY, COASTAL BREEZES EXCHANGE ENERGY BETWEEN THE HYDROSPHERE AND THE LITHOSPHERE.

MARINE CURRENTS

Hydrosphere

The hydrosphere is the name for all water in liquid form that is part of the climatic system. Most of the lithosphere is covered by liquid water, and some of the water even circulates through it.

3%
ALBEDO OF THE BODIES OF WATER

SOLAR RADIATION

About 50 percent of the solar energy reaches the surface of the Earth, and some of this energy is transferred directly to different layers of the atmosphere. Much of the available solar radiation leaves the air and circulates within the other subsystems. Some of this energy escapes to outer space.

ALBEDO

The percentage of solar radiation reflected by the climatic subsystems.

Sun

Essential for climatic activity. The subsystems absorb, exchange, and reflect energy that reaches the Earth's surface. For example, the biosphere incorporates solar energy via photosynthesis and intensifies the activity of the hydrosphere.

50%
ALBEDO OF LIGHT CLOUDS

SUN

Cryosphere

Represents regions of the Earth covered by ice. Permafrost exists where the temperature of the soil or rocks is below zero. These regions reflect almost all the light they receive and play a role in the circulation of the ocean, regulating its temperature and salinity.

80% ALBEDO OF RECENTLY FALLEN SNOW

Lithosphere

This is the uppermost solid layer of the Earth's surface. Its continual formation and destruction change the surface of the Earth and can have a large impact on weather and climate. For example, a mountain range can act as a geographic barrier to wind and moisture.

HEAT

HUMAN ACTIVITY

SMOKE
Particles that escape into the atmosphere can retain their heat and act as condensation nuclei for precipitation.

RETURN TO THE SEA

UNDERGROUND CIRCULATION

The circulation of water is produced by gravity. Water from the hydrosphere infiltrates the lithosphere and circulates therein until it reaches the large water reservoirs of lakes, rivers, and oceans.

ASHES
Volcanic eruptions bring nutrients to the climatic system where the ashes fertilize the soil. Eruptions also block the rays of the Sun and thus reduce the amount of solar radiation received by the Earth's surface. This causes cooling of the atmosphere.

GREENHOUSE EFFECT

Some gases in the atmosphere are very effective at retaining heat. The layer of air near the Earth's surface acts as a shield that establishes a range of temperatures on it, within which life can exist.

SOLAR ENERGY

OZONE LAYER

ATMOSPHERE

STRATOSPHERE

TROPOSPHERE

Climate Zones

Different places in the world, even if far removed from each other, can be grouped into climate zones—that is, into regions that are homogeneous relative to climatic elements, such as temperature, pressure, rain, and humidity. There is some disagreement among climatologists about the number and description of each of these regions, but the illustrations given on this map are generally accepted.

Ice cap

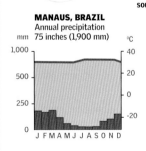

Human settlements

Fertile soil, stable climate

Fruit trees

Natural brush

Agriculture

Hudson Bay

Rocky Mountains

NORTH AMERICA

Appalachian Mountains

TEMPERATE

Characterized by pleasant temperatures and moderate rains throughout the year. Winters are mild, with long, frost-free periods. Temperate regions are ideal for most agricultural products.

HOUSTON, U.S.
Annual precipitation of 46 inches (1,170 mm)

mm
1,000
500
250
0

°C
40
20
0
-20

J F M A M J J A S O N D

59°F
(15°C)

IS THE AVERAGE ANNUAL TEMPERATURE OF THE EARTH.

CENTRAL AMERICA

Pacific Ocean

Atlantic Ocean

TROPICAL

High temperatures throughout the year, combined with heavy rains, are typical for this climate. About half of the world's population lives in regions with a tropical climate. Vegetation is abundant, and humidity is high because the water vapor in the air is not readily absorbed.

RAINFOREST OR JUNGLE

Tropical fruits and flowers

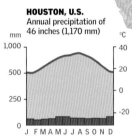

Plentiful water sources

Green and fertile soil

Layers of vegetation

Cordillera de los Andes

Amazon Basin

SOUTH AMERICA

Pampas region

Patagonia

MANAUS, BRAZIL
Annual precipitation 75 inches (1,900 mm)

mm
1,000
500
250
0

°C
40
20
0
-20

J F M A M J J A S O N D

DESERT
Intermittent water

Sea of dunes

Sparse vegetation

DRY

Lack of rain controls the arid climate in desert or semidesert regions, the result of the atmospheric circulation of air. In these regions, dry air descends, leaving the sky clear, with many hours of burning Sun.

Temperature and Rains

The temperature of the Earth depends on the energy from the Sun, which is not distributed equally at all latitudes. Only 5 percent of sunlight reaches the surface at the poles, whereas this figure rises to 75 percent at the Equator. Rain is an atmospheric phenomenon. Clouds contain millions of drops of water, which collide to form larger drops. The size of the drops increases until they are too heavy to be supported by air currents, and they fall as rain.

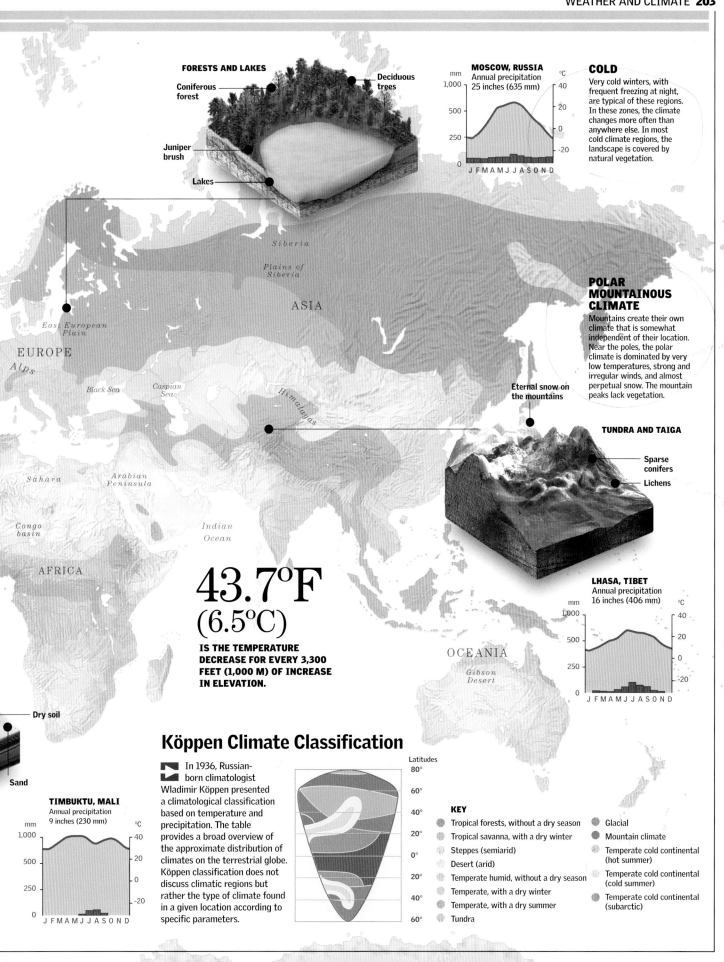

FORESTS AND LAKES

Coniferous forest

Deciduous trees

Juniper brush

Lakes

MOSCOW, RUSSIA
Annual precipitation
25 inches (635 mm)

mm
1,000
500
250
0

°C
40
20
0
-20

J F M A M J J A S O N D

COLD
Very cold winters, with frequent freezing at night, are typical of these regions. In these zones, the climate changes more often than anywhere else. In most cold climate regions, the landscape is covered by natural vegetation.

Siberia

Plains of Siberia

ASIA

East European Plain

EUROPE
Alps

Black Sea

Caspian Sea

Himalayas

POLAR MOUNTAINOUS CLIMATE
Mountains create their own climate that is somewhat independent of their location. Near the poles, the polar climate is dominated by very low temperatures, strong and irregular winds, and almost perpetual snow. The mountain peaks lack vegetation.

Eternal snow on the mountains

TUNDRA AND TAIGA

Sparse conifers

Lichens

Sahara

Arabian Peninsula

Congo basin

Indian Ocean

AFRICA

43.7°F
(6.5°C)

IS THE TEMPERATURE DECREASE FOR EVERY 3,300 FEET (1,000 M) OF INCREASE IN ELEVATION.

OCEANIA

Gibson Desert

LHASA, TIBET
Annual precipitation
16 inches (406 mm)

mm
1,000
500
250
0

°C
40
20
0
-20

J F M A M J J A S O N D

Dry soil

Sand

TIMBUKTU, MALI
Annual precipitation
9 inches (230 mm)

mm
1,000
500
250
0

°C
40
20
0
-20

J F M A M J J A S O N D

Köppen Climate Classification

In 1936, Russian-born climatologist Wladimir Köppen presented a climatological classification based on temperature and precipitation. The table provides a broad overview of the approximate distribution of climates on the terrestrial globe. Köppen classification does not discuss climatic regions but rather the type of climate found in a given location according to specific parameters.

Latitudes
80°
60°
40°
20°
0°
20°
40°
60°

KEY

- Tropical forests, without a dry season
- Tropical savanna, with a dry winter
- Steppes (semiarid)
- Desert (arid)
- Temperate humid, without a dry season
- Temperate, with a dry winter
- Temperate, with a dry summer
- Tundra

- Glacial
- Mountain climate
- Temperate cold continental (hot summer)
- Temperate cold continental (cold summer)
- Temperate cold continental (subarctic)

Atmospheric Dynamics

The atmosphere is a dynamic system. Temperature changes and the Earth's motion are responsible for horizontal and vertical air displacement. Here the air of the atmosphere circulates between the poles and the Equator in horizontal bands within different latitudes. Moreover, the characteristics of the Earth's surface alter the path of the moving air, causing zones of differing air densities. The relations that arise among these processes influence the climatic conditions of our planet.

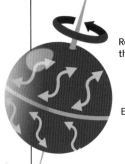

Rotation of the Earth

Equator

Coriolis Force

The Coriolis effect is an apparent deflection of the path of an object that moves within a rotating coordinate system. The Coriolis effect appears to deflect the trajectory of the winds that move over the surface of the Earth, because the Earth moves beneath the winds. This apparent deflection is to the right in the Northern Hemisphere and to the left in the Southern Hemisphere. The effect is only noticeable on a large scale because of the rotational velocity of the Earth.

FERREL CELL
A part of the air in the Hadley cells follows its course toward the poles to a latitude of 60° N and 60° S.

Intertropical Convergence Zone (ITCZ)

TRADE WINDS
These winds blow toward the Equator.

- Low-pressure area

+ High-pressure area

High and Low Pressure

Warm air rises and causes a low-pressure area (cyclone) to form beneath it. As the air cools and descends, it forms a high-pressure area (anticyclone). Here the air moves from an anticyclonic toward a cyclonic area as wind. The warm air, as it is displaced and forced upward, leads to the formation of clouds.

6 The masses of cold air lose their mobility.

1 Masses of cold air descend and prevent clouds from forming.

3 The wind blows from a high- toward a low-pressure area.

5 The rising air leads to the formation of clouds.

Jet-stream currents

A

B

2 The descending air forms an area of high pressure (anticyclone).

4 Warm air rises and forms an area of low pressure (cyclone).

Changes in Circulation

Irregularities in the topography of the surface, abrupt changes in temperature, and the influence of ocean currents can alter the general circulation of the atmosphere. These circumstances can generate waves in the air currents that are, in general, linked to the cyclonic zones. It is in these zones that storms originate, and they are therefore studied with great interest. However, the anticyclone and the cyclone systems must be studied together because cyclones are fed by currents of air coming from anticyclones.

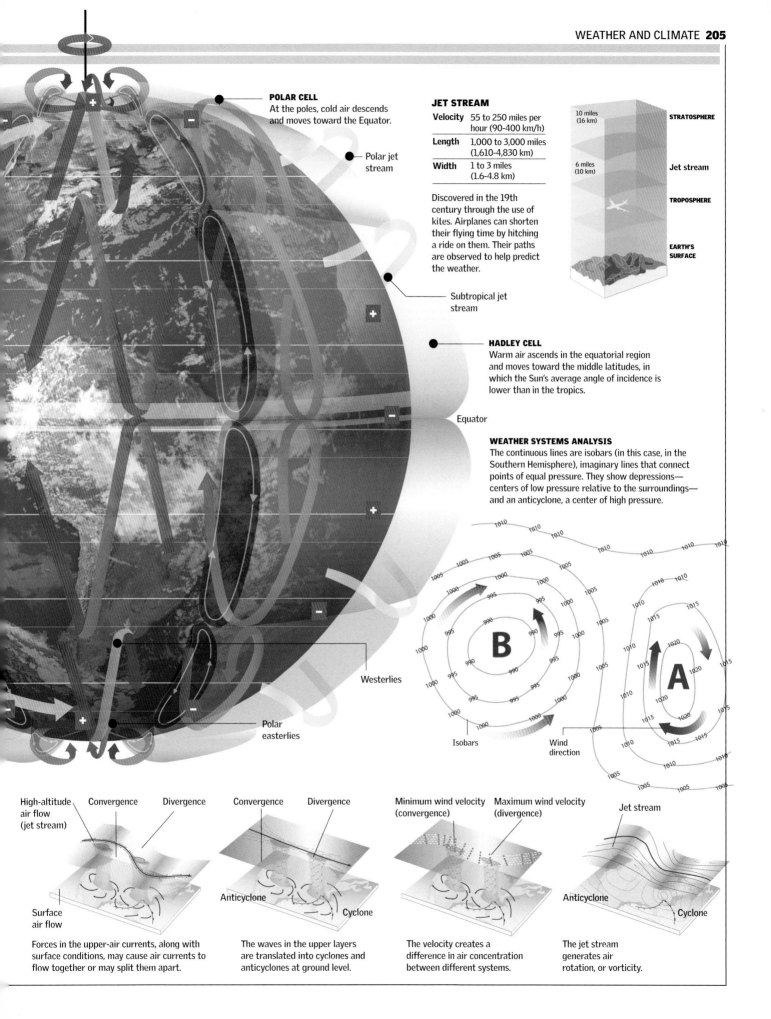

POLAR CELL
At the poles, cold air descends and moves toward the Equator.

Polar jet stream

JET STREAM

Velocity	55 to 250 miles per hour (90-400 km/h)
Length	1,000 to 3,000 miles (1,610-4,830 km)
Width	1 to 3 miles (1.6-4.8 km)

Discovered in the 19th century through the use of kites. Airplanes can shorten their flying time by hitching a ride on them. Their paths are observed to help predict the weather.

10 miles (16 km)

STRATOSPHERE

6 miles (10 km)

Jet stream

TROPOSPHERE

EARTH'S SURFACE

Subtropical jet stream

HADLEY CELL
Warm air ascends in the equatorial region and moves toward the middle latitudes, in which the Sun's average angle of incidence is lower than in the tropics.

Equator

WEATHER SYSTEMS ANALYSIS
The continuous lines are isobars (in this case, in the Southern Hemisphere), imaginary lines that connect points of equal pressure. They show depressions—centers of low pressure relative to the surroundings—and an anticyclone, a center of high pressure.

Westerlies

Polar easterlies

B

A

Isobars

Wind direction

High-altitude air flow (jet stream)   Convergence   Divergence

Surface air flow

Forces in the upper-air currents, along with surface conditions, may cause air currents to flow together or may split them apart.

Convergence   Divergence

Anticyclone

Cyclone

The waves in the upper layers are translated into cyclones and anticyclones at ground level.

Minimum wind velocity (convergence)   Maximum wind velocity (divergence)

The velocity creates a difference in air concentration between different systems.

Jet stream

Anticyclone

Cyclone

The jet stream generates air rotation, or vorticity.

Collision

When two air masses with different temperatures and moisture content collide, they cause atmospheric disturbances. When the warm air rises, its cooling causes water vapor to condense and the formation of clouds and precipitation. A mass of warm and light air is always forced upward, while the colder and heavier air acts like a wedge. This cold-air wedge undercuts the warmer air mass and forces it to rise more rapidly. This effect can cause variable, sometimes stormy, weather.

Cold Fronts

These fronts occur when cold air is moved by the wind and collides with warmer air. Warm air is driven upward. The water vapor contained in the air forms cumulus clouds, which are rising, dense white clouds. Cold fronts can cause the temperature to drop by 10° to 30°F (about 5°–15°C) and are characterized by violent and irregular winds. Their collision with the mass of ascending water vapor will generate rain, snow flurries, and snow. If the condensation is rapid, heavy downpours, snowstorms (during the cold months), and hail may result. In weather maps, the symbol for a cold front is a blue line of triangles indicating the direction of motion.

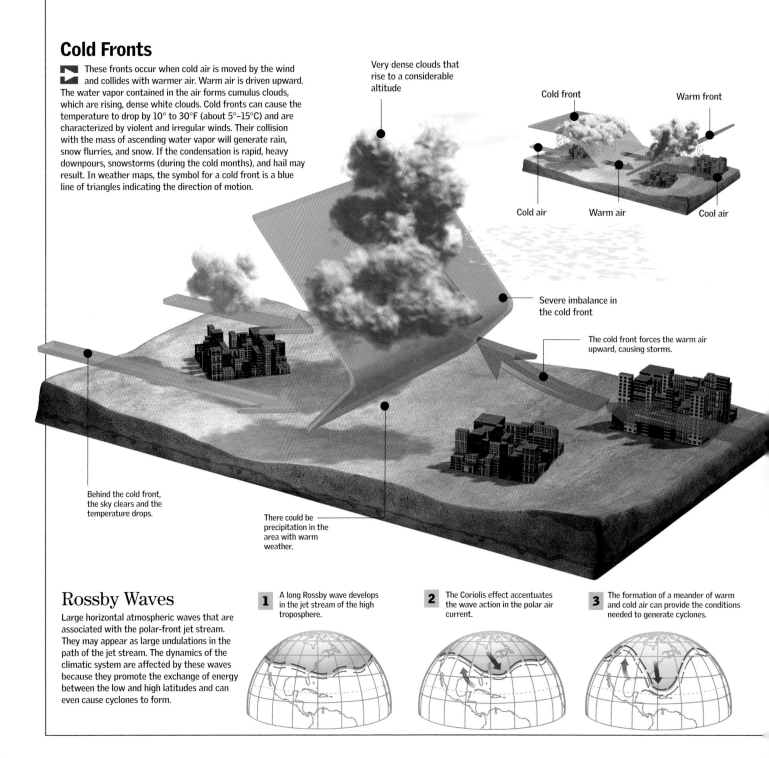

Very dense clouds that rise to a considerable altitude

Cold front

Warm front

Cold air

Warm air

Cool air

Severe imbalance in the cold front

The cold front forces the warm air upward, causing storms.

Behind the cold front, the sky clears and the temperature drops.

There could be precipitation in the area with warm weather.

Rossby Waves

Large horizontal atmospheric waves that are associated with the polar-front jet stream. They may appear as large undulations in the path of the jet stream. The dynamics of the climatic system are affected by these waves because they promote the exchange of energy between the low and high latitudes and can even cause cyclones to form.

1 A long Rossby wave develops in the jet stream of the high troposphere.

2 The Coriolis effect accentuates the wave action in the polar air current.

3 The formation of a meander of warm and cold air can provide the conditions needed to generate cyclones.

STATIONARY FRONTS

These fronts occur when there is no forward motion of warm or cold air—that is, both masses of air are stationary. This type of condition can last many days and produces only altocumulus clouds. The temperature also remains stable, and there is no wind except for some flow of air parallel to the line of the front. There could be some light precipitation.

Entire Continents

Fronts stretch over large geographic areas. In this case, a cold front causes storm perturbations in western Europe. But to the east, a warm front, extending over a wide area of Poland, brings light rain. These fronts can gain or lose force as they move over the Earth's surface, depending on the global pressure system.

Cold air   Warm air

Cool air

OCCLUDED FRONTS

When the cold air replaces the cool air at the surface, with a warm air mass above, a cold occlusion is formed. A warm occlusion occurs when the cool air rises above the cold air. These fronts are associated with rain or snow, cumulus clouds, slight temperature fluctuations, and light winds.

125 miles (200 km)

A WARM FRONT CAN BE 125 MILES (200 KM) LONG. A COLD FRONT USUALLY COVERS ABOUT 60 MILES (100 KM). IN BOTH CASES, THE ALTITUDE IS ROUGHLY 0.6 MILE (1 KM).

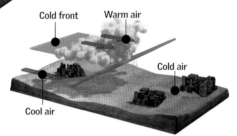

Cold front   Warm air

Cold air

Cool air

KEY
Surface cold front   Surface warm front

Warm Fronts

These are formed by the action of winds. A mass of warm air occupies a place formerly occupied by a mass of cold air. The speed of the cold air mass, which is heavier, decreases at ground level by friction, through contact with the ground. The warm front ascends and slides above the cold mass. This typically causes precipitation at ground level. Light rain, snow, or sleet are typically produced, with relatively light winds. The first indications of warm fronts are cirrus clouds, some 600 miles (1,000 km) in front of the advancing low pressure center. Next, layers of stratified clouds, such as the cirrostratus, altostratus, and nimbostratus, are formed while the pressure is decreasing.

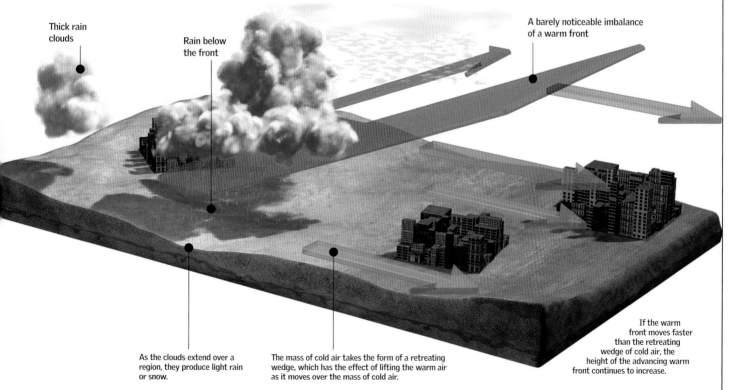

Thick rain clouds

Rain below the front

A barely noticeable imbalance of a warm front

As the clouds extend over a region, they produce light rain or snow.

The mass of cold air takes the form of a retreating wedge, which has the effect of lifting the warm air as it moves over the mass of cold air.

If the warm front moves faster than the retreating wedge of cold air, the height of the advancing warm front continues to increase.

Surface Factors

A mong meteorological phenomena, rain plays a very important role in the life of humans. Its scarcity causes serious problems, such as droughts, lack of food, and an increase in infant mortality. It is clear that an excess of water, caused by overabundant rain or the effects of gigantic waves, is also cause for alarm and concern. In Southwest Asia, there are

FLOODING
Abnormal flooding caused by El Niño in the desert regions of Chile and the later evaporation of water leave behind hexagonal deposits of potassium nitrate.

frequent typhoons and torrential rains during which millions of people lose their houses and must be relocated to more secure areas; however, they still run the risk of catching contagious diseases such as malaria. The warm current of El Niño also affects the lives and the economy of millions of people.

Living Water

The water in the oceans, rivers, clouds, and rain is in constant motion. Surface water evaporates, water in the clouds precipitates, and this precipitation runs along and seeps into the Earth. Nonetheless, the total amount of water on the planet does not change. The circulation and conservation of water is driven by the hydrologic, or water, cycle. This cycle begins with evaporation of water from the Earth's surface. The water vapor humidifies as the air rises. The water vapor in the air cools and condenses onto solid particles as microdroplets. The microdroplets combine to form clouds. When the droplets become large enough, they begin to fall back to Earth, and, depending on the temperature of the atmosphere, they return to the ground as rain, snow, or hail.

1 **EVAPORATION**
Thanks to the effects of the Sun, ocean water is warmed and fills the air with water vapor. Evaporation from humid soil and vegetation increases humidity. The result is the formation of clouds.

TRANSPIRATION
Perspiration is a natural process that regulates body temperature. When the body temperature rises, the sweat glands are stimulated, causing perspiration.

CONTRIBUTION OF LIVING BEINGS, ESPECIALLY PLANTS, TO

10% **THE WATER IN THE ATMOSPHERE**

THE HUMAN BODY IS 65% WATER.

2 **CONDENSATION**
In order for water vapor to condense and form clouds, the air must contain condensation nuclei, which allow the molecules of water to form microdroplets. For condensation to occur, the water must be cooled.

FORMATION OF DROPLETS
The molecules of water vapor decrease their mobility and begin to collect on solid particles suspended in the air.

Nucleus

GASEOUS STATE
The rays of the Sun increase the motion of atmospheric gases. The combination of heat and wind transforms liquid water into water vapor.

3 The water vapor escapes via micropores in the leaves' surface.

2 The water ascends via the stem.

1 The root absorbs water.

Root cells

All the molecules of water are freed.

CLOUDS

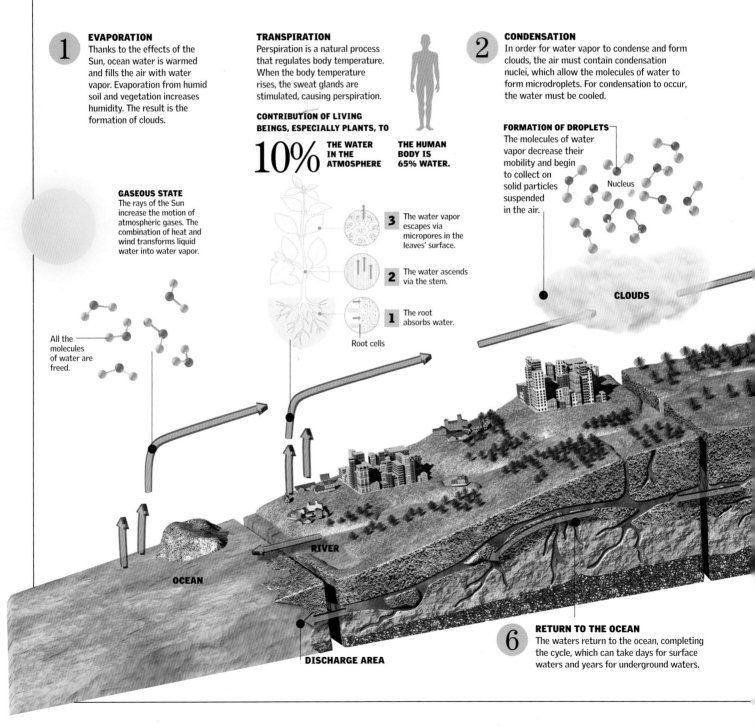

OCEAN

RIVER

DISCHARGE AREA

6 **RETURN TO THE OCEAN**
The waters return to the ocean, completing the cycle, which can take days for surface waters and years for underground waters.

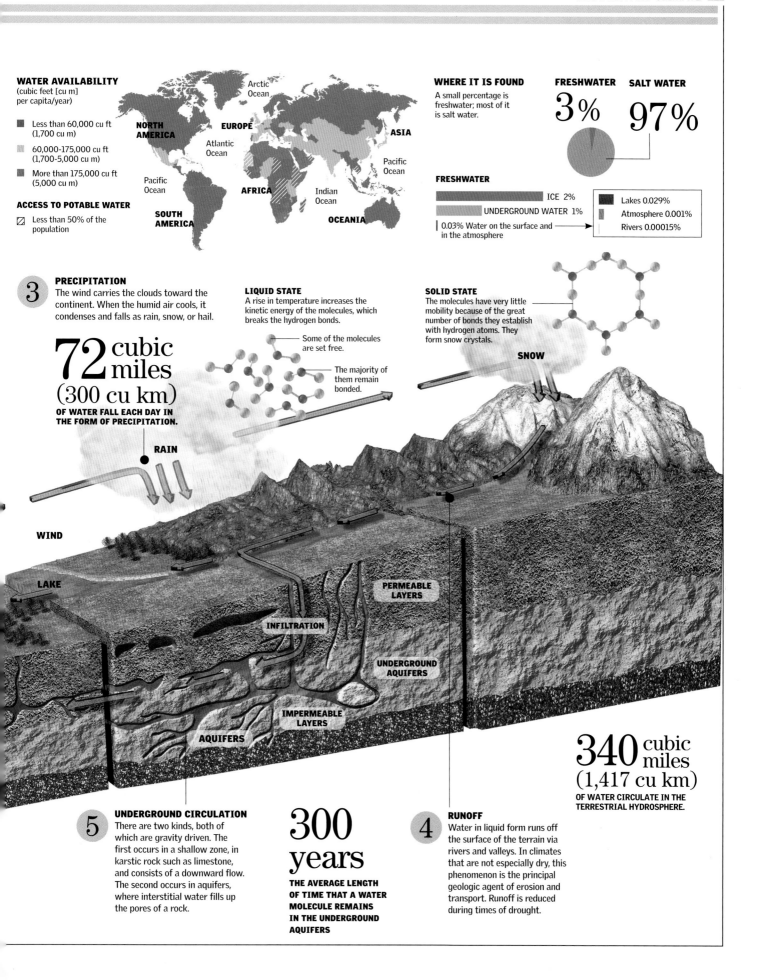

WATER AVAILABILITY
(cubic feet [cu m]
per capita/year)

- Less than 60,000 cu ft
  (1,700 cu m)
- 60,000-175,000 cu ft
  (1,700-5,000 cu m)
- More than 175,000 cu ft
  (5,000 cu m)

ACCESS TO POTABLE WATER

- Less than 50% of the
  population

Arctic
Ocean

**NORTH
AMERICA**

EUROPE

Atlantic
Ocean

ASIA

Pacific
Ocean

Pacific
Ocean

AFRICA

Indian
Ocean

**SOUTH
AMERICA**

OCEANIA

WHERE IT IS FOUND

A small percentage is
freshwater; most of it
is salt water.

FRESHWATER **SALT WATER**

3% 97%

FRESHWATER

ICE 2%

UNDERGROUND WATER 1%

0.03% Water on the surface and
in the atmosphere

Lakes 0.029%
Atmosphere 0.001%
Rivers 0.00015%

3 PRECIPITATION
The wind carries the clouds toward the
continent. When the humid air cools, it
condenses and falls as rain, snow, or hail.

LIQUID STATE
A rise in temperature increases the
kinetic energy of the molecules, which
breaks the hydrogen bonds.

- Some of the molecules
  are set free.
- The majority of
  them remain
  bonded.

SOLID STATE
The molecules have very little
mobility because of the great
number of bonds they establish
with hydrogen atoms. They
form snow crystals.

SNOW

72 cubic miles
(300 cu km)
**OF WATER FALL EACH DAY IN
THE FORM OF PRECIPITATION.**

RAIN

WIND

LAKE

**PERMEABLE
LAYERS**

INFILTRATION

**UNDERGROUND
AQUIFERS**

**IMPERMEABLE
LAYERS**

AQUIFERS

340 cubic miles
(1,417 cu km)
**OF WATER CIRCULATE IN THE
TERRESTRIAL HYDROSPHERE.**

5 UNDERGROUND CIRCULATION
There are two kinds, both of
which are gravity driven. The
first occurs in a shallow zone, in
karstic rock such as limestone,
and consists of a downward flow.
The second occurs in aquifers,
where interstitial water fills up
the pores of a rock.

300 years
**THE AVERAGE LENGTH
OF TIME THAT A WATER
MOLECULE REMAINS
IN THE UNDERGROUND
AQUIFERS**

4 RUNOFF
Water in liquid form runs off
the surface of the terrain via
rivers and valleys. In climates
that are not especially dry, this
phenomenon is the principal
geologic agent of erosion and
transport. Runoff is reduced
during times of drought.

Ocean Currents

Ocean water moves as waves, tides, and currents. There are two types of currents: surface and deep. The surface currents, caused by the wind, are great rivers in the ocean. They can be some 50 miles (80 km) wide. They have a profound effect on the world climate because the water warms up near the Equator, and currents transfer this heat to higher latitudes. Deep currents are caused by differences in water density.

The Influence of the Winds

TIDES AND THE CORIOLIS EFFECT
The Coriolis effect, which influences the direction of the winds, drives the displacement of marine currents.

Currents in the Northern Hemisphere travel in a clockwise direction.

In the Southern Hemisphere, the currents travel in a counterclockwise direction.

GEOSTROPHIC BALANCE
The deflection caused by the Coriolis effect on the currents is compensated for by pressure gradients between cyclonic and anticyclonic systems. This effect is called "geostrophic balance."

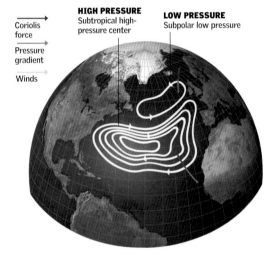

→ Coriolis force
→ Pressure gradient
→ Winds

HIGH PRESSURE
Subtropical high-pressure center

LOW PRESSURE
Subpolar low pressure

How Currents are Formed

Wind and solar energy produce surface currents in the water.

1 In the Southern Hemisphere, coastal winds push away the surface water so that cold water can ascend.

2 This slow ascent of deep water is called a "surge." This motion is modified by the Ekman spiral effect.

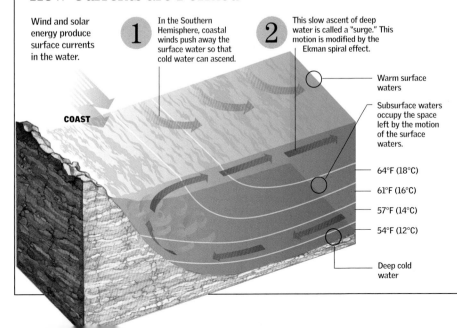

COAST

Warm surface waters

Subsurface waters occupy the space left by the motion of the surface waters.

64°F (18°C)

61°F (16°C)

57°F (14°C)

54°F (12°C)

Deep cold water

EKMAN SPIRAL
explains why the surface currents and deep currents are opposite in direction.

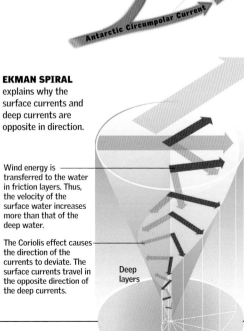

Wind energy is transferred to the water in friction layers. Thus, the velocity of the surface water increases more than that of the deep water.

The Coriolis effect causes the direction of the currents to deviate. The surface currents travel in the opposite direction of the deep currents.

Deep layers

Pacific Ocean

Alaska

North Pacific Current

California Current

Labrador

Gulf Stream

Atlantic Ocean

North Equatorial Countercurrent

Equatorial Countercurrent

South Equatorial Current

Canary Current

North Equatorial Countercurrent

Equatorial Countercur

South Equa

Peruvian Current

Brazil Current

Atlar Ocea

Pacific Ocean

Falkland Current

Antarctic Circumpolar Current

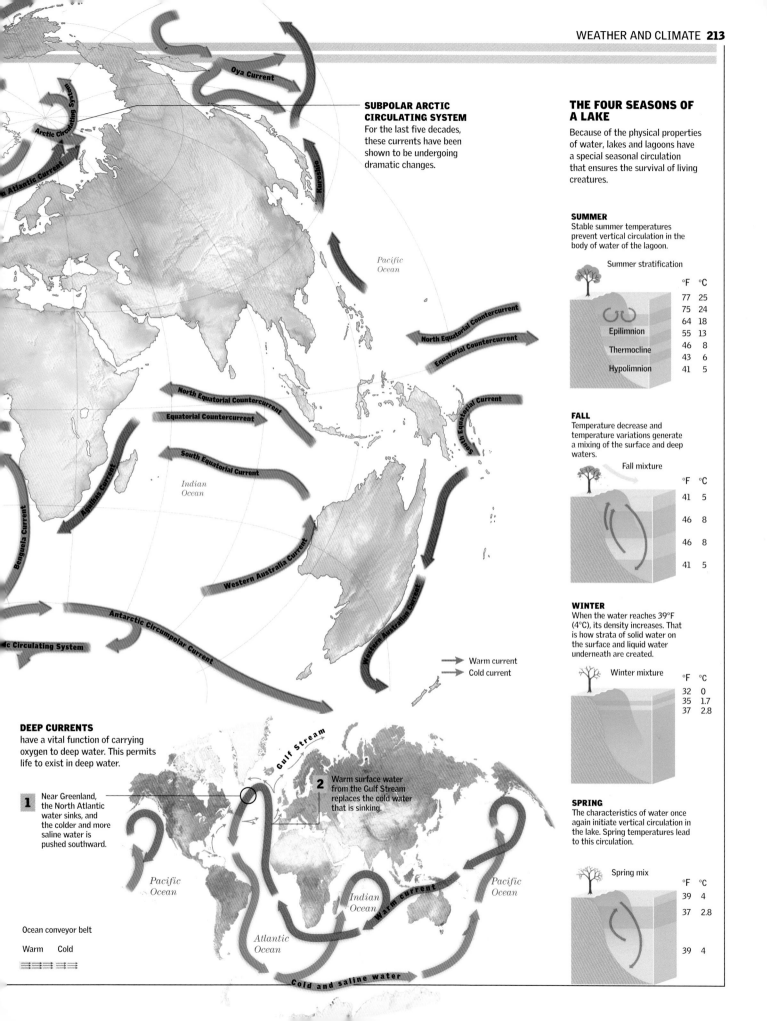

SUBPOLAR ARCTIC CIRCULATING SYSTEM

For the last five decades, these currents have been shown to be undergoing dramatic changes.

Oya Current

Arctic Circulating System

Kuroshio

Pacific Ocean

North Equatorial Countercurrent

Equatorial Countercurrent

North Equatorial Countercurrent

Equatorial Countercurrent

South Equatorial Current

South Equatorial Current

Indian Ocean

Agulhas Current

Benguela Current

Western Australia Current

Western Australian Current

Antarctic Circumpolar Current

Circulating System

→ Warm current
→ Cold current

DEEP CURRENTS

have a vital function of carrying oxygen to deep water. This permits life to exist in deep water.

1 Near Greenland, the North Atlantic water sinks, and the colder and more saline water is pushed southward.

Gulf Stream

2 Warm surface water from the Gulf Stream replaces the cold water that is sinking.

Pacific Ocean

Indian Ocean

Warm current

Pacific Ocean

Atlantic Ocean

Cold and saline water

Ocean conveyor belt

Warm   Cold

THE FOUR SEASONS OF A LAKE

Because of the physical properties of water, lakes and lagoons have a special seasonal circulation that ensures the survival of living creatures.

SUMMER
Stable summer temperatures prevent vertical circulation in the body of water of the lagoon.

Summer stratification

	°F	°C
	77	25
	75	24
	64	18
Epilimnion	55	13
Thermocline	46	8
	43	6
Hypolimnion	41	5

FALL
Temperature decrease and temperature variations generate a mixing of the surface and deep waters.

Fall mixture

	°F	°C
	41	5
	46	8
	46	8
	41	5

WINTER
When the water reaches 39°F (4°C), its density increases. That is how strata of solid water on the surface and liquid water underneath are created.

Winter mixture

	°F	°C
	32	0
	35	1.7
	37	2.8

SPRING
The characteristics of water once again initiate vertical circulation in the lake. Spring temperatures lead to this circulation.

Spring mix

	°F	°C
	39	4
	37	2.8
	39	4

An Obstacle Course

The mountains are geographical features with a great influence on climate. Winds laden with moisture collide with these vertical obstacles and have to rise up their slopes to pass over them. During the ascent, the air discharges water in the form of precipitation on the windward sides, which are humid and have dense vegetation. The air that reaches the leeward slopes is dry, and the vegetation usually consists of sparse grazing land.

The Effect of the Andes Mountains

1 HUMID WINDS
In the mountains, the predominant winds are moisture-laden and blow in the direction of the coastal mountains.

2 ASCENT AND CONDENSATION
Condensation occurs when a mass of air cools until it reaches the saturation point (relative humidity 100 percent). The dew point rises when the air becomes saturated as it cools and the pressure is held constant.

3 PRECIPITATION
A natural barrier forces the air to ascend and cool. The result is cloud formation and precipitation.

IN THE CLOUD

TEMPERATURE (IN °F [°C])	COMPOSITION
-40 to -4 (-40 to -20)	Ice crystals
-4 to 14 (-20 to -10)	Supercooled water
14 to 32 (-10 to 0)	Microdroplets of water
Greater than 32 (0)	Drops of water

HIGH LEVEL OF POLLUTION IN SANTIAGO
Partly because it is the most urbanized and industrialized city of Chile, the capital, Santiago, faces serious pollution problems. In addition, it is located in a valley with characteristics that do not help disperse the pollution produced by vehicles and factories.

MOIST ADIABATIC GRADIENT
The temperature decreases 1°F (0.6°C) for every 300 feet (100 m).

DEW POINT, OR CONDENSATION POINT

DRY ADIABATIC GRADIENT
The temperature declines 1.8°F (1°C) every 300 feet (100 m).

Height in feet (m): 16,400 (5,000) 18°F (-8°C); 27°F (-3°C); 13,000 (4,000) 36°F (2°C); 10,000 (3,000) 54°F (12°C); 6,500 (2,000) 72°F (22°C); 3,000 (1,000) 90°F (32°C) Surface

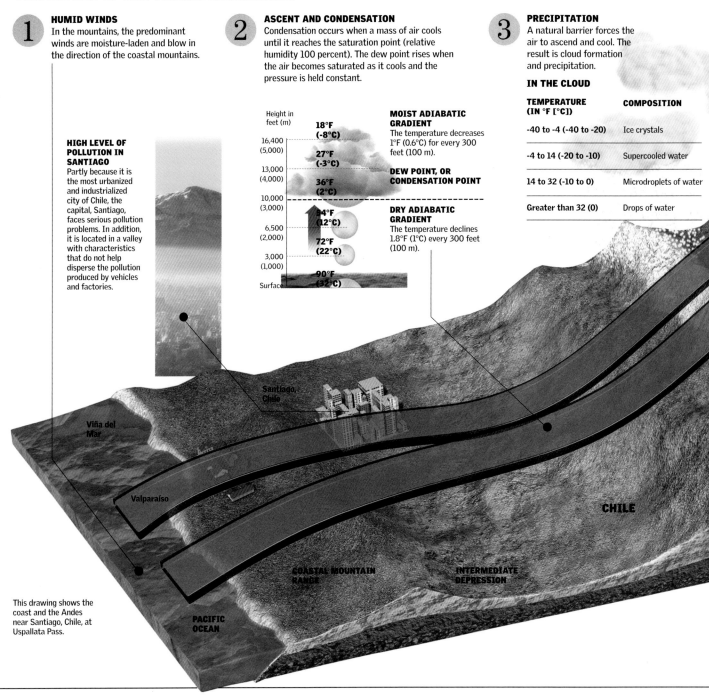

Santiago, Chile; Viña del Mar; Valparaíso; CHILE; COASTAL MOUNTAIN RANGE; INTERMEDIATE DEPRESSION; PACIFIC OCEAN

This drawing shows the coast and the Andes near Santiago, Chile, at Uspallata Pass.

MAJOR MOUNTAIN RANGES

Mountain	Elevation
Everest	29,035 feet (8,850 m)
Aconcagua	22,834 feet (6,960 m)
Dhaulagiri	26,795 feet (8,167 m)
Makalu	27,766 feet (8,463 m)
Nanga Parbat	26,660 feet (8,126 m)
Kanchenjunga	28,169 feet (8,586 m)
Ojos del Salado	22,614 feet (6,893 m)
Kilimanjaro	19,340 feet (5,895 m)

Rocky Mountains

Alps

Urals

Appalachians

Himalayas

ANDES

VEGETATION

13,000 FT (4,000 M)

Tundra. Its rate of growth is slow and only during the summer.

10,000 FT (3,000 M)

Taiga. The vegetation is conifer forest.

6,500 FT (2,000 M)

Mixed forest. Made up of deciduous trees and conifers.

3,000 FT (1,000 M)

Chaparral. Brush with thick and dry leaves.

0 feet (0 m)

Grazing. Thickets predominate: low, perennial grazing plants with an herbaceous appearance.

SNOW
Drops of super-cooled water combine to form ice crystals.

The crystals grow in size.

While they are falling, they combine with other crystals.

RAIN
The microdroplets increase in size and fall because of gravity.

When they fall, these drops collide with smaller ones.

Successive collisions increase the size of the drops.

4 DESCENDING WIND
A natural barrier forces the air to descend and warm up.

WESTERN SLOPES
receive most of the moisture, which leads to the growth of pine and other trees of coastal mountain ranges.

EASTERN SLOPES
The rays of the Sun fall directly upon these areas, making them more arid. There is little or no vegetation.

HOW OBSTACLES WORK
Obstacles, such as buildings, trees, and rock formations, decrease the velocity of the wind significantly and often create turbulence around them.

FRONT VIEW

Rotational flow

PLAN VIEW

Flow and counterflow

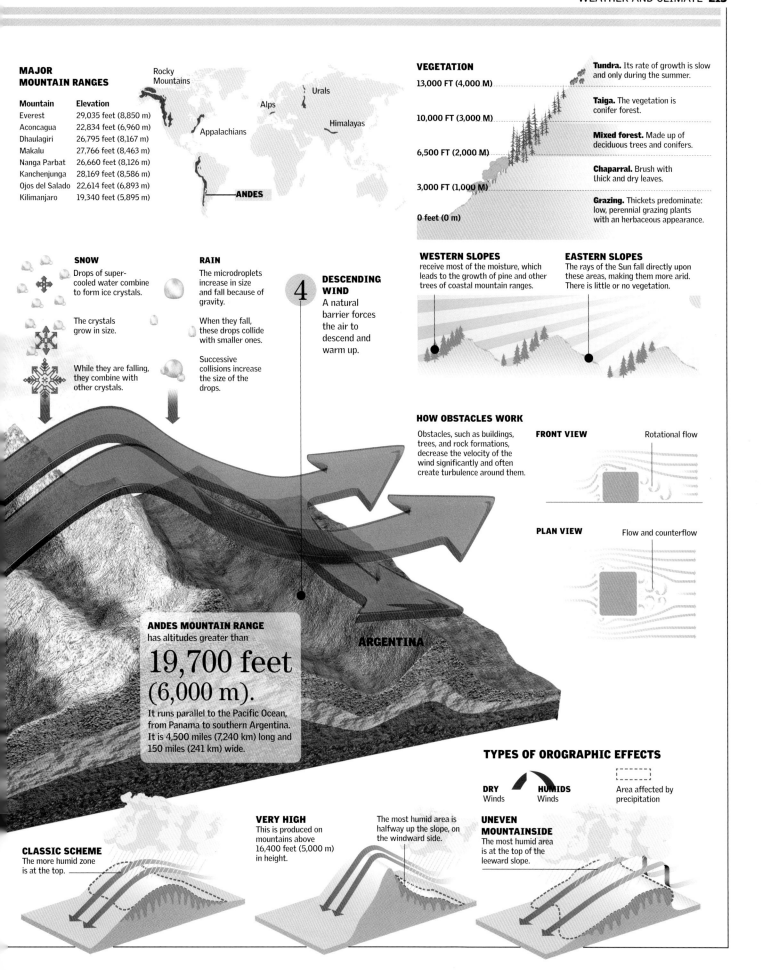

ANDES MOUNTAIN RANGE has altitudes greater than

19,700 feet (6,000 m).

It runs parallel to the Pacific Ocean, from Panama to southern Argentina. It is 4,500 miles (7,240 km) long and 150 miles (241 km) wide.

ARGENTINA

TYPES OF OROGRAPHIC EFFECTS

DRY Winds

HUMIDS Winds

Area affected by precipitation

CLASSIC SCHEME
The more humid zone is at the top.

VERY HIGH
This is produced on mountains above 16,400 feet (5,000 m) in height.

The most humid area is halfway up the slope, on the windward side.

UNEVEN MOUNTAINSIDE
The most humid area is at the top of the leeward slope.

The Land and the Ocean

Temperature distribution and, above all, temperature differences very much depend on the distribution of land and water surface. Differences in specific heat moderate the temperatures of regions close to great masses of water. Water absorbs heat and releases it more slowly than the land does, which is why a body of water can heat or cool the environment. Its influence is unmistakable. Moreover, these differences between the land and the sea are the cause of the coastal winds. In clear weather, the land heats up during the day, which causes the air to rise rapidly and form a low-pressure zone. This zone draws marine breezes.

MOUNTAIN WINDS

CHINOOK WINDS

These winds are dry and warm, sometimes quite hot, occurring in various places of the world. In the western United States, they are called chinooks and are capable of making snow disappear within minutes.

Humid winds are lifted over the slopes, creating clouds and precipitation on the windward side. These are called "anabatic" winds.

The dry and cool wind descends down the mountain slope on the leeward side. It is called "katabatic."

LEEWARD

WINDWARD

Winds	Characteristics	Location
Autan wind	Dry and mild	Southwestern France
Berg	Dry and warm	South Africa
Bora	Dry and cold	Northeastern Italy
Brickfielder	Dry and hot	Australia
Buran	Dry and cold	Mongolia
Harmattan	Dry and cool	North Africa
Levant	Humid and mild	Mediterranean region
Mistral	Dry and cold	Rhône Valley
Santa Ana	Dry and hot	Southern California
Sirocco	Dry and hot	Southern Europe and North Africa
Tramontana	Dry and cold	Northeast Spain
Zonda	Dry and mild	Western Argentina

WINDS OF THE MOUNTAINS AND VALLEYS

1 The Sun heats the soil of the valley and the surrounding air, which ascends by convection.

2 The air is cooled as it ascends, becomes more dense, and descends. Then it heats up again and repeats the cycle.

VALLEY

SLOPE

80% RECENT SNOW

75% THICK CLOUDS

15% ALBEDO OF MEADOWS

ABSORPTION OF HEAT

DAY

1 Cold air currents descend from the mountainside toward the floor of the valley, which is still hot.

2 The air currents are heated and ascend by convection. When they rise, they cool and once again descend along the mountainside.

MOUNTAINSIDE

VALLEY

NIGHT

RELEASE OF HEAT

WARM AIR WHIRLWINDS

Intense heat on the plains can generate a hot, spiral-formed column of air sometimes more than 300 feet (100 m) high.

1 Strong, high-speed winds move on top of weaker winds and cause the intermediate air to be displaced like a pencil on a table.

STRONG WIND

MILD WIND

2 A powerful air current lifts the spiral.

HEAT ISLANDS

Cities are complex surfaces. Concrete and asphalt absorb a large quantity of heat during sunny days and release it during the night.

ISOTHERMS IN A TYPICAL CITY (° F)

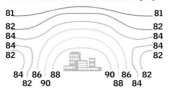

81   81
82   82
84   84
84   84
82   82

84   86   88   90   86   82
  82   90   88   84

CONTINENTALITY

In the interior of a landmass, there is a wide variation of daily temperatures, while on the coasts, the influence of the ocean reduces this variation. This continentality effect is quite noticeable in the United States, Russia, India, and Australia.

CONTINENTALITY INDEX

Less   More

DAILY VARIATION OF TEMPERATURES IN THE UNITED STATES

+ ALBEDO ▶ - ENERGY ABSORBED

25% WET SAND

3-5% WATER (WHEN THE SUN IS HIGH)

50% LIGHT CLOUDS

7-14% FORESTS

They absorb a significant amount of heat but remain cool because much energy is used to evaporate the moisture.

COASTAL BREEZES

1 **ON THE LAND**
During the day, the land heats up more rapidly than the ocean. The warm air rises and is replaced by cooler air coming from the sea.

Because it is opaque, the heat stays in the surface layers, which are heated and cooled rapidly.

IN THE OCEAN
From the coast, the ocean receives air that loses its heat near the water. As a result, the colder air descends toward the sea.

The heat penetrates into deeper layers thanks to the transparency of the water. A part of the heat is lost in evaporation of the water.

2 **ON THE LAND**
During the evening, the land radiates away its heat more rapidly than the water. The difference in pressure generated replaces the cold air of the coast with warm air.

When night falls, the land, which was hot, cools rapidly.

IN THE OCEAN
The loss of heat from the water is slower.

When night falls, the water is lukewarm (barely a degree more than the land).

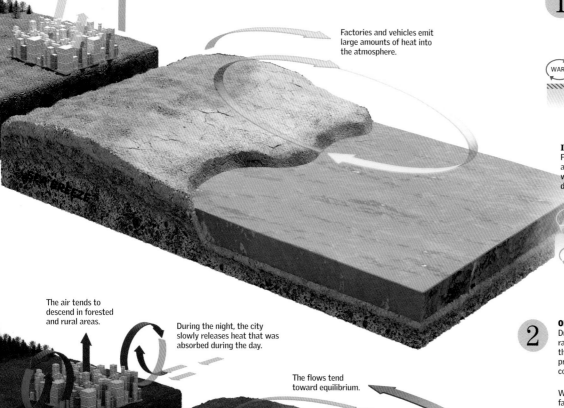

Factories and vehicles emit large amounts of heat into the atmosphere.

The air tends to descend in forested and rural areas.

During the night, the city slowly releases heat that was absorbed during the day.

The flows tend toward equilibrium.

KEY

→ WARM-AIR FLOW

→ COLD-AIR FLOW

Monsoons

The strong humid winds that usually affect the tropical zone are called "monsoons," an Arabic word meaning "seasonal winds." During summer in the Northern Hemisphere, they blow across Southeast Asia, especially the Indian peninsula. Conditions change in the winter, and the winds reverse and shift toward the northern regions of Australia. This phenomenon, which is also frequent in continental areas of the United States, is part of an annual cycle that, as a result of its intensity and its consequences, affects the lives of many people.

AREAS AFFECTED BY MONSOONS

This phenomenon affects the climates in low latitudes, from West Africa to the western Pacific. In the summer, the monsoon causes the rains in the Amazon region and in northern Argentina. There in the winter rain is usually scarce.

Predominant direction of the winds during the month of July

THE MONSOON OF NORTH AMERICA

Pre-monsoon. Month of May.

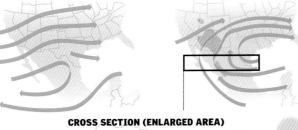

Monsoon. Month of July.

CROSS SECTION (ENLARGED AREA)

Rays of the Sun

Descent of the air from high altitudes

Descent of the air from high altitudes

Transport of water vapor

Western Sierra Madre

Transport of water vapor

Pacific Ocean

Gulf of California

Gulf of Mexico

How monsoons are created in India

End of the monsoon → | Beginning of the monsoon → | Cold and dry winds | Cold and humid winds | Cyclone (low pressure) | Anticyclone (high pressure)

1 THE CONTINENT COOLS

After the summer monsoon, the rains stop and temperatures in Central and South Asia begin to drop. Winter begins in the Northern Hemisphere.

NORTHERN HEMISPHERE
It is winter. The rays of the Sun are oblique, traveling a longer distance through the atmosphere to reach the Earth's surface. Thus, they are spread over a larger surface, so the average temperature is lower than in the Southern Hemisphere.

Rays of the Sun

SOUTHERN HEMISPHERE
It is summer. The rays of the Sun strike the surface at a right angle; they are concentrated in a smaller area, so the temperature on average is higher than in the Northern Hemisphere.

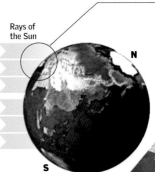

2 FROM THE CONTINENT TO THE OCEAN

The masses of cold and dry air that predominate on the continent are displaced toward the ocean, whose waters are relatively warmer.

Arabian Sea

3 OCEAN STORMS

A cyclone located in the ocean draws the cold winds from the continent and lifts the somewhat warmer and more humid air, which returns toward the continent via the upper layers of the atmosphere.

Limit of the Intertropical Convergence Zone (ITCZ)

INTERTROPICAL INFLUENCE

The circulation of the atmosphere between the tropics influences the formation of monsoon winds. The trade winds that blow toward the Equator from the subtropical zones are pushed by the Hadley cells and deflected in their course by the Coriolis effect. Winds in the tropics occur within a band of low pressure around the Earth called the Intertropical Convergence Zone (ITCZ). When this zone is seasonally displaced in the warm months of the Northern Hemisphere toward the north, a summer monsoon occurs.

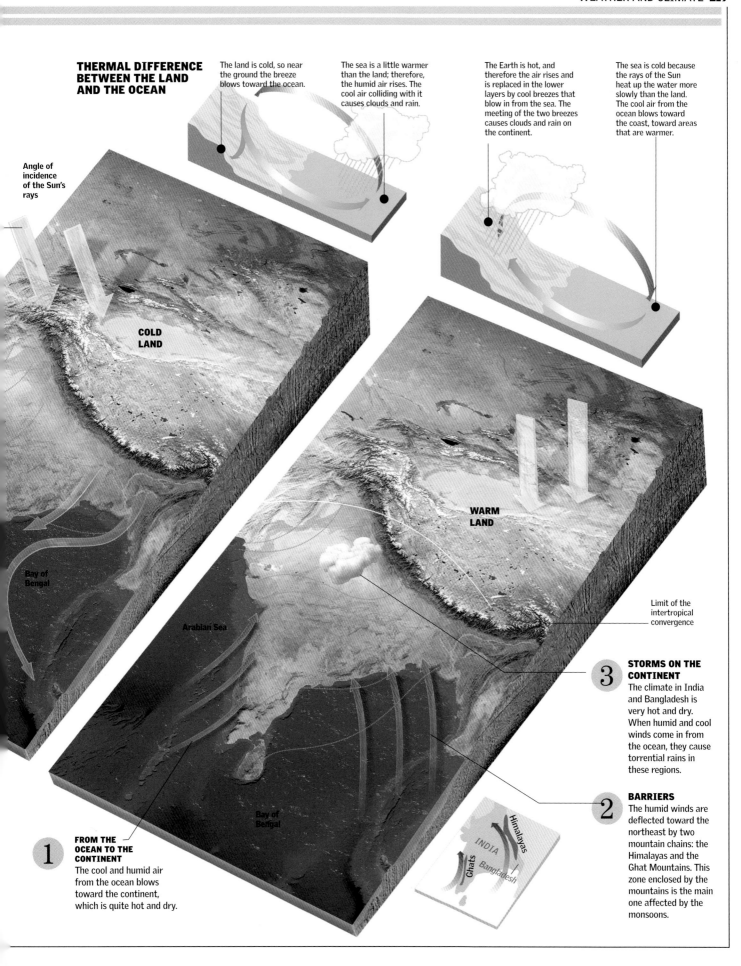

THERMAL DIFFERENCE BETWEEN THE LAND AND THE OCEAN

The land is cold, so near the ground the breeze blows toward the ocean.

The sea is a little warmer than the land; therefore, the humid air rises. The cool air colliding with it causes clouds and rain.

The Earth is hot, and therefore the air rises and is replaced in the lower layers by cool breezes that blow in from the sea. The meeting of the two breezes causes clouds and rain on the continent.

The sea is cold because the rays of the Sun heat up the water more slowly than the land. The cool air from the ocean blows toward the coast, toward areas that are warmer.

Angle of incidence of the Sun's rays

COLD LAND

WARM LAND

Bay of Bengal

Arabian Sea

Bay of Bengal

Limit of the intertropical convergence

3 **STORMS ON THE CONTINENT**
The climate in India and Bangladesh is very hot and dry. When humid and cool winds come in from the ocean, they cause torrential rains in these regions.

2 **BARRIERS**
The humid winds are deflected toward the northeast by two mountain chains: the Himalayas and the Ghat Mountains. This zone enclosed by the mountains is the main one affected by the monsoons.

1 **FROM THE OCEAN TO THE CONTINENT**
The cool and humid air from the ocean blows toward the continent, which is quite hot and dry.

Himalayas
INDIA
Ghats
Bangladesh

Meteorological Phenomena

Tropical cyclones (called hurricanes, typhoons, or cyclones in different parts of the world) cause serious problems and often destroy everything in their path, uprooting trees, damaging buildings, and causing deaths. The Gulf of Mexico is one of the areas of the planet continually affected by hurricanes. For this reason, the government

HURRICANE ALERT
This image of Hurricane Elena, captured by
the Space Shuttle on September 1, 1985,
allowed meteorologists to evaluate its
scope before it reached the Gulf of Mexico.

authorities organize preparedness exercises
so that the population knows what to do.
To understand how hurricanes function and
improve forecasts, investigators require detailed
information from the heart of the storm. The use
of artificial satellites that send clear pictures has
contributed greatly to detecting and tracking
strong winds, preventing many disasters.

Capricious Forms

Clouds are masses of large drops of water and ice crystals. They form because the water vapor contained in the air condenses or freezes as it rises through the troposphere. How the clouds develop depends on the altitude and the velocity of the rising air. Cloud shapes are divided into three basic types: cirrus, cumulus, and stratus. They are also classified as high, medium, and low depending on the altitude they reach above sea level. They are of meteorological interest because they indicate the behavior of the atmosphere.

TYPES OF CLOUDS

NAME	MEANING
Cirrus	Filament
Cumulus	Agglomeration
Stratus	Blanket
Nimbus	Rain

Troposphere

The layer closest to the Earth and in which meteorological phenomena occur, including the formation of clouds

EXOSPHERE

300 miles (500 km)

MESOSPHERE

50 miles (80 km)

STRATOSPHERE

30 miles (50 km)

TROPOSPHERE

6 miles (10 km)

0

HOW THEY ARE FORMED

Clouds are formed when the rising air cools to the point where it cannot hold the water vapor it contains. In such a circumstance, the air is said to be saturated, and the excess water vapor condenses. Cumulonimbus clouds are storm clouds that can reach a height of 43,000 feet (13,000 m) and contain more than 150,000 tons of water.

CONVECTION
The heat of the Sun warms the air near the ground, and because it is less dense than the surrounding air, it rises.

CONVERGENCE
When the air coming from one direction meets air from another direction, it is pushed upward.

GEOGRAPHIC ELEVATION
When the air encounters mountains, it is forced to rise. This phenomenon explains why there are often clouds and rain over mountain peaks.

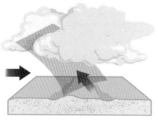

PRESENCE OF A FRONT
When two masses of air with different temperatures meet at a front, the warm air rises and clouds are formed.

T R O P O

6 MILES (10 KM)

-67°F (-55°C)
Temperature in the upper part of the troposphere

HIGH CLOUDS

CIRROSTRATUS
A very extensive cloud that eventually covers the whole sky and has the form of a transparent, fibrous-looking veil

2.5 MILES (4 KM)

14°F (-10°C)
The temperature of the middle part of the troposphere

MEDIUM CLOUDS

CUMULONIMBUS
A storm cloud. It portends intense precipitation in the form of rain, hail, or snow. Its color is white.

CUMULUS
A cloud that is generally dense with well-defined outlines. Cumulus clouds can resemble a mountain of cotton.

1.2 MILES (2 KM)

50°F (10°C)
Temperature of the lower part of the troposphere

LOW CLOUDS

59°F (15°C)
Temperature at the Earth's surface

0 MILES (0 KM)

H E R E

CIRRUS
A high, thin cloud with white, delicate filaments composed of ice crystals

CIRROCUMULUS
A cloud formation composed of very small, granulated elements spaced more or less regularly

ALTOCUMULUS
A formation of rounded clouds in groups that can form straight or wavy rows

1802
THE YEAR THAT BRITISH METEOROLOGIST LUKE HOWARD CARRIED OUT THE FIRST SCIENTIFIC STUDY OF CLOUDS

ALTOSTRATUS
Large, nebulous, compact, uniform, slightly layered masses. Altostratus does not entirely block out the Sun. It is bluish or gray.

STRATOCUMULUS
A cloud that is horizontal and very long. It does not blot out the Sun and is white or gray in color.

NIMBOSTRATUS
Nimbostratus portends more or less continuous precipitation in the form of rain or snow that, in most cases, reaches the ground.

STRATUS
A low cloud that extends over a large area. It can cause drizzle or light snow. Stratus clouds can appear as a gray band along the horizon.

The Inside
The altitude at which clouds are formed depends on the stability of the air and the humidity. The highest and coldest clouds have ice crystals. The lowest and warmest clouds have drops of water. There are also mixed clouds. There are ten classes of clouds depending on their height above sea level. The highest clouds begin at a height of 2.5 miles (4 km). The mid-level begins at a height of 1.2 to 2.5 miles (2–4 km) and the lowest at 1.2 miles (2 km) high.

1.2 to 5 miles (2-8 km)
THICKNESS OF A STORM CLOUD

150,000 tons of water
CAN BE CONTAINED IN A STORM CLOUD.

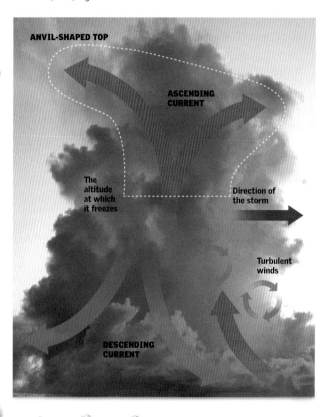

ANVIL-SHAPED TOP

ASCENDING CURRENT

The altitude at which it freezes

Direction of the storm

Turbulent winds

DESCENDING CURRENT

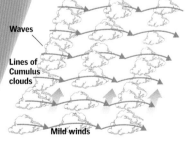

Waves

Lines of Cumulus clouds

Mild winds

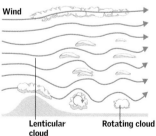

Wind

Lenticular cloud

Rotating cloud

SPECIAL FORMATIONS

CLOUD STREETS
The form of the clouds depends on the winds and the topography of the terrain beneath them. Light winds usually produce lines of Cumulus clouds positioned as if along streets. Such waves can be created by differences in surface heating.

LENTICULAR CLOUDS
Mountains usually create waves in the atmosphere on their lee side, and on the crest of each wave lenticular clouds are formed that are held in place by the waves. Rotating clouds are formed by turbulence near the surface.

The Rain Announces Its Coming

The air inside a cloud is in continuous motion. This process causes the drops of water or the crystals of ice that constitute the cloud to collide and join together. In the process, the drops and crystals become too big to be supported by air currents and they fall to the ground as different kinds of precipitation. A drop of rain has a diameter 100 times greater than a droplet in a cloud. The type of precipitation depends on whether the cloud contains drops of water, ice crystals, or both. Depending on the type of cloud and the temperature, the precipitation can be liquid water (rain) or solid (snow or hail).

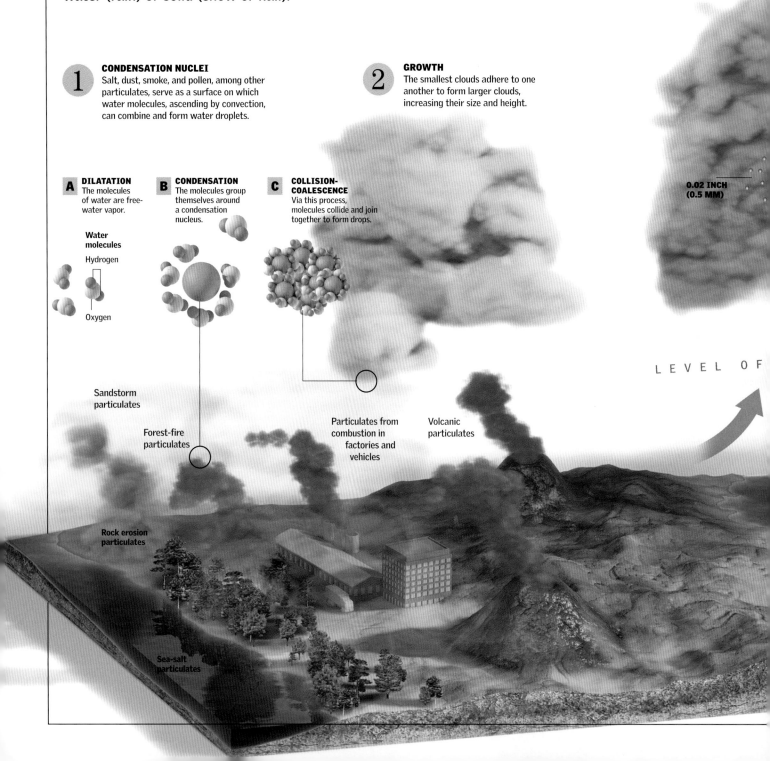

1 CONDENSATION NUCLEI
Salt, dust, smoke, and pollen, among other particulates, serve as a surface on which water molecules, ascending by convection, can combine and form water droplets.

2 GROWTH
The smallest clouds adhere to one another to form larger clouds, increasing their size and height.

A DILATATION
The molecules of water are free-water vapor.

Water molecules

Hydrogen

Oxygen

B CONDENSATION
The molecules group themselves around a condensation nucleus.

C COLLISION-COALESCENCE
Via this process, molecules collide and join together to form drops.

0.02 INCH
(0.5 MM)

Sandstorm particulates

Forest-fire particulates

Particulates from combustion in factories and vehicles

Volcanic particulates

LEVEL OF

Rock erosion particulates

Sea-salt particulates

3 **MATURATION**
Mature clouds have very strong ascending currents, leading to protuberances and rounded formations. Convection occurs.

4 **RAIN**
The upper part of the cloud spreads out like an anvil, and the rain falls from the lower cloud, producing descending currents.

5 **DISSIPATION**
The descending currents are stronger than the ascending ones and interrupt the feeding air, causing the cloud to disintegrate..

• **4 miles
(6.4 km)**

-22°F (-30°C)
When the air cools, it descends and is then heated again, repeating the cycle.

• **6 miles
(10 km)**

ANVIL-SHAPED

Low, thin clouds contain tiny droplets of water and therefore produce rain.

COALESCENCE
The microdroplets continue to collide and form bigger drops.

STORM CLOUD

The air cools. The water vapor condenses and forms microdroplets of water.

Heavier drops fall onto a lower cloud as fine rain.

• **0.6-1.2 miles
(1–2 km)**

**0.02 INCH
(0.5 MM)** When they begin to fall, the drops have a size of 0.02 inch (0.5 mm), which is reduced as they fall because they break apart.

**0.04 INCH
(1 MM)**

C O N D E N S A T I O N

68°F
(20°C)
The hot air rises.

**0.04 INCH
(1 MM)**

**0.07 INCH
(1.8 MM)**

• **0 miles
(0 km)**

26,875 trillion   molecules occupy 0.00006 cubic inch (1 cu mm) under normal atmospheric conditions.

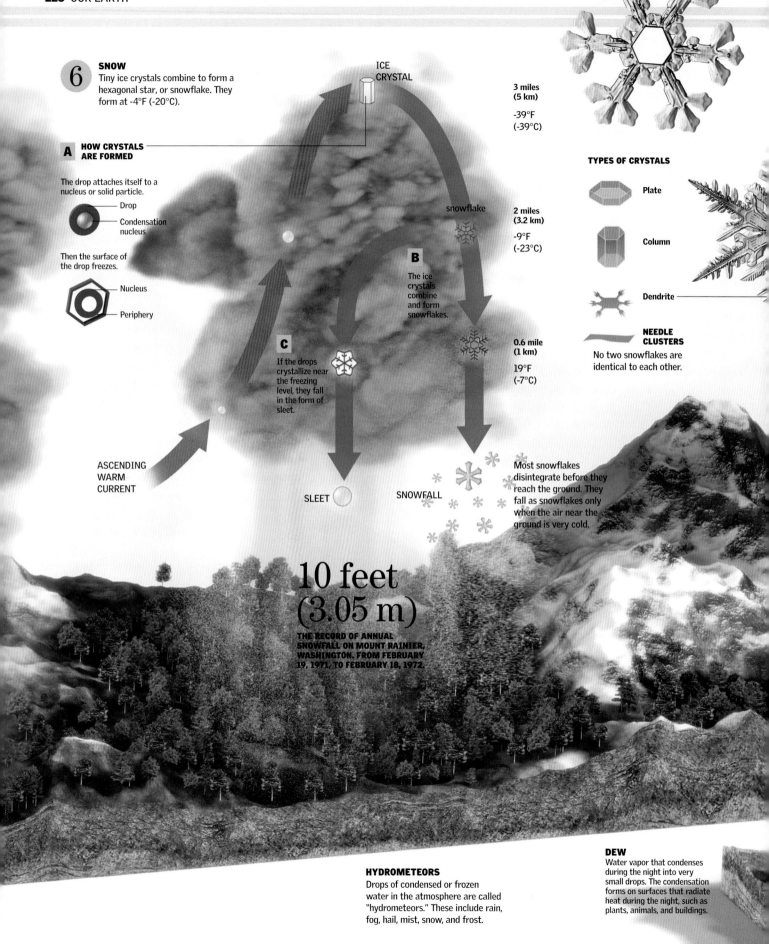

6 **SNOW**
Tiny ice crystals combine to form a hexagonal star, or snowflake. They form at -4°F (-20°C).

ICE CRYSTAL

A **HOW CRYSTALS ARE FORMED**

The drop attaches itself to a nucleus or solid particle.

- Drop
- Condensation nucleus

Then the surface of the drop freezes.

- Nucleus
- Periphery

C
If the drops crystallize near the freezing level, they fall in the form of sleet.

ASCENDING WARM CURRENT

snowflake

B
The ice crystals combine and form snowflakes.

SLEET

SNOWFALL

3 miles (5 km)
-39°F (-39°C)

2 miles (3.2 km)
-9°F (-23°C)

0.6 mile (1 km)
19°F (-7°C)

Most snowflakes disintegrate before they reach the ground. They fall as snowflakes only when the air near the ground is very cold.

TYPES OF CRYSTALS

- Plate
- Column
- Dendrite

NEEDLE CLUSTERS
No two snowflakes are identical to each other.

10 feet (3.05 m)

THE RECORD OF ANNUAL SNOWFALL ON MOUNT RAINIER, WASHINGTON, FROM FEBRUARY 19, 1971, TO FEBRUARY 18, 1972.

HYDROMETEORS
Drops of condensed or frozen water in the atmosphere are called "hydrometeors." These include rain, fog, hail, mist, snow, and frost.

DEW
Water vapor that condenses during the night into very small drops. The condensation forms on surfaces that radiate heat during the night, such as plants, animals, and buildings.

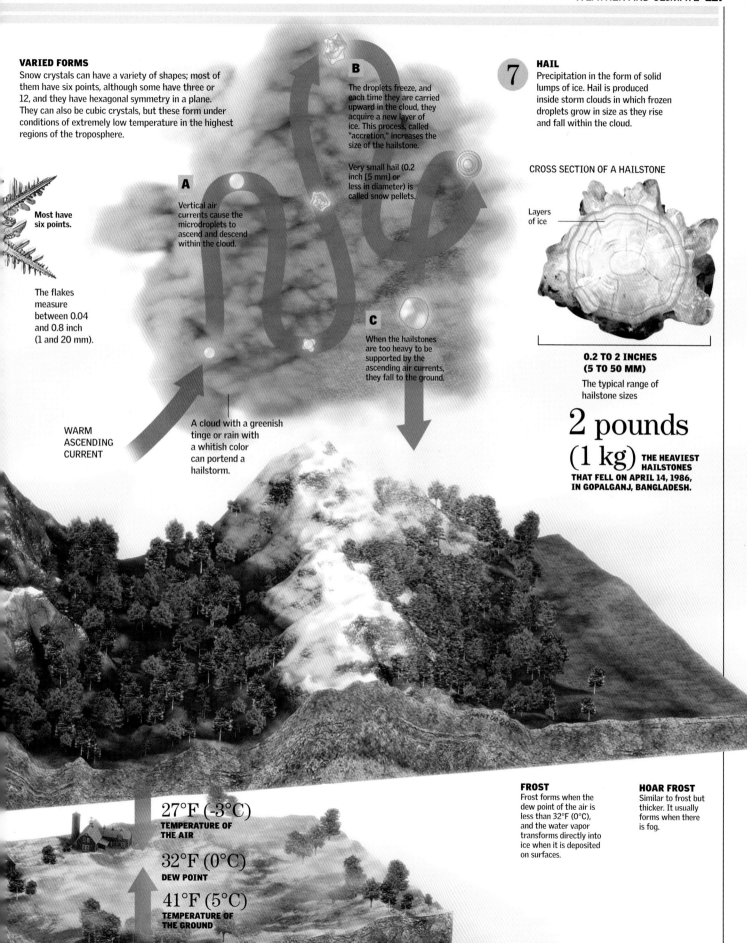

VARIED FORMS
Snow crystals can have a variety of shapes; most of them have six points, although some have three or 12, and they have hexagonal symmetry in a plane. They can also be cubic crystals, but these form under conditions of extremely low temperature in the highest regions of the troposphere.

Most have six points.

The flakes measure between 0.04 and 0.8 inch (1 and 20 mm).

A

Vertical air currents cause the microdroplets to ascend and descend within the cloud.

B

The droplets freeze, and each time they are carried upward in the cloud, they acquire a new layer of ice. This process, called "accretion," increases the size of the hailstone.

Very small hail (0.2 inch [5 mm] or less in diameter) is called snow pellets.

C

When the hailstones are too heavy to be supported by the ascending air currents, they fall to the ground.

WARM ASCENDING CURRENT

A cloud with a greenish tinge or rain with a whitish color can portend a hailstorm.

7 HAIL
Precipitation in the form of solid lumps of ice. Hail is produced inside storm clouds in which frozen droplets grow in size as they rise and fall within the cloud.

CROSS SECTION OF A HAILSTONE

Layers of ice

0.2 TO 2 INCHES (5 TO 50 MM)
The typical range of hailstone sizes

2 pounds
(1 kg) THE HEAVIEST HAILSTONES
THAT FELL ON APRIL 14, 1986, IN GOPALGANJ, BANGLADESH.

27°F (-3°C)
TEMPERATURE OF THE AIR

32°F (0°C)
DEW POINT

41°F (5°C)
TEMPERATURE OF THE GROUND

FROST
Frost forms when the dew point of the air is less than 32°F (0°C), and the water vapor transforms directly into ice when it is deposited on surfaces.

HOAR FROST
Similar to frost but thicker. It usually forms when there is fog.

Lost in the Fog

When atmospheric water vapor condenses near the ground, it forms fog and mist. The fog consists of small droplets of water mixed with smoke and dust particles. Physically the fog is a cloud, but the difference between the two lies in their formation. A cloud develops when the air rises and cools, whereas fog forms when the air is in contact with the ground, which cools it and condenses the water vapor. The atmospheric phenomenon of fog decreases visibility to distances of less than 1 mile (1.6 km) and can affect ground, maritime, and air traffic. When the fog is light, it is called mist. In this case, visibility is reduced to 2 miles (3.2 km).

160 feet
(50 m)

THE DENSEST FOG AFFECTS VISIBILITY AT THIS DISTANCE AND HAS REPERCUSSIONS ON CAR, BOAT, AND AIRPLANE TRAFFIC. IN MANY CASES, VISIBILITY CAN BE ZERO.

OROGRAPHIC BARRIER
Fog develops on leeward mountain slopes at high altitudes and occurs when the air becomes saturated with moisture.

4

OROGRAPHIC FOG

DEW
The condensation of water vapor on objects that have radiated enough heat to decrease their temperature below the dew point

Fog and Visibility

Visibility is defined as a measure of an observer's ability to recognize objects at a distance through the atmosphere. It is expressed in miles and indicates the visual limit imposed by the presence of fog, mist, dust, smoke, or any type of artificial or natural precipitation in the atmosphere. The different degrees of fog density have various effects on maritime, land, and air traffic.

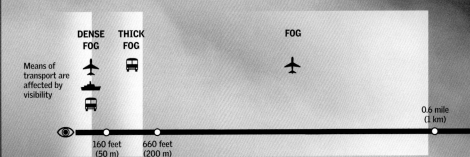

Means of transport are affected by visibility

| DENSE FOG | THICK FOG | | FOG |
| 160 feet (50 m) | 660 feet (200 m) | 0.6 mile (1 km) | 1.2 mile (2 km) |

Types of Fog

Radiation fog forms during cold nights when the land loses the heat that was absorbed during the day. Frontal fog forms when water that is falling has a higher temperature than the surrounding air; the drops of rain evaporate, and the air tends to become saturated. These fogs are thick and persistent. Advection fog occurs when humid, warm air flows over a surface so cold that it causes the water vapor from the air to condense.

1 RADIATION FOG
This fog appears only on the ground and is caused by radiation cooling of the Earth's surface.

FOG

2 FRONTAL FOG
Formed ahead of a warm front

FOG

3 ADVECTION FOG
Formed when a mass of humid and cool air moves over a surface that is colder than the air

FOG

The air becomes saturated as it ascends.

ASCENDING AIR

MIST
Mist consists of salt and other dry particles imperceptible to the naked eye. When the concentration of these particles is very high, the clarity, color, texture, and form of objects we see are diminished.

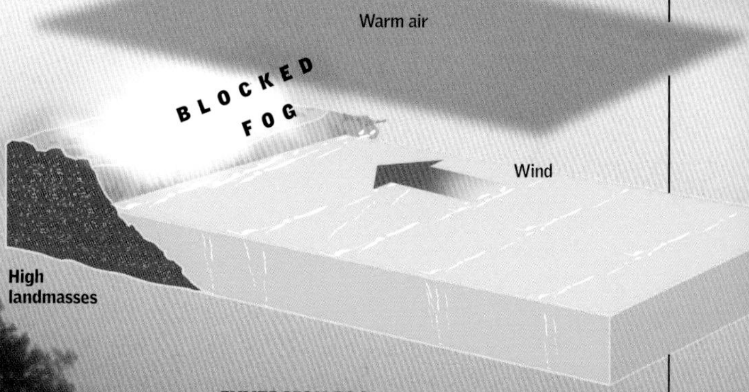

Warm air

BLOCKED FOG

Wind

High landmasses

INVERSION FOG
When a current of warm, humid air flows over the cold water of an ocean or lake, an inversion fog can form. The warm air is cooled by the water, and its moisture condenses into droplets. The warm air traps the cooled air below it, near the surface. High coastal landmasses prevent this type of fog from penetrating very far inland.

6 miles
(10 km)
Normal visibility

1.9 mile
(3 km)

Brief Flash

Electrical storms are produced in large cumulonimbus-type clouds, which typically bring heavy rains in addition to lightning and thunder. The storms form in areas of low pressure, where the air is warm and less dense than the surrounding atmosphere. Inside the cloud, an enormous electrical charge accumulates, which is then discharged with a zigzag flash between the cloud and the ground, between the cloud and the air, or between one cloud and another. This is how the flash of lightning is unleashed. Moreover, the heat that is released during the discharge generates an expansion and contraction of the air that is called "thunder."

THUNDER
This is the sound produced by the air when it expands very rapidly, generating shock waves as it is heated.

Cold air   Very hot air   Very hot air   Cold air

1 ORIGIN
Lightning originates within large cumulonimbus storm clouds. Lightning bolts can have negative or positive electric charges.

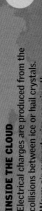

Cold air

Warm air

TYPES OF LIGHTNING
Lightning can be distinguished primarily by the path taken by the electrical charges that cause them.

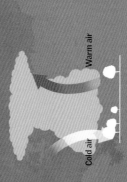

CLOUD-TO-AIR
The electricity moves from the cloud toward an air mass of opposite charge.

CLOUD-TO-CLOUD
A lightning flash can occur within a cloud or between two oppositely charged areas.

CLOUD-TO-GROUND
Negative charges of the cloud are attracted by the positive charges of the ground.

2 INSIDE THE CLOUD
Electrical charges are produced from the collisions between ice or hail crystals. Warm air currents rise, causing the charges in the cloud to shift.

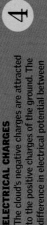

SEPARATION
The charges become separated, with the positive charges accumulating at the top of the cloud and the negative charges at the base.

3 ELECTRICAL CHARGES
The cloud's negative charges are attracted to the positive charges of the ground. The difference in electrical potential between the two regions produces the discharge.

INDUCED CHARGE
The negative charge of the base of the cloud induces a positive charge in the ground below it.

4 DISCHARGE
The discharge takes place from the cloud toward the ground after the stepped leader, a channel of ionized air, extends down to the ground.

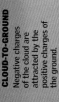

8,700 miles per second
(14,000 km/s) speed

Lightning bolt: 8,700 miles per second (14,000 km/s)

Airplane: 0.2 mile per second (0.3 km/s)

F1 car: 0.06 mile per second (0.1 km/s)

100 million volts
IS THE ELECTRICAL POTENTIAL OF A LIGHTNING BOLT.

A WINDMILL GENERATES 200 VOLTS.

110 VOLTS IS CONSUMED BY A LAMP.

5 RETURN STROKE
In the final phase, the discharge rises from the Earth to the cloud.

DISCHARGE SEQUENCE

Channel   1st phase   2nd phase   3rd phase

1st return   2nd return   3rd return

A
The lightning bolt propagates through an ionized channel that branches out to reach the ground. Electrical charges run along the same channel in the opposite direction.

B
If the cloud has additional electrical charges, they are propagated to the ground through the channel of the first stroke and generate a second return stroke toward the cloud.

C
This discharge, as in the second stroke, does not have branches. When the return discharge ceases, the lightning flash sequence comes to an end.

POINT OF IMPACT

65 feet (20 m)

This is the radius of a lightning bolt's effective range on the surface of the Earth.

LIGHTNING RODS

The primary function of lightning rods is to facilitate the electrostatic discharge, which follows the path of least electrical resistance.

Tip of the conductor

Lightning rod

A lightning rod is an instrument whose purpose is to attract a lightning bolt and channel the electrical discharge to the ground so that it does no harm to buildings or people. A famous experiment by Benjamin Franklin led to the invention of this apparatus. During a lightning storm, he flew a kite into clouds, and it received a strong discharge. That marked the birth of the lightning rod, which consists of an iron rod placed on the highest point of the object to be protected and connected to the ground by a metallic, insulated conductor. The principle of all lightning rods, which terminate in one or more points, is to attract and conduct the lightning bolt to the ground.

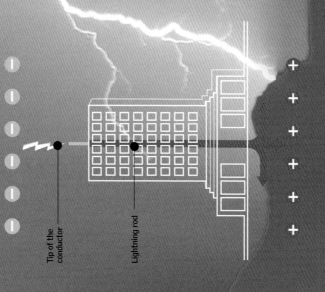

When Water Accumulates

ater is a vital element for life, but in excess it leads to serious consequences for people and their economic activity. Flooding occurs when certain areas that are normally dry are covered with water for a more or less prolonged period. The most important causes are excessive rains, the overflow of rivers and lakes, and giant waves that wash over the coast. Such waves can be the result of unusually high tides caused by strong surface winds or by submarine earthquakes. Walls, dikes, dams, and embankments are used to help prevent flooding.

Flooded Land

When land is flooded for days or months, the air in the soil is replaced by water, which prevents the buildup of oxygen, thus affecting the biological activity of plants and the soil itself. In the latter case, if the water does not have sufficient salt, the incomplete decomposition of organic matter and the significant washing away of nutrients make the soil more acidic. If the water contains a great deal of salt, the salt will remain in the soil, causing a different problem: salinization.

Reduction

THE COMPONENTS OF THE SOIL THAT ARE OXIDIZED CAN BE REDUCED AND THUS CHANGE THEIR PROPERTIES.

FLOOD CONTROL
With the construction of dikes and embankments, the flow of rivers prone to flooding is largely contained.

Floodplains

Floodplains are areas adjacent to rivers or streams that are subject to recurrent flooding.

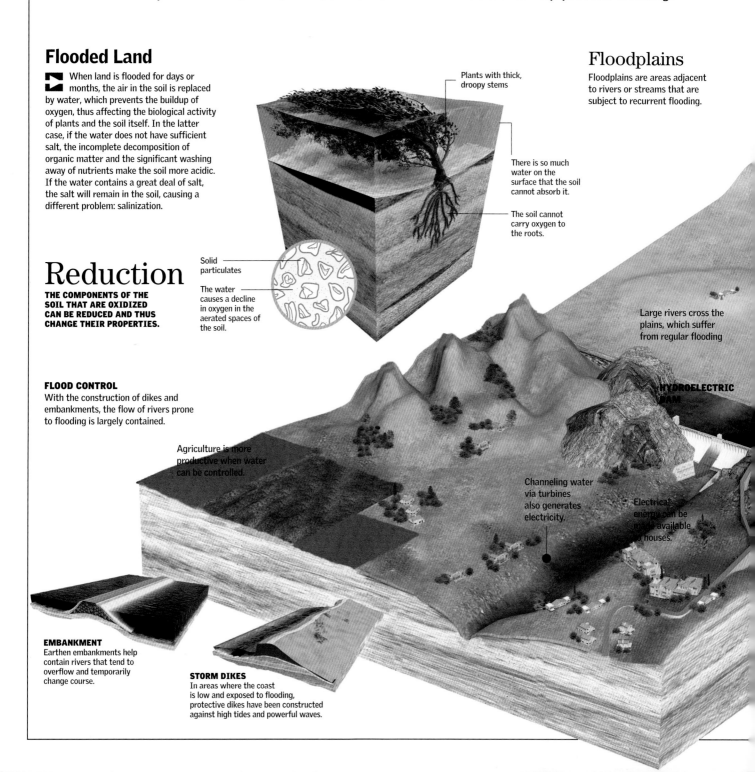

Plants with thick, droopy stems

There is so much water on the surface that the soil cannot absorb it.

The soil cannot carry oxygen to the roots.

Solid particulates

The water causes a decline in oxygen in the aerated spaces of the soil.

Large rivers cross the plains, which suffer from regular flooding

HYDROELECTRIC DAM

Agriculture is more productive when water can be controlled.

Channeling water via turbines also generates electricity.

Electrical energy can be made available to houses.

EMBANKMENT
Earthen embankments help contain rivers that tend to overflow and temporarily change course.

STORM DIKES
In areas where the coast is low and exposed to flooding, protective dikes have been constructed against high tides and powerful waves.

Torrential Rains

Caused by low pressure systems, instability of the air mass, and high humidity

Torrential rains raise the level of the water in the rivers and the riverbeds.

SNOW increases runoff into the rivers.

Little or no rain penetrates into the valley slopes covered with pines.

Principal river

Tributary river

LOW-LYING TERRAIN
The main river cannot contain the increased flow of the tributary rivers.

Houses and trees covered with water

Natural course of the river

250,000
VICTIMS OF FLOODING IN THE BAY OF BENGAL, BANGLADESH, IN 1970

TRANSFORMERS
Their job is to transform the voltage of the electric current.

DAM
stores water to divert it or to regulate its flow outside the riverbed.

FILTERING GRATES
prevent the passage of unwanted objects in the water used to produce hydroelectric power.

Elevation of the reservoir

HYDROELECTRIC PLANTS
Use the force and velocity of running water to turn turbines. There are two types: runoff river (which uses the natural kinetic energy of the river's running waters) and reservoir (where the water accumulates behind dams and is then released under increased pressure to the power plant).

Electrical power lines

ELECTRICAL GENERATOR
Equipment that produces electricity by converting the mechanical energy of the rotating turbine into electrical energy

Lethal Force

Tornadoes are the most violent storms of nature. They are generated by electrical storms (or sometimes as the result of a hurricane), and they take the form of powerful funnel-shaped whirlwinds that extend from the sky to the ground. In these storms, moving air is mixed with soil and other matter rotating at velocities as high as 300 miles per hour (480 km/h). They can uproot trees, destroy buildings, and turn harmless objects into deadly airborne projectiles. A tornado can devastate a whole neighborhood within seconds.

How They Form

Tornadoes begin to form when a current of warm air ascends inside a cumulonimbus cloud and begins to rotate under the influence of winds in the upper part of the cloud. From the base of the column, air is sucked toward the inside of the turning spiral. The air rotates faster as it approaches the center of the column. This increases the force of the ascending current, and the column continues to grow until it stretches from high in the clouds to the ground. Because of their short duration, they are difficult to study and predict.

6 miles
(10 km)
MAXIMUM HEIGHT THAT IT CAN ATTAIN

0.6 mile (1 km)
Maximum diameter

TOP
The top of the tornado remains inside the cloud.

300 miles per hour
(480 km/h)
MAXIMUM VELOCITY THE TORNADO WINDS CAN ATTAIN

VORTEX
Column of air that forms the lower part of a tornado; a funnel that generates violent winds and draws in air. It usually acquires the dark color of the dust it sucks up from the ground, but it can be invisible.

MULTIPLE VORTICES
Some tornadoes have a number of vortices.

1 BEGINNING OF A TORNADO
When the winds meet, they cause the air to rotate in a clockwise direction in the Southern Hemisphere and in the reverse direction in the Northern Hemisphere.

2 ROTATION
The circulation of the air causes a decrease in pressure at the center of the storm, creating a central column of air.

Strong wind

Mild Wind

Spinning funnel of air

Convection

Where and When

Most tornadoes occur in agricultural areas. The humidity and heat of the spring and summer are required to feed the storms that produce them. In order to grow, crops require both the humidity and temperature variations associated with the seasons.

- ● Tornadoes
- ● Agricultural areas

3:00 P.M.–9:00 P.M.
The period of the day with the highest probability of tornado formation

1,000 tornadoes are generated on average annually in the United States.

125 miles (200 km)
THE LENGTH OF THE PATH ALONG THE GROUND OVER WHICH A TORNADO CAN MOVE

SPIRALING WINDS
First a cloud funnel appears that can then extend to touch the ground.

Some tornadoes are so powerful that they can rip the roofs off houses.

The tornado generally moves from the southwest to the northeast.

3 DESCENT
The central whirling column continues to descend within the cloud, perforating it in the direction of the ground.

4 THE OUTCOME
The tornado reaches the Earth and depending on its intensity can send the roofs of buildings flying.

PATH
Normally, the tornado path is no more than 160 to 330 feet (50–100 m) wide.

Cumulonimbus

Warm and humid wind

Cold and dry wind

Storm

Humid wind

FUJITA SCALE
The Fujita-Pearson scale was created by Theodore Fujita to classify tornadoes according to the damage caused by the wind, from the lightest to the most severe.

WIND VELOCITY MILES PER HOUR (KM/H)	40-72 (64-116)	73-112 (117-180)	113-157 (181-253)	158-206 (254-332)	207-260 (333-418)	261-320 (420-515)
CATEGORY	F0	F1	F2	F3	F4	F5
EFFECTS	Damage to chimneys; tree branches broken	Mobile homes ripped from their foundations	Mobile homes destroyed, trees felled	Roofs and walls demolished, cars and trains overturned	Solidly built walls blown down	Houses uprooted from their foundations and dragged great distances

Anatomy of a Hurricane

A hurricane, with its ferocious winds, banks of clouds, and torrential rains, is the most spectacular meteorological phenomenon of the Earth's weather. It is characterized by an intense low-pressure center surrounded by cloud bands arranged in spiral form; these rotate around the eye of the hurricane in a clockwise direction in the Southern Hemisphere and in the opposite direction in the Northern Hemisphere. While tornadoes are brief and relatively limited, hurricanes are enormous and slow-moving, and their passage usually takes many lives.

DAY 1
A jumble of clouds is formed.

1 **BIRTH**
Forms over warm seas, aided by winds in opposing directions, high temperatures, humidity, and the rotation of the Earth

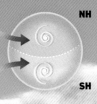

NH

SH

Hurricanes in the Northern Hemisphere rotate counterclockwise, and those in the Southern Hemisphere rotate clockwise.

FRINGES OF STORM CLOUDS
rotate violently around the central zone.

THE EYE
Central area, has very low pressure

Descending air currents

The air wraps around the eye.

81°F
(27°C)

IS LIKELY THE MINIMUM SEA-SURFACE TEMPERATURE CAPABLE OF SUSTAINING TROPICAL CYCLONES.

Strong ascendant currents

Cloud bands in the form of a spiral

EYE WALL
The strongest winds are formed.

VAPOR
Rises warm from the sea, forming a column of clouds. It rises 3,900 feet (1,200 m) in the center of the storm.

The trade winds are pulled toward the storm.

DAY 2
The clouds
begin to rotate.

DAY 3
The spiral
form becomes
more defined.

HURRICANE   TYPHOON

Equator   CYCLONE

DANGER ZONE
The areas that are vulnerable to hurricanes in the United States include the Atlantic coast and the coast along the Gulf of Mexico, from Texas to Maine. The Caribbean and the tropical areas of the western Pacific, including Hawaii, Guam, American Samoa, and Saipan, are also zones frequented by hurricanes.

DAY 6
Now mature, it
displays a visible eye.

DAY 12
The hurricane
begins to break
apart when it
makes landfall.

2 **DEVELOPMENT**
Begins to ascend, twisting
in a spiral around a low-
pressure zone

19 miles per hour (30 km/h)
VELOCITY AT WHICH IT APPROACHES THE COAST

FRICTION
When the hurricane reaches
the mainland, it moves more
slowly; it is very destructive in
this stage, since it is here that
populated cities are located.

3 **DEATH**
As they pass from the sea to
the land, they cause enormous
damage. Hurricanes gradually
dissipate over land from the
lack of water vapor.

The high-altitude
winds blow from
outside the storm.

**PATH OF THE
HURRICANE**

92 feet high (28 m)
MAXIMUM HEIGHT REACHED BY THE WAVES

1

2

3

4

5

WIND ACTIVITY

Light winds give
it direction and
permit it to grow.

The
winds flow
outward.

CLASSIFICATION OF HURRICANE SCALE
Saffir-Simpson category

	DAMAGE	SPEED miles per hour (km/h)	HIGH TIDE feet (m)
CLASS 1	**MINIMUM**	74 to 95 (119 to 153)	4 to 5 (1.2 to 1.5)
CLASS 2	**MODERATE**	96 to 110 (154 to 177)	6 to 8 (1.8 to 2.4)
CLASS 3	**EXTENSIVE**	111 to 130 (179 to 209)	9 to 12 (2.7 to 3.6)
CLASS 4	**EXTREME**	131 to 155 (211 to 250)	13 to 18 (4.0 to 5.5)
CLASS 5	**CATASTROPHIC**	More than 155 (250)	More than 18 (5.5)

Meteorology

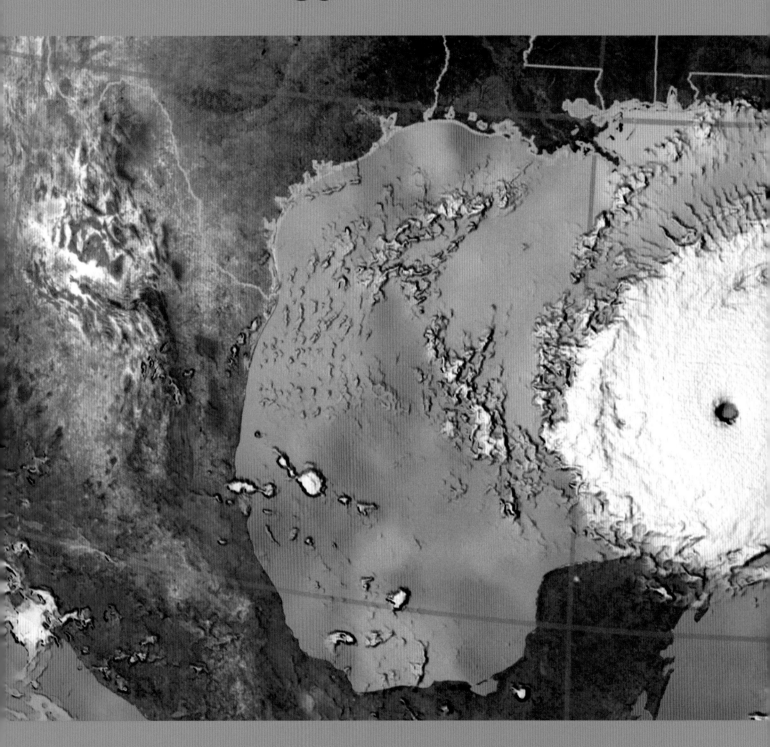

The use of satellites orbiting the Earth, recording the coming of rain, air currents, and clouds, allows us to know with some hours of advance warning if a severe storm is heading toward a certain point on the planet. Counting on this type of precise information about when and where tropical cyclones will occur, for example, has

RITA, SEPTEMBER 2003
The image from the GOES-12
satellite shows the configuration
of Hurricane Rita in the eastern
portion of the Gulf of Mexico.

allowed government officials to coordinate the evacuation of people from the affected zones. The surface of the planet is also monitored by a system of meteorological stations placed hundreds of miles from each other. These collect information from and send information to all areas of the world so that meteorologists can prepare maps, graphics, and predictions.

Compilation of Information

Most of the information available regarding climatic data comes from the record that meteorologists everywhere in the world keep regarding cloud cover, temperature, the force and direction of the wind, air pressure, visibility, and precipitation. Then from each meteorological station, the data is sent by radio or satellite, and this makes it possible to make forecasts and maps.

Radar

ANEROID BAROMETER

measures atmospheric pressure. Changes are shown by the pointers.

Scale

Spring

Spiral spring

Metal drum

Levers   Chains

Atmospheric pressure

Vacuum

760 mm (30 in)

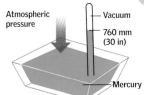

Mercury

MERCURY BAROMETER

An instrument used to measure atmospheric pressure. It consists of a glass tube full of mercury, with the open end submerged in a reservoir.

BAROGRAPH

measures the atmospheric pressure and records its changes over time.

Workplace

A typical meteorological station checks the temperature, humidity, wind velocity and direction, solar radiation, rain, and barometric pressure. In some places, soil temperature and flow of nearby rivers are also monitored. The compilation of this data makes it possible to predict different meteorological phenomena.

The light strikes and is concentrated as it traverses the sphere.

HELIOPHANOGRAPH

An instrument used to measure the number of hours of sunlight. It consists of a glass sphere that acts as a lens to concentrate sunlight. The light is projected onto a piece of cardboard behind the sphere. The cardboard is burned according to the intensity of the light.

IMPRESSION

The concentrated rays of sunlight burn cardboard placed behind the glass sphere.

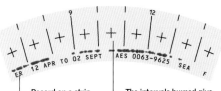

ER   12 APR TO 02 SEPT   AES 0063-9625   SEA   F

Record on a strip of cardboard graduated in hours

The intervals burned give a count of the hours of sunlight during the day.

EVAPORIMETER

As its name indicates, it measures the effective evaporation of water from a mass of liquid in the open air, from its loss from the surface through transformation to water vapor.

WEATHER VANE

shows which way the wind is blowing. It is a perfectly balanced mechanical system.

Indicates the direction of the wind

Three equally spaced cups record the intensity of the wind.

DATA RECORDER

records the data obtained.

MAXIMUM THERMOMETER

shows the highest temperature of the day. The capillary with mercury is calibrated in the bulb.

Bulb with mercury

Bulb with alcohol

ANEMOMETER

measures the speed of the wind. This instrument is activated by the wind, which turns three hemispherical cups mounted on a vertical rod firmly placed in the ground.

MINIMUM THERMOMETER

indicates the lowest temperature of the day. It has a fork-shaped bulb.

METEOROLOGICAL SHELTER

It is built of wood or fiberglass on a base that insulates it from the soil and protects certain instruments (thermometers, psychrometers, and others) from solar radiation. Screens in the windows ensure good ventilation.

Double circulation of the air to prevent the heating of the instruments when the radiation is very intense

Psychrometer

Maximum and minimum thermometers

Hygrothermograph

Slats allow the air to flow through freely without creating currents.

HYGROTHERMOGRAPH

simultaneously records the air temperature and relative humidity. A thermograph and a hygrograph independently make records on paper of the daily variations in temperature and humidity.

PSYCHROMETER

measures the relative humidity of the air. It consists of two thermometers and two bulbs (one dry and one covered with muslin that is always kept damp).

Dry-bulb thermometer

Wet-bulb thermometer

Container of distilled water

Weather vane

Anemometer

Data recorder   Solar panel

Control unit

Weather Station

Meteorologists collect data at different heights. They use various instruments at ground level: a thermometer for temperature, a hygrometer for humidity, and a barometer for atmospheric pressure.

In the Northern Hemisphere, the doors should be oriented toward the north to prevent the Sun's rays from striking the instruments when observations are being made.

Thermometer

Mouth

Drum

Recording pen

Siphon

Collector container

Wooden platform

Rain Meter

Automatic Weather Station

An automatic meteorological station uses electrical sensors to record temperature, humidity, wind velocity and direction, atmospheric pressure, and rainfall, among other parameters. The readings are processed by microprocessors and transmitted via an automatic system. This station functions autonomously, 24 hours a day, powered by solar energy (solar panels) or wind energy.

RAIN METER

This is used to keep a chronological record of the amount of water falling as rain.

RAIN GAUGE

The precipitation that falls on the ground in the form of rain is collected by the rain gauge.

Instantaneous Maps

Weather maps represent at any given moment the state of the atmosphere at different altitudes. These maps are made based on the information provided by meteorological stations and are useful for specialists. The data collected by them include various values for pressure and temperature that make it possible to forecast the probability of precipitation, whether the weather will remain stable, or if it will change because a weather front is moving in.

NOMENCLATURE
Every meteorological map carries a label that indicates the date and time it was made.

12 indicates the hour and Z Greenwich Mean Time.

This map is prepared with the initial values of Tuesday, September 2.

It indicates the initial values.

1686
is the year in which English astronomer Edmond Halley made the first meteorological map.

SYMBOLS
There are a number of different symbols to represent different kinds of fronts.

WARM A warm air mass with local storms is advancing.

COLD A cold air mass with rain is advancing.

STATIONARY Moderately bad weather and little change of temperature

OCCLUDED FRONT It is mixed; it will act first as a warm front and then as a cold front.

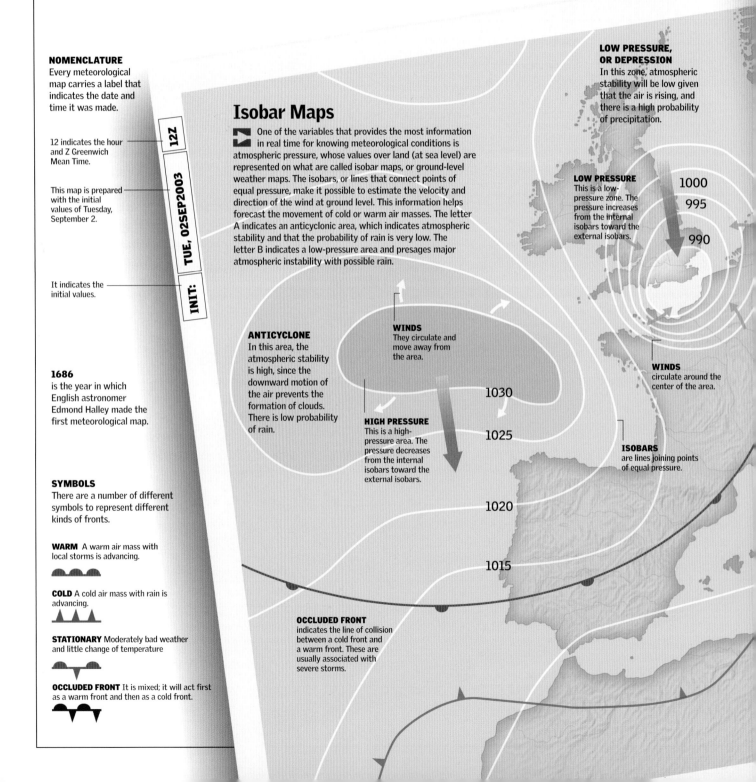

Isobar Maps

One of the variables that provides the most information in real time for knowing meteorological conditions is atmospheric pressure, whose values over land (at sea level) are represented on what are called isobar maps, or ground-level weather maps. The isobars, or lines that connect points of equal pressure, make it possible to estimate the velocity and direction of the wind at ground level. This information helps forecast the movement of cold or warm air masses. The letter A indicates an anticyclonic area, which indicates atmospheric stability and that the probability of rain is very low. The letter B indicates a low-pressure area and presages major atmospheric instability with possible rain.

LOW PRESSURE, OR DEPRESSION
In this zone, atmospheric stability will be low given that the air is rising, and there is a high probability of precipitation.

LOW PRESSURE
This is a low-pressure zone. The pressure increases from the internal isobars toward the external isobars.

ANTICYCLONE
In this area, the atmospheric stability is high, since the downward motion of the air prevents the formation of clouds. There is low probability of rain.

WINDS
They circulate and move away from the area.

HIGH PRESSURE
This is a high-pressure area. The pressure decreases from the internal isobars toward the external isobars.

WINDS
circulate around the center of the area.

ISOBARS
are lines joining points of equal pressure.

OCCLUDED FRONT
indicates the line of collision between a cold front and a warm front. These are usually associated with severe storms.

INIT: TUE, 02SEP2003 12Z

1000
995
990
1030
1025
1020
1015

Upper-air Map

Another type of map, which is used to analyze upper-air weather conditions, is an upper-level, or geopotential, map. On these maps, contour lines connect points located at the same altitude for a certain pressure level (normally 500 hectopascals [hPa]) and correlate with the temperature of the air in the higher layers of the troposphere (at 16,400 feet [5,000 meters] altitude on the 500 hPa map). The temperature is represented in each region of the troposphere by lines called "isotherms."

WINDS
The direction and intensity of the winds are indicated by a segment with a circle at its end, which indicates the direction from which the wind is blowing. On this segment, perpendicular lines are traced that indicate the velocity of the wind in knots, where one knot equals 1.2 miles per hour (1.9 km/h).

SYMBOLS
The direction of the wind is represented by these symbols:

POSITION
The line indicates the direction of the wind. It can be north, northeast, east, southeast, south, southwest, west, or northwest.

BAD WEATHER
Instability and high probability of abundant rain

LOW-PRESSURE TROUGH
This phenomenon increases the probability of bad weather. A low-pressure trough has a low geopotential value.

HIGH-PRESSURE RIDGE
Area of high geopotential values in which the chances of rain are slight

GOOD WEATHER
Atmospheric stability and low expectation of precipitation

OVERCAST SKY
A black circle indicates an overcast sky and a white circle a clear sky.

WIND VELOCITY
A short line indicates five knots, a longer line indicates 10 knots, and a terminal triangle indicates more than 40 knots.

LOW-PRESSURE TROUGH AXIS

HIGH-PRESSURE RIDGE AXIS

UPPER-LEVEL MAPS
The contour lines traced in these charts connect points of equal geopotential height, which define high-pressure ridges and low-pressure troughs. The wind direction is parallel to these lines. These charts are used to prepare weather forecasts.

250 HPA ● — 36,100 FEET (11,000 METERS)

500 HPA ● — 18,000 FEET (5,500 METERS)

700 HPA ● — 9,800 FEET (3,000 METERS)

850 HPA ● — 4,900 FEET (1,500 METERS)

SURFACE ● — 0 FEET (0 METERS)

500 HPA
The first pressure value that represents a geopotential of 500 hectopascals (hPa)

600 596 592 588 584 580 576 572 568 564 560 556 552 548 544 540 536 532 528 524 520 516 512 508 504 500 496 492 488 484 480 476

Rain, Cold, or Heat

Knowing ahead of time what the weather will be is sometimes a question of life or death. The damage resulting from a torrential rain or a heavy snowfall can be avoided thanks to the forecasts of meteorologists. The forecasts they make are based on information gathered from many sources, including instruments on the ground, in the air, and at sea. Despite the use of sophisticated information systems, the weather can be forecast only for the next few hours or days. Nonetheless, it is very useful in helping to prevent major catastrophes.

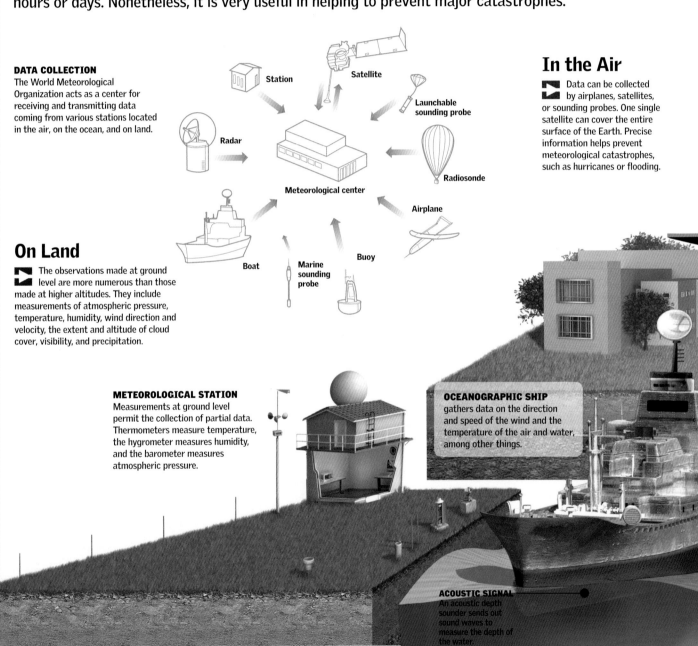

DATA COLLECTION
The World Meteorological Organization acts as a center for receiving and transmitting data coming from various stations located in the air, on the ocean, and on land.

Station

Satellite

Launchable sounding probe

Radar

Radiosonde

Meteorological center

Airplane

Boat

Marine sounding probe

Buoy

In the Air

Data can be collected by airplanes, satellites, or sounding probes. One single satellite can cover the entire surface of the Earth. Precise information helps prevent meteorological catastrophes, such as hurricanes or flooding.

On Land

The observations made at ground level are more numerous than those made at higher altitudes. They include measurements of atmospheric pressure, temperature, humidity, wind direction and velocity, the extent and altitude of cloud cover, visibility, and precipitation.

METEOROLOGICAL STATION
Measurements at ground level permit the collection of partial data. Thermometers measure temperature, the hygrometer measures humidity, and the barometer measures atmospheric pressure.

OCEANOGRAPHIC SHIP
gathers data on the direction and speed of the wind and the temperature of the air and water, among other things.

ACOUSTIC SIGNAL
An acoustic depth sounder sends out sound waves to measure the depth of the water.

On the Sea

Boats, buoys, and autonomous underwater vehicles help measure water temperature, salinity, density, and reflected sunlight. All the information gathered is sent to a meteorological center.

AUTONOMOUS UNDERWATER VEHICLE
Images related to the physical properties of the ocean water, such as the temperature, salinity, and density, are relayed to operators and its location and depth tracked via the Global Positioning System (GPS).

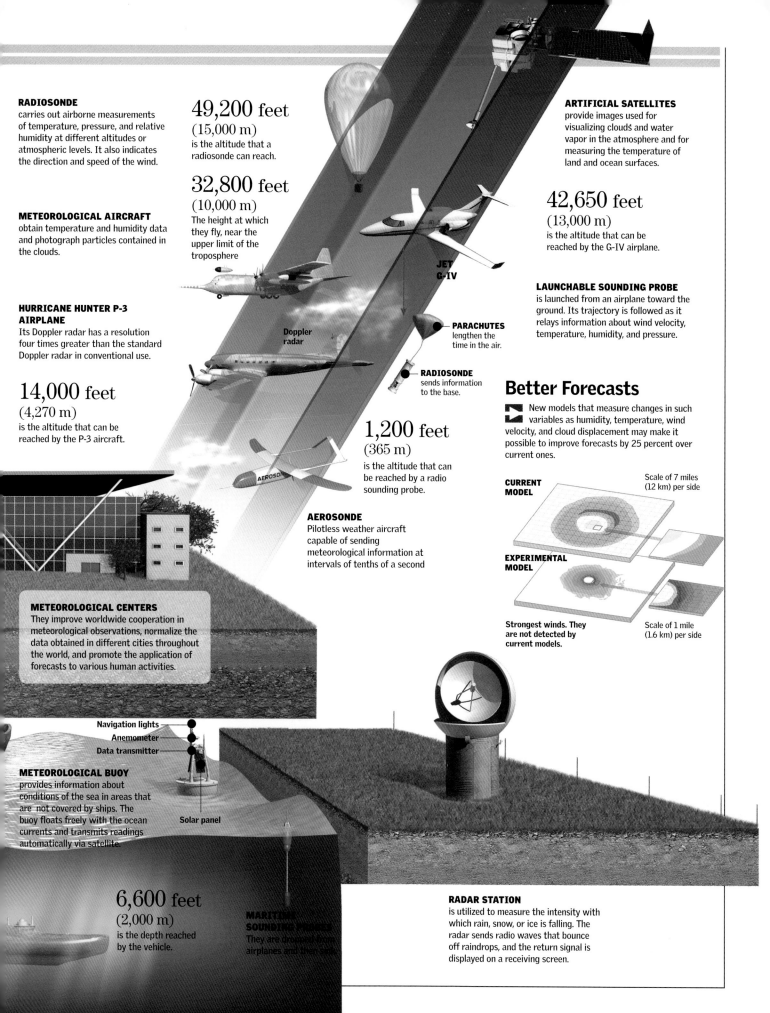

RADIOSONDE
carries out airborne measurements of temperature, pressure, and relative humidity at different altitudes or atmospheric levels. It also indicates the direction and speed of the wind.

METEOROLOGICAL AIRCRAFT
obtain temperature and humidity data and photograph particles contained in the clouds.

HURRICANE HUNTER P-3 AIRPLANE
Its Doppler radar has a resolution four times greater than the standard Doppler radar in conventional use.

14,000 feet
(4,270 m)
is the altitude that can be reached by the P-3 aircraft.

49,200 feet
(15,000 m)
is the altitude that a radiosonde can reach.

32,800 feet
(10,000 m)
The height at which they fly, near the upper limit of the troposphere

Doppler radar

JET G-IV

PARACHUTES
lengthen the time in the air.

RADIOSONDE
sends information to the base.

1,200 feet
(365 m)
is the altitude that can be reached by a radio sounding probe.

AEROSONDE
Pilotless weather aircraft capable of sending meteorological information at intervals of tenths of a second

ARTIFICIAL SATELLITES
provide images used for visualizing clouds and water vapor in the atmosphere and for measuring the temperature of land and ocean surfaces.

42,650 feet
(13,000 m)
is the altitude that can be reached by the G-IV airplane.

LAUNCHABLE SOUNDING PROBE
is launched from an airplane toward the ground. Its trajectory is followed as it relays information about wind velocity, temperature, humidity, and pressure.

Better Forecasts
New models that measure changes in such variables as humidity, temperature, wind velocity, and cloud displacement may make it possible to improve forecasts by 25 percent over current ones.

CURRENT MODEL

Scale of 7 miles (12 km) per side

EXPERIMENTAL MODEL

Scale of 1 mile (1.6 km) per side

Strongest winds. They are not detected by current models.

METEOROLOGICAL CENTERS
They improve worldwide cooperation in meteorological observations, normalize the data obtained in different cities throughout the world, and promote the application of forecasts to various human activities.

Navigation lights
Anemometer
Data transmitter

METEOROLOGICAL BUOY
provides information about conditions of the sea in areas that are not covered by ships. The buoy floats freely with the ocean currents and transmits readings automatically via satellite.

Solar panel

6,600 feet
(2,000 m)
is the depth reached by the vehicle.

MARITIME SOUNDING PROBES
They are dropped from airplanes and then sink.

RADAR STATION
is utilized to measure the intensity with which rain, snow, or ice is falling. The radar sends radio waves that bounce off raindrops, and the return signal is displayed on a receiving screen.

GLOSSARY

A'a
Type of lava flow in which the surface consists of solid fragments of slag. After hardening, the surface remains rough, covered with numerous sharp and chipped solid debris.

Accretion
Growth of an ice crystal in the atmosphere by direct capture of water droplets when the temperature is below 32°F (0°C).

Active Volcano
Volcano that erupts lava and gas at regular intervals.

ADP
Acronym of the chemical compound adenosine diphosphate.

Adventitious Root
Root that appears in unusual places, such as on the stem.

Aftershock
Small temblor or quake produced as rock settles into place after a major earthquake.

Air Mass
Extensive volume in the atmosphere whose physical properties, in particular the temperature and humidity in a horizontal plane, show only small and gradual differences. An air mass can cover an area of a few million square miles and can have a thickness of several miles.

Albedo
A measure of the percentage of radiation reflected by a surface.

Algae
Organisms of the Protist kingdom, at one time considered plants, but without roots, stems, or leaves. They live in water or in humid areas. They can be pluricellular or unicellular.

Amorphous
Mineral with fractured surfaces, instead of crystalline faces. Noncrystalline.

Anemometer
Instrument for measuring wind velocity.

Angiosperms
From the Greek *angion* (recipient) and *sperm* (seed). Plants with flowers whose seeds are contained in structures that develop into fruits.

Anther
Structure of the stamen composed of two locules (ovaries) and four pollen sacs.

Anticline
A fold of sedimentary strata sloping upward like an arch.

Anticyclone
Region where the atmospheric pressure is relatively high compared with neighboring regions. Normally, the air above an anticyclone descends, which prevents clouds from forming at medium and high levels of the atmosphere. Hence, an anticyclonic system is associated with good weather.

Antimatter
Matter formed from subatomic particles with shared properties. Its electrical charge is opposite that of normal matter.

Aphelion
The point in a celestial body's orbit farthest from the Sun. The Earth reaches aphelion on or about July 4, when it is 95,000,000 miles (152,900,000 km) from the Sun.

Aseismic
The characteristic of a building designed to withstand oscillations, or of areas with no seismic activity.

Aseismic Region
Tectonically stable region of the Earth, where there are almost no earthquakes. For example, the Arctic region is aseismic.

Asexual Reproduction
Process through which a single progenitor generates descendants identical to itself.

Ashfall
Phenomenon in which gravity causes ash (or other pyroclastic material) to fall from a smoke column after an eruption. The distribution of the ash is a function of wind direction.

Asteroids
Minor bodies of the solar system, formed by rock, metal, or a mixture of both. Most asteroids orbit the Sun between the orbits of Mars and Jupiter. Their size ranges from dozens of feet to hundreds of miles.

Asthenosphere
Layer inside the Earth, below the lithosphere. It is part of the upper mantle and is composed of easily deformable rock.

Astronomy
Science that studies the universe. It is concerned with the physical characteristics, movements, distances, formation, and interactions of galaxies, stars, planets, moons, comets, asteroids, and other celestial bodies.

Atmosphere
Layer of gas retained around a planet by its gravity. It is also the outer layer of matter in a star, where the energy produced in the star's interior is emitted in the form of radiation.

Atmospheric Pressure
The pressure or weight exerted by the atmosphere at a specific point. Its measurement can be expressed in various units: hectopascals, millibars, inches, or millimeters of mercury (Hg). It is also called "barometric pressure."

Atom
The smallest part of an element that partakes of all the element's properties. It is generally composed of three subatomic particles: the neutron, the proton, and the electron.

ATP
Adenosine triphosphate. Molecule produced by the mitochondria, which functions as the main source of energy for cells.

Aurora
Luminous phenomenon, with red and green layers, visible in the skies of the polar regions. The auroras are caused by the collision of solar particles with the Earth's atmosphere.

Austral
Related to the Southern Hemisphere.

Avalanche
Rapid movement of enormous volumes of rock and other materials caused by instability on the flanks of the volcano. The cause of this instability could be the intrusion of magma into the structure of the volcano, by a large earthquake, or by the weakening of the volcano's structure by hydrothermal variation, for example.

Bacteria
Microscopic and unicellular life-form found in air, water, plants, animals, and on the Earth's crust.

Ballistic (Fragment)
A lump of rock expelled forcefully by a volcanic eruption and that follows a ballistic or parabolic trajectory.

Baltic
Of or pertaining to the Baltic Sea, or to the territories along it.

Barometer
An instrument for measuring atmospheric pressure. A decrease in pressure usually means that storms are on the way. Increasing pressure indicates good weather.

Batholith
Massive body of magma that results from an intrusion between preexisting layers.

Beaufort Scale
A scale invented at the beginning of the 19th century by a British sailor, Francis Beaufort, for estimating and reporting wind velocity. It is based on the different shapes taken by water waves at different wind velocities, and its graduation goes from 0 to 12. There is also a Beaufort Scale for application on land, based on observations of the wind's effect on trees and other objects.

Berry
Simple fleshy fruit formed by one or more carpels.

Big Bang
Cosmological theory asserting that the universe began to exist as a result of a great explosion that occurred some 14 billion years ago.

Black Hole
Celestial body so dense that not even light can escape its gravity.

Bryophytes
Group of small flowerless plants that comprise the hepaticae, anthocerotae, and mosses.

Caldera
Large, round depression left when a volcano collapses onto its magma chamber.

Cambium
Interior part of the root and the stem of a plant that forms xylem on one side and phloem on the other. It makes stems grow thicker.

Canyon
Deep, narrow valley formed by fluvial erosion.

Carat
Unit of weight used in jewelry, variable in time and place, equivalent to 0.007 ounce (0.2 g).

Carbon
One of the most common elements in the universe, produced by stars. All known life is carbon-based.

Carpel
Female part that bears the ovules of a flower. The grouping of carpels forms the gynoecium.

Cave
Subterranean cavity formed through the chemical action of water on soluble, generally calcareous, ground.

Cell
Smallest vital unit of an organism. Plant cells have a wall that is more or less rigid.

Cellular Membrane
Flexible cover of all living cells. It contains cytoplasm and regulates the exchange of water and gases with the exterior.

Cellulose
Fibrous carbohydrate that a plant produces as part of its structural material. Main component of the cell wall.

Cementation
Process by which sediment both loses porosity and is lithified through the chemical precipitation of material in the spaces between the grains.

Cementation Zone
Place where lithification occurs. Water infiltrates the area, fills up the spaces between the grains of sediment, and transforms loose sediment into a solid mass.

Chasm, or Rift
Wide valley formed as a consequence of the

extension of the crust at the boundaries of diverging tectonic plates.

Chemical Compound
Substance formed by more than one element.

Chemical Element
Substance that contains only one type of atom.

Chitin
Polysaccharide that contains nitrogen. It is present in the cell walls of mushrooms.

Chlorophyll
Pigment contained in the chloroplasts of plant cells. It captures the energy of light during photosynthesis.

Chloroplast
Microscopic sac, located on the inside of green-plant cells, where the chemical processes of photosynthesis take place.

Chromosphere
The lowest layer of the Sun's atmosphere. It emits a pinkish-red light that can be seen only when the brighter photosphere is obscured during a total eclipse.

Cirrus
Wispy cloud formations at altitudes greater than 16,400 feet (5,000 m).

Class
Taxonomic group superior to Order and inferior to Phylum. For example, the Charophyceae Class includes green algae related to higher plants.

Clay
Fine-grained sediments formed by the chemical decomposition of some rocks. It is malleable when wet and hardens as it dries.

Climate
The average state of the meteorological conditions of a location considered over a long period of time. The climate of a location is determined by climatological factors: latitude, longitude, altitude, topography, and continentality.

Cloud
A visible mass of small particles, such as droplets of water and/or crystals of ice, suspended in the air. A cloud is formed in the atmosphere because of the condensation of water vapor onto solid particles of smoke, dust, ashes, and other elements called "condensation nuclei."

Coal
Combustible black rock of organic origin. It is produced through the decomposition of plant materials that accumulate in swamps or shallow marine waters.

Coalescence
The process of growth of drops of water in a cloud. Two drops collide and remain joined after the collision, constituting a bigger drop. This is one of the mechanisms that explains the growth of the size of drops in a cloud until precipitation (rain) is produced.

Comet
Object made of ice and rock dust. When a comet approaches the Sun, the growing heat causes the ice to evaporate, forming a gaseous head and a tail of dust and gas pointing away from the Sun.

Constellation
Group of stars in the sky. Constellations tend to bear the names of mythological characters or creatures. To astronomers, the constellations demarcate various regions of the sky.

Contact Metamorphism
Large-scale transformation of a rock into another type of rock. This happens mostly as a consequence of a sudden temperature increase.

Continentality
The tendency of the interior regions of the continents to have more extreme temperature changes than coastal zones.

Convection
The process by which a heated surface transfers energy to the material (air, water, etc.) above it. This material becomes less dense and rises. Cooler material descends to fill in the void. Air rising as a result of the heating of the ground by the Sun's rays.

Convection Currents
Vertical and circular movement of rock material in the mantle but found exclusively in the mantle.

Convergent Boundary
Border between two colliding tectonic plates.

Core
In a planet, a solid, high-pressure central mass; in a star, the central region undergoing nuclear fusion; in a galaxy, the innermost light-years.

Coriolis Force
A fictitious or apparent force that applies when the Earth is used as a reference frame for motion. It depends upon the latitude and the velocity of the object in motion. In the Northern Hemisphere, the air is deflected toward the right side of its path, and in the Southern Hemisphere, the air is deflected toward the left side of its path. This force is strongest at the poles and does not exist at the Equator.

Corona
Upper atmosphere of the Sun. It is visible as a pearly halo during a total solar eclipse.

Cosmos
Another name for the universe.

Cotyledon
First leaf of flowering plants, found on the inside of the seed. Some store food and remain buried while the plant germinates.

Crack
Fissure or cavity in the rock that results from tension. It can be completely or partially filled with minerals.

Crater
Circular depression formed by the impact of a meteorite on the surface of a natural satellite or a planet.

Crust
Rocky layer of the surface of a planet or natural satellite.

Crystal
Organized, regular, and periodically repeated arrangement of atoms.

Cyclone
A climatic low-pressure system.

Cytoplasm
Compartment of the cells of eukaryotes, marked by the cellular membrane and the membranes of the organelles of the cell.

Deciduous
Describes a plant that loses all its leaves in specific seasons of the year.

Density
Degree of solidity of a body (its mass divided by its volume).

Deposit
A natural accumulation of a rock or mineral. If it is located at the site where it formed, the deposit is called "primary." Otherwise, it is called "secondary."

Desert
A hot or cold zone where annual precipitation is less than 1 inch (25 mm).

Dew
Condensation in the form of small drops of water formed on grass and other small objects near the ground when the temperature has dropped to the dew point. This generally happens during the night.

Dicotyledon
Flowering plant whose seed has two cotyledons.

Dike
An earthwork for containing or channeling a river or for protection against the sea. Also, tabular igneous intrusion that crosses through layers of surrounding rock.

Diploid
Cell with two complete sets of chromosomes.

DNA
Deoxyribonucleic acid. Double helix molecule with codified genetic information.

Dolostone
Carbonated sedimentary rock that contains at least 50 percent or more carbonate, of which at least half appears as dolomite.

Dome
Cup-shaped bulge with very steep sides, formed by the accumulation of viscous lava. Usually, a dome is formed by andesitic, dacitic, or rhyolitic lava, and the dome can reach a height of many hundreds of feet.

Drizzle
A type of light liquid precipitation composed of small drops with diameters between 0.007 and 0.019 inch (0.18 and 0.5 mm). Usually, drizzle falls from stratus-type clouds that are found at low altitudes and can be accompanied by fog, which significantly decreases visibility.

Drought
An abnormally dry climatic condition in a specific area where the lack of water is prolonged and which causes a serious hydrological imbalance.

Drupe
Simple fleshy fruit that develops from hypogynous flowers—flowers in which the ovary lies above the point where the other flower parts are attached. It has one seed in its interior. Examples include the olive, peach, and almond.

Duration of Earthquake
Time during which the shaking or tremor of an earthquake is perceptible to humans. This period is always less than that registered by a seismograph.

Earthquake
The sudden and violent release of energy and vibrations in the Earth that generally occurs along the edges of tectonic plates.

Eclipse
Visual concealment of one celestial body by another. A lunar eclipse occurs when the Moon passes into the Earth's shadow, and a solar eclipse takes place when the Earth passes into the Moon's shadow.

Ecliptic
Imaginary line around the sky along which the Sun moves during the year. The orbits of the Earth and the other planets generally lie along the ecliptic.

Ecosystem
Grouping of the organisms of a community and the nonbiological components associated with their environment.

Element
A basic substance of nature that cannot be diminished without losing its chemical properties. Each element (such as hydrogen, helium, carbon, oxygen) has its own characteristics.

Elliptical Orbit
Orbit shaped like a flattened circle. All orbits are elliptical. A circle is a special form of an ellipse.

El Niño
The anomalous appearance, every few years, of unusually warm ocean conditions along the tropical west coast of South America.

Embryo
Product of an egg cell fertilized by a sperm cell; it can develop until it constitutes an adult organism.

Enzyme
Protein that helps to regulate the chemical processes in a cell.

Eon
The largest unit of time on the geologic scale, of an order of magnitude greater than an era.

Epicenter
Point on the Earth's surface located directly above the focus of an earthquake.

Epicentral Area
Region around the epicenter of an earthquake, usually characterized by being the area where the earth movement and shaking is most intense and the earthquake damage is greatest.

Epicentral Distance
Distance along the Earth's surface from the

point where an earthquake is observed to the epicenter.

Epidermis
The most external cellular layers of stems and leaves.

Epiphyte
Plant that grows and supports itself on the surface of another plant but does not take water or nutrients from it.

Era
Division of time in the Earth's history. Geologists divide eras into periods.

Erosion
Action in which the ground is gradually worn down over long periods by moving water, glaciers, wind, or waves.

Evaporation
Physical process by which a liquid (such as water) is transformed into its gaseous state (such as water vapor). The reverse process is called "condensation."

Exfoliation
The tendency for certain minerals to fracture along regular planes within their crystalline structure.

Exosphere
The outermost layer of the Earth's atmosphere.

Extinct Volcano
Volcano that shows no signs of activity for a long period of time, considered to have a very low probability of erupting.

Fault
Fracture involving the shifting of one rock mass with respect to another.

Fertilization
Fusion of the special reproductive cells (contained in the pollen and in the ovules) in order to give rise to a new plant.

Filament
Structure, in the form of a thread, that forms the support of a flower's stamen.

Focus
Internal zone of the Earth, where seismic waves are released, carrying the energy held by rocks under pressure.

Fog
Visible manifestation of drops of water suspended in the atmosphere at or near ground level; this reduces the horizontal visibility to less than a mile. It originates when the temperature of the air is near the dew point, and sufficient numbers of condensation nuclei are present.

Fold
Bending and deformation of rock strata due to the compression caused by the movements of tectonic plates.

Force
Something that changes the motion or shape of a body.

Forecast
A statement about future events. The weather forecast includes the use of objective models based on a number of atmospheric parameters combined with the ability and experience of the meteorologist. It is also called "weather prediction."

Fossil
Any trace of an old life-form. It can be the petrified remains of an organism or an impression of an organism left in rock.

Fossil Fuel
Fuel formed from the partially decomposed remains of deceased organisms. These mixtures of organic compounds are extracted from the subsoil with the goal of producing energy through combustion. They are coal, oil, and natural gas.

Fracture
Break of a mineral along an irregular surface. It can be conchoidal, hooked, smooth, or earthy.

Front
The transition or contact zone between two masses of air with different meteorological characteristics, which almost always implies different temperatures. For example, a front occurs at the area of convergence between warm humid air and dry cold air.

Frost
A covering of ice crystals on a cold object.

Fruit
Ovary or group of ovaries of a flower, transformed and mature. It contains the seeds.

Fumarole
Emission of steam and gas, usually at high temperatures, from fractures or cracks in the surface of a volcano or from a region with volcanic activity. Most of the gas emitted is steam, but fumarole emissions can include gases such as CO_2, CO, SO_2, H_2S, CH_4, HCl, among others.

Galactic Filament
Structure formed by superclusters of galaxies stretching out through great portions of space. Filaments are the largest structures in the universe and are separated by great voids.

Galaxy
Collection of billions of stars, nebulae, dust, and interstellar gas held together by gravity.

Galaxy Cluster
Group of galaxies linked together by gravity.

Gem
Mineral or other natural material that is valued for its beauty and rarity. It can be polished and cut to produce jewels.

Gene
Unit of information of a chromosome. Sequence of nucleotides in the DNA molecule that carries out a specific function.

Genetic Drift
Phenomenon produced in small populations that demonstrates that the frequency of alleles (alternative forms of a gene) can vary by chance or throughout generations.

Geode
Spherical, rocky cavity covered with well-formed crystals.

Geology
Study of the Earth, its shape, and its composition. Rocks, minerals, and fossils offer information that helps us reconstruct the history of the planet.

Geothermal Energy
Energy produced from steam generated by heated water from within Earth's interior.

Germination
Process in which a plant begins to grow from a seed or a spore.

Geyser
Spring that periodically expels hot water from the ground.

Glacier
A large mass of ice formed through the accumulation of recrystallized and compacted snow occurring either on a mountain or over a large area on a landmass. Ice moves slowly and both excavates rock and carries debris.

Gondwana
Southern portion of Pangea, which at one time included South America, Africa, Australia, India, and Antarctica.

Granite
Intrusive igneous rock composed mainly of quartz and feldspar. It can be polished and used in decoration.

Gravity
Attractive force between bodies, such as between the Earth and the Moon.

Gust
A rapid and significant increase in wind velocity. The maximum velocity of the wind must reach at least 16 knots (18 miles per hour [29 km/h]), and the difference between the peaks and calm must be at least 10 knots (12 miles per hour [19 km/h]). It generally lasts less than 20 seconds.

Gymnosperm
Plants with seeds that are not sealed in an ovary. Examples are conifers (pine, fir, larch, cypress).

Gynoecium
Grouping of carpels of a flower that make up the female sexual organ of angiosperms.

Hail
Precipitation that originates in convective clouds, such as the cumulonimbus, in the form of masses or irregular pieces of ice. Typically hail has a diameter of 0.2 to 2 inches (5 to 50 mm) but may grow significantly larger. The smallest ice fragments—whose diameter is 0.2 inch (5 mm) or less—are called small hailstones, or "graupel." Strong upward currents are required inside the clouds for hail to be produced.

Haploid
From the Greek *haplous* (singular): cell with one set of chromosomes, unlike diploids. It is characteristic of the gametes, the gametophytes, and some mushrooms.

Hardness
Resistance offered by a mineral to scratching and abrasion. One mineral is said to be harder than another if the former can scratch the latter.

Hectopascal
A pressure unit equal to 100 pascals and equivalent to 1 millibar—a millibar being equivalent to 0.031 inch (0.9 mm) of ordinary mercury. The millibar (mb) was the technical unit used to measure pressure until recently, when the hectopascal was adopted. The pascal is the unit for pressure in the MKS (Metres, Kilograms and Seconds) system, corresponding to the pressure exerted by the unit force (1 newton) on a unit surface (11 square feet—1 square meter); 1,000 hPa = 1,000 mb = 1 bar = 14.5 pounds per square inch (1.02 kg per sq cm).

Helium
The second most common and second lightest element in the universe. It is a product of the Big Bang and of nuclear fusion of stars.

High
A prefix describing cloud formations at an altitude between 6,560 and 16,400 feet (2,000 and 5,000 m).

Host
Plant from which another organism (parasite) obtains food or shelter.

Hot Spot
Point of concentrated heat in the mantle that rises to Earth's surface far from the boundaries between tectonic plates.

Humidity
The amount of water vapor contained in the air.

Hurricane
The name for a tropical cyclone with sustained winds of 64 knots (74 miles per hour [119 km/h]) or more, which develops in the North Atlantic, the Caribbean, the Gulf of Mexico, and the Pacific Northeast. This storm is called a "typhoon" in the western Pacific and a "cyclone" in the Indian Ocean.

Hydrogen
The most common and lightest element in the universe; the main component of stars and galaxies.

Hygrometer
An instrument used to measure the moisture content in the environment.

Hyphae
Interwoven filaments that form the mycelia of fungi.

Ice
The solid state of water. It is found in the form of ice crystals, snow, or hail in the atmosphere.

Igneous Rocks
Rocks formed directly from the cooling of magma. If they solidify inside the crust, they are said to be "plutonic" (or intrusive); if they solidify on the surface, they are said to be "volcanic" (or extrusive).

Impermeable Rock
Rock through which liquids cannot be filtered.

Incandescent
A property of metal that has turned red or white because of heat.

Inflorescence
Groupings of flowers in a specific form on a peduncle (stalk).

Infrared Radiation
Heat radiation, with a wavelength between visible light and radio waves.

Interstellar Space
Space between the stars.

Intrusion
A large mass of rock that forms in empty spaces underground when magma infiltrates strata, cools, and solidifies.

Jet Streams
Air currents high in the troposphere (about 6 miles [10 km] above sea level), where the wind velocity can be up to 200 miles per hour (90 meters per second). This type of structure is seen in subtropical latitudes in both hemispheres, where the flow is toward the east, reaching its maximum intensity during the winter.

Kimberlite
Type of rock usually associated with diamonds and other minerals coming from the depths of the Earth.

Kingdom
Taxonomic group superior to a phylum and inferior to a domain, such as the kingdom Plantae.

Kuiper Belt
Region of the solar system that is home to millions of frozen objects, such as comets. It stretches from the orbit of Neptune to the inner limit of the Oort cloud.

Lahar
Mudflows produced on the slopes of volcanoes when unstable layers of ash and debris become saturated with water and flow downhill.

Lapilli
Fragments of rock with a diameter between 0.06 and 1.3 inches (1.5 and 3.2 mm) expelled during a volcanic eruption.

Latitude
A system of imaginary parallel lines that encircle the globe north and south of the Equator. The poles are located at 90° latitude north and south and the Equator at 0° latitude.

Lava
Magma, or molten rock, that reaches the Earth's surface.

Lava Bombs
Masses of lava that a volcano expels, which have a diameter equal to or greater than 1.2 inches (3 cm).

Lava Flow
River of lava that flows out of a volcano and runs along the ground.

Legume
Simple fruit of some species that come from one carpel divided in two. Examples are garbanzos and peas.

Light
Electromagnetic radiation with a wavelength visible to the human eye.

Lightning
A discharge of the atmosphere's static electricity occurring between a cloud and the ground.

Light-Year
Standard astronomical measurement unit equivalent to the distance traveled by light, or any form of electromagnetic radiation, in one year. Equivalent to 6,000,000,000,000 miles (10,000,000,000,000 km).

Limestone
Rock containing at least 50% calcite. It can also have dolomite, aragonite, and siderite.

Liquefaction
Transformation of ground from solid to fluid state through the action of an earthquake.

Lithosphere
Exterior, rigid layer of the Earth formed by the crust and upper mantle.

Luster
Level of light reflection on the surface of a crystal.

Magma
Mass of molten rock deep below the surface, which includes dissolved gas and crystals. When magma has lost its gases and reaches the surface, it is called "lava." If magma cools within the Earth's crust, it forms "plutonic rocks."

Magma Chamber
Section within a volcano where incandescent magma is found.

Magmatic Rock
Rock that forms when magma cools off and solidifies. Magmatic intrusive rocks solidify underground, while the extrusive ones solidify on the surface.

Magnetic Field
The area near a magnetic body, electric current, or changing electric field. Planets, stars, and galaxies have magnetic fields that extend into space.

Magnetism
Property of some minerals that allows them to be attracted by a magnet and to change the direction of a compass needle.

Magnetosphere
Sphere that surrounds a planet with a magnetic field strong enough to protect the planet from the solar wind.

Malleability
Mechanical property of a mineral that makes it possible for the mineral to be molded and formed into a sheet through repeated blows without breaking.

Mantle
Layer that lies between the crust and the core of a planet.

Marble
Metamorphosed limestone rock composed of compacted calcite and dolomite. It can be polished.

Mass
Measure of the amount of matter in an object.

Matter
The substance of a physical object, it occupies a portion of space.

Meiosis
Type of cellular division in which two successive divisions of the diploid nucleus of a cell give rise to four haploid nuclei. As a result, gametes or spores are produced.

Meristem
Region of tissue consisting of cells that produce other cells through cellular division.

Mesosphere
The layer of the Earth's atmosphere that lies above the stratosphere.

Metal
Any element that shines, conducts electricity, and is malleable.

Metamorphic Rock
Type of rock resulting from the application of high pressure and temperature on igneous and sedimentary rocks.

Meteorite
Rocky or metallic object that strikes the surface of a planet or satellite, where it can form a crater.

Meteorology
The science and study of atmospheric phenomena. Some of the subdivisions of meteorology are agrometeorology, climatology, hydrometeorology, and physical, dynamic, and synoptic meteorology.

Mid-Ocean Ridge
An elongated mountain range on the ocean floor, which varies between 300 and 3,000 miles (483 and 4,830 km) in breadth.

Milky Way
The galaxy to which the Sun and the solar system belong. It is visible as a pale band of light that crosses our night sky.

Mineral
Inorganic solid of natural origin that has an organized atomic structure.

Mist
Microscopic drops of water suspended in the air, or humid hygroscopic particles, which reduce visibility at ground level.

Mohs Scale
A tool designed to test the hardness of a given mineral by comparing it to ten known minerals, from the softest to the hardest. Each mineral can be scratched by those following it.

Molecule
Smallest unit of a pure substance that has the composition and chemical properties of the substance. It is formed by one or more atoms.

Monocotyledon
Flowering plant with only one cotyledon. Examples are the onion, orchid, and palm.

Monsoon
A seasonal wind that causes heavy rains in tropical and subtropical regions.

Moon
The Earth's natural satellite is called the Moon. The natural satellites of other planets are commonly known as moons and have their own proper names.

Mycelium
Interwoven mass of hyphae of a fungus.

NADP
Acronym of the chemical compound Nicotinamide Adenine Dinucleotide Phosphate in its oxidized form.

NADPH
Acronym of the chemical compound Nicotinamide Adenine Dinucleotide Phosphate in its reduced form.

Nebulae
Clouds of gas and dust in space. Nebulae can be seen when they reflect starlight or when they obstruct light from sources behind them.

Neck
Column of lava that has solidified inside a volcano.

Nectar
Sweet liquid, produced by flowers and some leaves, that attracts insects and birds, which serve as pollinating agents.

Neutron
Electrically neutral subatomic particle. It makes up part of an atom's nucleus (with the exception of ordinary hydrogen).

Node
Axillary bud, the part of the stem of a plant where one or more leaves appear.

Normal
The standard value accepted for a meteorological element as calculated for a specific location over a specific number of years. The normal values refer to the distribution of data within the limits of the common occurrence. The parameters can include temperature (high, low, and divergences), pressure, precipitation (rain, snow, etc.), winds (velocity and direction), storms, cloud cover, percentage of relative humidity, and so on.

Normal Fault
Fracture in rock layers where the ground is being stretched and the block over the fault plane shifts downward, relative to the block under the fault plane.

Nova
Star that increases greatly in brightness for several days or weeks and then slowly fades. Most novae probably occur in binary-star systems in which a white dwarf draws in matter from its companion star.

Nuclear Fusion
Nuclear reaction in which relatively light elements (such as hydrogen) form heavier elements (such as helium). Nuclear fusion is the source of energy that makes stars shine.

Nucleic Acid
A molecule that carries genetic information about the cell.

Nucleus
The part of the cell that contains the DNA, which carries the genetic material.

Ocean Current
The movement of water in the ocean caused by the system of planetary winds. Ocean currents transport warm or cold water over long distances around the planet.

Ocean Trench
Long, narrow, extremely deep area of the ocean floor formed where the edge of an oceanic tectonic plate sinks beneath another plate.

Orographic Rain
Rain that results from the cooling of humid air as it crosses over a mountain range.

Ovary
The part of a flower consisting of one or more carpels and containing the ovules. Fertilized, it will form all or part of the fruit.

Ovule
The part of the ovary in flowering plants that contains the female sexual cells. After fertilization it transforms into seed.

Oxidation Zone
Deposit of minerals with oxidizing properties, formed through the effect of meteorization or weathering.

Oxygen
Chemical element vital to life and to the expansion of the universe. Oxygen makes up 21 percent of the Earth's atmosphere.

Ozone Layer
A layer of the atmosphere situated 20 to 30 miles (32 to 48 km) above the Earth's surface between the troposphere and the stratosphere. It acts as a filtering mechanism for ultraviolet radiation.

Pahoehoe Lava
Lava with a smooth surface that has a ropelike form.

Parasite
An organism that lives at the expense of another, from which it obtains its nutrients.

Particle
In particle physics, a tiny, individual component of matter with characteristic mass, electrical charge, and other properties.

Pelean Eruption
Type of volcanic eruption with a growing dome of viscous lava that may be destroyed when it collapses because of gravity or brief explosions. Pelean eruptions produce pyroclastic flows or burning clouds. The term comes from Mt Pelée in Martinique.

Perihelion
The point in a celestial body's orbit closest to the Sun. The Earth reaches perihelion on or about January 4, when it is 92,000,000 miles (148,000,000 km) from the Sun.

Permeable Layers
Strata of the Earth's crust that allow water to reach deeper layers.

Petal
Modified leaves that form the corolla.

Phloem
Vessels that conduct the sap throughout the entire plant.

Photon
Elemental particle responsible for electromagnetic radiation. Photons are the most common particles in the universe.

Photosynthesis
Process through which the energy of light is used to produce carbohydrates from carbon dioxide and water.

Piezoelectric
Property that some minerals have to produce a difference in potential when subjected to compression, traction, or torsion.

Planet
Roughly spherical object made of rocks or gas orbiting a star. A planet cannot generate its own light but reflects the light of its parent star.

Plate Tectonics
Theory that the Earth's outer layer consists of separate plates that interact in various ways, causing earthquakes and forming volcanoes, mountains, and the crust itself.

Plinian Eruption
Extremely violent and explosive type of volcanic eruption that continuously expels large quantities of ash and other pyroclastic materials into the atmosphere, forming an eruption column typically 5 to 25 miles (8 to 40 km) high. The term honors Pliny the Younger, who observed the eruption of Mt Vesuvius (Italy) in AD 79.

Pollen
Fine powder of plants with seeds whose grains contain the male sexual cells.

Pollination
Passage of pollen from the male organ of a flower to the female organ of the same flower or another.

Precipitation
A liquid or solid, crystallized or amorphous particle that falls from a cloud or system of clouds and reaches the ground.

Primary (P) Wave
Seismic wave that alternately compresses and stretches the ground along its direction of travel.

Protein
Macromolecule composed of one or more chains of amino acids. They define the physical characteristics of an organism and regulate its chemical reactions when they act as enzymes.

Proton
Subatomic particle with positive electrical charge. It forms part of the nucleus of an atom.

Pumice
Pale volcanic rock full of holes, which give it a low density. Its composition is usually acidic (rhyolitic). The holes are formed by volcanic gases that expand as volcanic material rises to the surface.

Pyroclastic Flow
Dense, hot mix of volcanic gas, ash, and rock fragments that flows rapidly down the sides of a volcano.

Pyroelectric
Property that some nonconductor minerals have to create difference in power transmissions from differences in temperature.

Quartzite
Metamorphic rock formed by the consolidation of quartz sandstone. It is extremely hard. Quartzite can also be a sedimentary rock, which is sandstone with a very high content of quartz; it is very hard and it has light color.

Radiation
The process by which energy propagates through a specific medium (or a vacuum) via wave phenomena or motion. Electromagnetic radiation, which emits heat and light, is one form of radiation. Other forms are sound waves.

Reverse Fault
Fractures in rock layers where the ground is being compressed, which generally causes the upper edge to rise above the lower part in a plane inclined between 45 and 90 degrees from the horizontal.

Rhizoids
Cellular formation or filament in the form of a thin and branching tube that attaches mosses to the soil.

Rhizome
Horizontal subterranean stem.

Richter Scale
Measures the magnitude of an earthquake or of the energy it releases. The scale is logarithmic, such that an earthquake of magnitude 8 releases ten times as much energy as a magnitude 7 quake. An earthquake's magnitude is estimated based on measurements taken by seismic instruments.

Rift Zone
Area where the crust is splitting and stretching, as shown by cracks in the rock. Such areas are produced by the separation of tectonic plates, and their presence causes earthquakes and recurrent volcanic activity.

Rock
Natural aggregate of one or more minerals (sometimes including noncrystalline substances) that constitute an independent geologic unit.

Root
Organ that fixes a plant to the soil and absorbs water and minerals from it.

Sap
Watery liquid that contains the products of photosynthesis and is transported by the phloem.

Seaquake
An earthquake at the bottom of the ocean, causing a violent agitation of ocean waves, which in some cases reach coastal areas and cause flooding.

Secondary (S) Wave
Transverse or cross-section wave with motion perpendicular to the direction of its travel.

Sedimentary Rock
Rock that forms through accumulation of sediments that, when subjected to physical and chemical processes, result in a compacted and consolidated material. Sediment can form on riverbanks, at the bottom of precipices, in valleys, lakes, and seas. Sedimentary rock accumulates in successive layers, or strata.

Sediments
Rock fragments or remains of plants or animals deposited at the bottom of rivers, lakes, or oceans by water, wind, or ice.

Seed
Structure consisting of the embryo of a plant, a reserve of food called the "endosperm," and a protective cover called the "testa."

Seedling
First sprouting of the embryo of a seed, formed by a short stem and a pair of young leaves.

Seismic Event
Shaking of the ground caused by an abrupt and violent movement of a mass of rock along a fault, or fracture, in the crust. Active volcanoes cause a wide variety of seismic events.

Seismic Wave
Wavelike movement that travels through the Earth as a result of an earthquake or an explosion.

Seismic Zone
Limited geographic area within a seismic region, with similar seismic hazard, seismic risk, and earthquake-resistant design standards.

Seismograph
Instrument that registers seismic waves or tremors in the Earth's surface during an earthquake.

Seismology
Branch of geology that studies tremors in the Earth, be they natural or artificial.

Sepal
Modified leaf that forms the outer covering of a flower that protects the bud before it opens.

Sexual Reproduction
Reproduction based on the fertilization of a female cell by a male cell; it produces descendants different from both progenitors.

Shield Volcano
Large volcano with gently sloping flanks formed by fluid basaltic lava.

Silicates
They make up about 95 percent of the Earth's crust. Their tetrahedral structure, with one silicon and four oxygen ions, creates different types of configurations through the union of the ions. According to their composition, members of this mineral group are differentiated into light and dark.

Silicon
One of the most common materials, and a component of many minerals.

Slate
Bluish black, fine-grained metamorphic rock. It can be easily divided into sheets.

Snow
Precipitation in the form of white or transparent frozen ice crystals, often in the form of complex hexagons. In general, snow falls from stratiform clouds, but it can also fall from cumulus clouds, usually in the form of snowflakes.

Solar Flare
Immense explosion produced on the surface of the Sun by the collision of two loops of the solar magnetic field.

Solar Mass
Standard unit of mass against which other objects in the universe can be compared. The Sun has 333,000 times as much mass as the Earth.

Solution
Mixture of two or more chemical substances. It can be liquid, solid, or gaseous.

Sori
Set of sporangia found on the underside of fern leaves.

Space
The medium through which all celestial bodies move.

Spectrum
The result of dispersing the electromagnetic radiation of an object so that the wavelengths of which it is composed can be seen. Dark lines that originate from elements that are present and punctuate the spectrum at specific wavelengths reveal the composition of the object.

Speed of Light
The distance traveled by light in a vacuum in one second (approximately 186,000 miles, or 300,000 km). No object can move faster than the speed of light.

Sporangia
Structure in which spores are formed.

Spore
Reproductive structure formed by one cell, capable of originating a new organism without fusing with another cell.

Stalactite
Internal structure of a cave. It is conical and hangs from the cave ceiling.

Stalagmite
Internal structure of a cave. It is conical and rises from the cave floor.

Stamen
Element of the male reproductive apparatus of a flower that carries pollen. It is formed by a filament that supports two pollen sacs on its upper part.

Star
Enormous sphere of gas (generally hydrogen) that radiates light and heat. The Sun is a star.

Star Cluster
Group of stars linked together by gravity. Open clusters are scattered groups of several hundred stars. Globular clusters are dense spheres of several million old stars.

Stem
Part of a plant that holds up the leaves or the reproductive structures.

Stigma
Upper part of the female reproductive apparatus of a flower. The receptor of pollen, it connects with the ovary.

Stratosphere
The layer of the atmosphere situated above the troposphere.

Stratus
Low clouds that form layers. They often produce drizzle.

Subduction
Process by which the oceanic lithosphere sinks into the mantle along a convergence boundary. The Nazca Plate is undergoing subduction beneath the South American Plate.

Subduction Zone
Long, narrow region where one plate of the crust is slipping beneath another.

Sunspots
Dark, relatively cool spots on the surface of the Sun. They tend to be located on either side of the solar equator and are created by the solar magnetic field.

Supernova
Explosion of a massive star at the end of its life.

Surface Wave
Seismic wave that travels along the Earth's surface. It is perceived after the primary and secondary waves.

Tectonic Plates
Large, rigid sections of the Earth's outer layer. These plates sit on top of a more ductile and plastic layer of the mantle, the asthenosphere, and they drift slowly at an average rate of 1 inch (2.5 cm) or more per year.

Tenacity
The level of toughness that a mineral offers to fracture, deformation, crushing, bending, or pulverization.

Thallus
Plantlike body of brown seaweed. Also the long, rigid part that holds up the reproductive structures of some fungi.

Thermometer
An instrument for measuring temperature. The different scales used in meteorology are Celsius, Fahrenheit, and Kelvin (or absolute).

Thrust Fault
A fracture in rock layers that is characterized by one boundary that slips above another at an angle of less than 45 degrees.

Thylakoid
Small, flat sac that makes up part of the internal membrane of a chloroplast. Site where solar energy is transformed into chemical energy as part of the process of photosynthesis.

Tide
The effect of the gravitational pull of one astronomical object upon the surface of another. Ocean tides on Earth are an example.

Tissue
Group of identical cells with the same function.

Tornado
A column of air that rotates with great violence, stretching between a convective cloud and the surface of the Earth. It is the most destructive phenomenon in the atmosphere. Tornadoes can occur, under the right conditions, anywhere on Earth, but they appear most frequently in the central United States, between the Rocky Mountains and the Appalachian Mountains.

Transform Fault
Fault in which plate boundaries cause friction by sliding past each other in opposite directions.

Tremor
Seismic event perceived on the Earth's surface as a vibration or shaking of the ground, without causing damage or destruction.

Tropical Cyclone
A cyclone without fronts, it develops over tropical waters and has a surface circulation organized and defined in a counterclockwise direction. A cyclone is classified, according to the intensity of its winds, as a tropical disturbance (light ground-level winds), tropical depression (maximum ground-level winds of 38 miles per hour [61 km/h]), tropical storm (maximum winds in the range of 39 to 73 miles per hour [63 to 117 km/h]), or hurricane (maximum ground-level winds exceeding 74 miles per hour [119 km/h]).

Troposphere
The layer of the atmosphere closest to the ground, its name means "changing sphere," and this layer is where most changes in weather take place. This is also where most of the phenomena of interest in meteorology occur.

Tsunami
Word of Japanese origin that denotes a large ocean wave caused by an earthquake.

Tuber
Modified, thickened underground stem where the plant accumulates reserves of food substances.

Turbulence
Disorderly motion of air composed of small whirlwinds that move within air currents. Atmospheric turbulence is produced by air in a state of continuous change. It can be caused by thermal or convective currents, by differences in terrain and in the velocity of the wind, by conditions along a frontal zone, or by a change in temperature and pressure.

Unstable
Tendency to change from one state into another less energetic one. Radioactive elements decay into more stable elements.

Van Allen Belt
Radiation zone surrounding the Earth, where the Earth's magnetic field traps solar particles.

Vascular
Describes plants with a complex structure and highly organized cells for transporting water and nutrients to all parts of the plant.

Viscous
Measure of a material's resistance to flow in response to a force acting on it. The higher the silicon content of the lava, the higher the viscosity.

Volcanic Glass
Natural glass formed when molten lava cools rapidly without crystallizing. A solid-like substance made of atoms with no regular structure.

Volcanic Ring
Chain of mountains or islands located near the edges of the tectonic plates and that is formed as a result of magma activity associated with subduction zones.

Volcano
Mountain formed by lava, pyroclastic materials, or both.

Volcanology
Branch of geology that studies the form and activity of volcanoes.

Vulcanian Eruption
Type of volcanic eruption characterized by the occurrence of explosive events of brief duration that expel material into the atmosphere to heights of about 49,000 feet (15 km). This type of activity is usually linked to the interaction of groundwater and magma (phreatomagmatic eruption).

Wavelength
Distance between the peaks of any wave of electromagnetic radiation. Radiation with a short wavelength (such as X rays) has more energy than radiation with a longer wavelength (such as radio waves).

Weather
The state of the atmosphere at a given moment, as it relates to its effects on human activity. This process involves short-term changes in the atmosphere in contrast to the great climatic changes that imply more long-term changes. The terms used to define weather include cloudiness, humidity, precipitation, temperature, visibility, and wind.

Weathering
The breaking down of a material by sustained physical or chemical processes.

Windward
The direction from which the wind is blowing.

Xylem
Part of a plant's vascular system. It transports water and minerals from the roots to the rest of the plant.

Zenith
Point in the sky 90° above the horizon (that is, immediately above an observer).

Zodiac
Twelve constellations through which the Sun, the Moon, and the planets appear to move.

INDEX